Teaching Shakespeare with Film and Television

Al Pacino as King Richard III in the 1996 film *Looking for Richard*. Courtesy of FOX Searchlight Pictures and Youth Media International.

Teaching Shakespeare with Film and Television

A Guide

H. R. COURSEN

GREENWOOD PRESS
Westport, Connecticut • London

Library of Congress Cataloging-in-Publication Data

Coursen, Herbert R.
    Teaching Shakespeare with film and television : a guide / H.R.
Coursen.
        p.   cm.
    Includes bibliographical references (p.) and index.
    ISBN 0–313–30066–6 (alk. paper)
    1. Shakespeare, William, 1564–1616—Study and teaching—Audio-
visual aids.   2. Shakespeare, William, 1564–1616—Film and video
adaptations.   3. English drama—Study and teaching—Audio-visual
aids.   I. Title.
PR2987.C68   1997
822.3´3—dc21   96–49732

British Library Cataloguing in Publication Data is available.

Library of Congress Catalog Card Number: 96–49732
ISBN: 0–313–30066–6

First published in 1997

Greenwood Press, 88 Post Road West, Westport, CT 06881
An imprint of Greenwood Publishing Group, Inc.

Printed in the United States of America

The paper used in this book complies with the
Permanent Paper Standard issued by the National
Information Standards Organization (Z39.48–1984).

10 9 8 7 6 5 4 3 2 1

Copyright Acknowledgments

The author and publisher gratefully acknowledge permission to reprint
material from the following:

Shakespeare and the Classroom, a periodical published by Ohio Northern
University, for reviews cited in chapters 6 and 10 of this book.

Duffy, Robert A. "Gade, Olivier, Richardson: Visual Strategy in *Hamlet*
Adaptation." *Literature/Film Quarterly* 4, no. 2 (1976), 141–52.

Mullin, Michael. "Tony Richardson's *Hamlet*: Script and Screen."
Literature/Film Quarterly 4, no. 2 (1976), 123–33.

Contents

Contents

For Jim

Preface

This book is designed for all teachers—from high school through college—who use film and television in the teaching of Shakespeare. Students too will find the book useful since it suggests ways of using the many available and newly arriving cassettes, and lists materials that supplement the use of film and television in teaching the plays. The book not only suggests how to write and do research in a rapidly expanding and exciting field of inquiry but provides examples of such writing and research, from the review of a single production to the comparison of several versions of the same character or scene as depicted in productions emerging from different decades.

The book makes distinctions about the media that must be understood before any evaluation of a specific production can be attempted. In spite of their conflation on cassette, film and television are not the same medium, either physically or conceptually. The concept of script is discussed, that is, the words that are to be interpreted by actors and directors and placed in a context that becomes the world of the production.

That world is to a large extent defined by the *space* available in which to construct it. Kenneth Branagh's 70-mm film of *Hamlet* occupies a wide screen in the cinema and is therefore able to fill the frame with detail. Laertes's rebellion, for example, is a full-scale military attack in what looks like regimental strength. The Nunnery Scene occurs in a huge hall of mirrored doors, with Claudius and Polonius lurking behind one of the doors, a two-way mirror. The scale is huge and would be totally inappropriate to the restricted field of depth of a television screen, where close-ups, two-shots, and the occasional three-shot are the norm.

The book suggests ways of using weaker productions—and there are many—for teaching purposes. Too often teachers have been stuck with bad productions that make Shakespeare seem like far less than the exciting playwright he continues to be. How do we translate that disadvantage into effective teaching strategies?

One of the most difficult tasks for any teacher of English is to elicit good writing from students. The approach through film and television will produce good writing, and this book suggests how to encourage it by showing how to talk about production. It covers defining a director's approach to a given script, looking at ways of framing the action, using some of the newer critical paradigms, and dealing with camera technique. The goal here is to give the teacher and the student mastery over material that otherwise becomes coercive and controlling.

Since Shakespeare pervades the English-speaking culture, the book looks briefly at some of the many offshoots from Shakespeare into popular films, including *Star Trek, LA Story,* and *The Last Action Hero.* Other examples abound, of course. This book also looks at an approach to Shakespeare that many teachers have begun to use: the trial format. Since a trial of Hamlet exists on cassette, it is examined in detail.

The book lists major resources available: film and television productions and books that will inform the approach in ways that go beyond this effort.

Part I ends with an evaluation of recent work in the area of Shakespeare on film. This field is rapidly expanding as new films come into being, and it includes the popular press as it responds to new films. It follows, then, that teachers must be alert to the influx of material into the discourse. One useful student assignment, for example, is to gather the reviews of a particular film and write a paper on critical response to it. The student learns not just about what was said but about the criteria for judgment. Is a new Shakespeare film, for example, being judged against other films emerging at a particular moment, or against other Shakespeare films? In other words, is a court of critical appeal apparent, and, if so, what is it?

Part II provides examples of critical inquiry. Is Malvolio a subject of comedy? The generic approach is still useful even if seemingly obsolete in today's critical armories. What is the effect of editing on the finished film? The recent *Othello* makes Othello not just Iago's victim but the editor's as well. What of allusion to a prior work, as in the case of Branagh's charming little film, *A Midwinter's Tale*? How does setting dictate what can happen there? Edzard's *As You Like It* and Loncraine's *Richard III* are cases in point. How does a film's opening sequence dictate what follows? Over seventy years of *Hamlet* films provide some responses, and the approach of another *Hamlet* in December 1996 leaves the question open-ended. How does history itself, or the passage of time, affect content? Several different Pistols, from film and television versions of *Henry V,* suggest some answers.

In each case—genre, editing, allusion, setting, opening, and historicist—
the examples provided in the book do not exhaust the almost infinite number of areas for exploration that open out from this basic approach to
teaching Shakespeare. The field is vast and growing. This book shows how
to make it one's own and thus how to participate fully in an exciting adventure that becomes central to teaching and learning, and our imaginative lives
as well.

I

THEORIES, TECHNIQUES, AND RESOURCES

As I write, in mid-1996, several films based on Shakespearean scripts have already appeared, and several more are on the way. A front-page story in *Variety* earlier this year reports "H'wood Going Over-Bard in Quest for Will Power" (Cox 1996, 22–28). Kenneth Branagh, one of the chief agents behind the explosion of Shakespeare films, reports that "around the world now, when people are studying Shakespeare, they pull out the latest video version. That's confirmed by my mailbag" (Cox 1996, 115).

As gratifying as this sudden influx of new material is to those of us who have worked in the area of Shakespeare on film, it is a mixed blessing. Unless the materials are used intelligently, they will become just a few rounds of the media bombardment to which we and our students are being subjected. When the films become cassettes, as they are all destined to be, they can all too easily become part of the "culture" that Bill Moyers describes: "You can turn off your own television set, but you cannot turn off the environment of television. It goes on without you. It's not just the networks, it's the music video, the movie, the trailer—it's the culture that mediates between us and the world" (PBS, 10 January 1995).

People set a problem and then proclaim themselves experts and say, "I can solve it for you!" Much of the cold war emerged from the simultaneous creation of and solution to a problem. Vietnam remains an example.

But a problem does exist: not just the media but our understanding of them and the uses we put them to. To use *"film* as a blanket term for all formats," says Hardy Cook, as Jo McMurtry does in her very useful *Shakespeare Films in the Classroom*, is to mislead the student by "leveling . . . the distinctions . . . between productions conceived for the 'big' screen and for television, or between productions that interpret the plays visually, eliminating much of the language in the interest of images and productions that essentially record stage performances. . . . These are distinctions that I find very useful" (Cook 1994, 77). So do I.

In a recent book on teaching Shakespeare, we are told that "for [the execution of Cawdor] the Roman Polanski film is the best because the camera shows many full-body shots so students can see where actors move—it even shows Cawdor hanging. The Royal Shakespeare Company and the BBC productions . . . show more closeups" (Renino 1993, 211). But the latter two are television productions, not films. The Royal Shakespeare version uses intense close-ups, even a chiaroscuro tonality. The Polanski film uses a field of depth and location shooting unavailable to television, which is largely studio bound. In the Polanski film we see Cawdor. We do not in the script. We even hear him cry, "God save the King!" before he plunges, neck locked to a chain, from a precipice. We watch the chain snap taut. This scene, like the murder of Duncan, the nakedness of Lady Macbeth, and Donalbain's seeking out of the Weird Sisters at the end, are added by Polanski or, in the case of Lady Macbeth's nightgown, subtracted.

To conflate film and television, not to ask students to make distinctions between the media, to ignore the ways in which a given production deviates, by addition or subtraction, from an inherited script, to neglect to ask what a script *is* is to smudge distinctions just when they should be explored and to deny students a crucial aspect of their education: that is, an understanding of how the media work. And what happens when Shakespeare is translated to television or film? We are told that "video is excellent for teaching Shakespeare . . . because . . . students come to us with thousands of hours of TV and movie watching under their belts" (LoMonico 1994, 219–20). Perhaps it is under their belts, but can they describe the experience analytically, or plain the difference between a light-sensitive medium and a cathode ray tube being bombarded with electrons, begin to explore the differences between what can happen on a large movie screen and a much smaller television set, talk intelligently about the differences in expectation between watching a show at home on television and going to a cinema complex to see a film? Being a frequent flyer does not mean that one knows how to fly the airplane, and one can drown without knowing the formula H_2O.

Teachers are encouraged to permit students to see four different *Othellos* "on film" (Newlin and Poole 1995, 178). The productions suggested are the Suzman, the BBC, the Bard, and the Welles. Only one of these is a film. The Suzman is a tape of an actual stage production, the Bard a version of stage production designed for television, and the BBC a studio television production. The Welles is a film that uses a lot of black-and-white texture in the sets, as Anthony Davies (1988) and Jack Jorgens (1977) demonstrate. It employs deep-field work that is likely to be lost on cassette. If we do not permit students to question the material and technical means whereby Shakespeare is translated and transmitted or if we assume that they already know, we rob them of a central segment of their ongoing education. Here the teacher is told to "ask one or two people to follow along, in the text to see what lines have been cut" (Newlin and Poole 1995, 178). That is hardly a valid response to the issue of editing, particularly when it comes to shaping a film script.

What we observe on the screen—film or television—and not on a printed page is a relationship between word and image. Stephen Hearst observes of television that

a written text on the right-hand side of any script page which makes complete sense in itself is a bad text. What are the pictures there for? . . . The words, except in exceptional circumstances, need to follow the pictures. . . . Pictures have their own grammar, their own logic . . . and cannot easily be kept waiting. . . . To such a picture you could speak no more than about 25 words. . . . [L]anguage seems to play a secondary role in television. (1978, 4–5)

As Peter Hall suggests, in Shakespeare, "what is meant is said. Even his stage action is verbalized before or after the event. This is bad screen writing. A good film script relies on contrasting visual images. What is spoken is of secondary importance. And so potent is the camera in convincing us that we are peering at reality, that dialogue is best underwritten or elliptical" (1969). The great Russian filmmaker Grigori Kozintsev agrees, calling "half of the text of any play a diffused remark that the author wrote in order to acquaint actors as thoroughly as possible with the heart of the action to be played" (1966, 215). In other words, actors and directors collaborate with the original work. This is particularly true of film.

All of us spend time with film and television, so it is not a foreign world (as "Shakespeare" tends to be for many students). Working with film and television is challenging, partly because film asks for some critical vocabulary, partly because television tries to hide from objective analysis, and partly because the scripts themselves do not meet student demand that they be taught only from inside their own cultural experience, which sometimes means that students be "taught" what they already know. Still, education should involve challenges, for student and teacher, and this field is interesting and not difficult.

George W. Slover (1990), using Paul Ricoeur's idea that reading aims at ownership of a text and always involves extensions of self-understanding, argues for vigorous revival of a pedagogy in which students speak and act Shakespeare's text—to reverse the growing dependency on videos. Assisted by informed teaching, speaking and acting foster personal engagement with Shakespeare's language and its power to enliven the body and the imagination, a process subverted by ready-made video images. Slover's teaching model uses *Romeo and Juliet* 1.1.1–75 for illustration and shows that enactments become the points of departure for debate on interpretation, for writing and formal language study. As opposed to video-centered teaching, enactment contributes importantly to gains in literacy but presupposes radical reform in teaching teachers Shakespeare.

Slover would counter or slow the trend noted by biopsychologist Sherry Dingman of Marist College, who suggests that

children today are developing awesome capabilities in their right cerebral hemispheres at the expense of left-hemisphere skills. The left cerebral cortex is specialized to process language and abstract functions such as translating a narrative from a book into a visual image in the mind. The right cerebral cortex is specialized to process visual imagery, such as video. The faster and more intense the visual information, the more work and practice the right brain gets. The result is a generation of children who may be deficient in left-hemisphere skills, and who can become addicted to the fast-action visual feast. By contrast, the "camera angle" in a classroom or a book never changes. This helps explain why children seem to pay more attention to videogames and electronic media than they do when they read or listen to a lecture. . . . Does this mean the brain is changing in an evolutionary sense? Not that obviously. The genetic blueprint takes thousands of years to vary significantly. But for all practical purposes our culture has changed the way the brain develops. (Schwartz 1995, 28)

Slover is absolutely right to oppose plopping students down in front of, say, the BBC *Romeo and Juliet* (Zeffirelli, we must remember, included "brief nudity," and still does, and students, if they see that film at all, often get a further edited version in their classrooms) and pretending that we are doing anything but avoiding our responsibilities. "Shakespeare's plays," Brian Gibbons says, "are designed deliberately to expand the mind—to generate a sense of concentrated vigorous life in emotions and ideas, to promote as multiple an awareness as possible of differing facts of a story; and that this aim, already discernible in Shakespeare's earliest work, is at the core of his development, and of his power and distinctiveness as an artist" (1993). Gibbons gives us a major reason that we do not want to base our pedagogy on a single interpretation of any given script.

Slover nicely defines the irony "that television should furnish the remedy for the condition [students' lack of understanding of their language and lack of skill in using it] of which it is, at least in part, the cause" (1990). Peter Reynolds argues, "Systematic incorporation of television and videotape into our teaching should be used to *reinforce* verbal literacy, not as a substitution for, or distraction from, reading and writing skills" (1991). But is not production the goal of a script? Are not the words on the page intended for translation into formats that once included only stage, and only a very specific stage at one point, but that now include many different stages and media undreamed of in Shakespeare's dramaturgy? In other words, performance is the goal. Must that mean only student performance? To have students look at productions other than their own can be an extension of what they have worked out with the script. To encourage students to make their own tapes or, if copyright is a problem, to cue up excerpts for presentation to a seminar, tapes or excerpts based on something in a script that has attracted the students can give the students mastery over the material and show them how many valid options exist within the script: "*If* you have tears" (where have they been until now?). "If *you* have tears" (the way the line scans, suggesting, *I* have wept, can you?). "If you *have* tears" (are you totally devoid of compassion?). "If you have *tears*" (along with the other manifestations of grief). Charlton Heston, in a very undistinguished version of *Julius Caesar,* says, "You gentle Romans," cynically as he picks up the voices of the crowd, not as part of his opening appeal to the crowd that he will transform into a mob. We are unlikely to accept that reading as an option unless we hear an actor make the choice.

Furthermore, while most Fortinbras's say, "Take up the bodies," Q2 has him say, "Take up the body." Presumably Fortinbras means Hamlet's body and is using that body and the funeral he will give it as transitional elements in his own elevation. That makes sense of his conjectural "coronation" of Hamlet ("He was likely, had he been put on . . .") and shows Fortinbras as a skillful politician, aware that he is moving from "body natural" (I) to "body politic" (we) and that Hamlet's "voice," which Horatio has promised, is important in Fortinbras's gaining "the election." The textual difference gives students a choice to make and permits teachers to show how Fortinbras cleverly contains and redirects the violence of "the field [which] here shows much amiss" to his own advantage and within the premises defined by Kantorowitz in his seminal *The King's Two Bodies.*

Those of us who are interested in film and video should teach from that expertise while admitting its limitations. One of the strengths of the approach through video is that it allows for working outward from the image on the screen to other approaches, even including the textual. The two basic reasons for using video are that (1) plays with more than one version on cassette can be contrasted in style, scenic emphasis, characterization, and interpretation of lines and (2) television and other media (film, and stage, and types of stage) must be examined. The alternative is the tube as baby-sitter for all ages, as opposed to the good audience for Shakespeare that will encourage more good Shakespeare into being. When students recognize, for example, that television is a "fourth-wall" medium, they begin to understand that the medium, if not totally the message, defines what can occur within it. They also begin to recognize that our own expectations condition what can occur within the space of performance.

Comparing and contrasting the same scene in two or more versions of the same script teaches the student to look for detail. Suddenly his or her writing moves out of the wallow of adolescent generalization and into a mature exploration and evaluation of distinctions that directors and actors

are making—and that students are also making. The often sudden crystal-
lization of a student's prose can be remarkable when the topic is his or hers:
the chalice in *Hamlet,* the Third Murderer, battle scenes in Olivier's *Henry
V* and *Richard III,* Jane Howell's *Henry VI* and *Richard III,* and Branagh's
Henry V, the depiction of Caliban and of Ariel, the use of animation for a
Shakespearean script, and so on.

The recent debate in Great Britain over standardized testing for all students focuses many of the issues in teaching Shakespeare. Shakespeare in
Great Britain is a function of "the sensitive reader apprehending the meaning of the isolated play," says John Collick. "The pupil's response is carefully
engineered, and very definite distinctions are created between correct and
incorrect interpretations. Not surprisingly the 'correct' response tends to
endorse the ideology of a capitalist economy" (1989, 4). "Teaching Shakespeare is not," asserts Jane Coles, "about studying character-theme-and-plot
in individual plays. This view simply invites thoughtless rehashes of Brad-
leyan analysis and willfully ignores all literary theory post-Leavis" (1992).
The process works, according to James Wood, this way:

Cultural materialism does not believe in radical texts; it believes in radical readers.
To sit in a theatre, inspired, surrounded by people similarly moved, people asked by
Shakespeare to reinvent their lives, to "take upon us the mystery of things, / as if we
were god's spies," is to know that Shakespeare's meanings are not static, not fixed,
but radical, stealthy and searing. (1993)

Rosalind King, however, delivers a denunciation of newer critical modes for
political impotence:

The greatest indictment of the various schools and "isms" that form the more prominent faces of contemporary literary criticism is that, despite the avowed political
stance that most of them adopt, none is actually capable of responding to the greatest political challenge that the subject "literary criticism" has yet had to face, at least
in this country—namely the British Government's attempt to control it through the
use of testing based on particular limited interpretations of an equally limited range
of select texts. (1993)

John Major, a Tory politician, chimes in with a bracing list: "People say
there is too much jargon in education. So let me give you some of my own.
Knowledge. Discipline. Tables. Sums. Dates. Shakespeare. British history.
Standard English. Grammar. Spelling. Marks. Tests" (Gibson 1993, 2). The
problem may be that such items are seen as a goal, or end product, as opposed to elements that lead to further learning. "Shakespeare," at least, is
not something we "have" and seems to be on the wrong list for more reasons than can be briefly adduced.

A recent article makes the sweeping statement that "researchers have con-
cluded that watching any TV show is a meaninglessly passive activity"

(Tashman 1994, 21). Any TV show? Yes, says Paul Robinson. "It can't" educate, he says. "Complete ignorance really would be preferable, because ignorance at least preserves a mental space that might someday be filled with real knowledge, or some approximation of it" (1978, 14). What about television as an element in the educational process, as opposed to "educator"? "On a recent Sunday, Joanna Cleveland made sure she had a supply of chips and soda at home because her daughter, Meghan, was expecting friends. The teenagers, sophomores at South Portland [Maine] High, spent the afternoon talking, joking and having a marvelous time—all over a video of 'Julius Caesar' " (Lau 1994, 1A). TV as static medium induces passivity. Like any other machine, it has to have a purpose, and in most cases the content of the machine does not provide purpose, even on a cathode tube. A radar screen showing a line of thunder storms, for example, does not recommend response. Response is dictated by the observer. Watching *Julius Caesar* as part of a course on Shakespeare is not a meaninglessly passive activity. As David Hale argues, "Reading video instead of watching television becomes a vital supplement to reading Shakespeare" (1995, 22).

One goal in having students look at Shakespeare on different media is to get them to examine the nature of the media themselves. As one who remembers World War II vividly, I am haunted by the possibility that the German people might have understood how they were being manipulated—by Leni Reifenstahl's *Triumph of the Will*, for example—if they had had a grasp of how the media work. This is probably an ongoing fear, and a growing one, since we seem to be educating the manipulators, the people with a stake in the system of indoctrination, as Noam Chomsky would say, and making sure that the proliferating underclass lacks any vestiges of formal education. "Political pitchmen," says Russell Baker, "turned politics into television 40 years ago." It follows, as Baker suggests, that "candidates are merely products being marketed to gullible masses" and that "a candidate cannot be elected unless he stops acting human and starts behaving like a product" (1996, A19). It follows that those who watch television are consumers and no more than that.

When students recognize that television is an outgrowth of radio, they can begin to understand some of the assumptions and limitations of TV. If they know that films come from the silent screen, they can answer other questions. Special effects, so important to recent films, from *Raiders of the Lost Ark* to *Frankenstein*, are a product of the silent screen, though techniques have become more sophisticated since 1925. But elaborate special effects, so powerful in the darkened auditorium that faces a huge screen, are diminished on television, where the field of depth is shallow. Television has a normalizing tendency, so that the supernatural tends to become, on television, the product of a single disturbed psyche, as opposed to an aberration in the cosmos. Television should be a good medium for Shakespeare because, coming from radio as it does and having a small screen, it can and must contain more words than film. Television, however, unlike film, cannot contain the larger scenes of a Shakespearean script or suggest the supernatural, as film obviously can. The shots in television are simpler and tend, with the development of standard techniques, to incorporate a close-up, a reaction shot, and a two-shot in their three-camera format. Films made for television tend toward televisual values—their camera techniques, "naturalism," and shallow field. All of these considerations impinge on the question of Shakespeare on film or on television and on the complicated issue of televised live performance of a Shakespeare play, of which many examples are available. Does the fact of an audience help recreate a sense of live performance? Does stage performance, with its tendency toward exaggeration and projection, translate to a medium where "microacting" tends to be the rule? Can the three-camera format work with a stage production? We cannot begin to evaluate the production until we examine the medium in which the script is transmitted. These may seem like very sophisticated questions, but they can elicit enthusiasm and intelligent response from students. Film and TV are, after all, the media they claim for their own. Teachers can enlist that claim and energize it within agendas that help students deconstruct effectively as opposed to self-destructing.

Many teachers in the late 1970s and early 1980s did sit their students down to stare at some very bad BBC-TV productions. The students were bored, and the teachers were in the false position of trying to defend, say, that terrible *Romeo and Juliet* or that cramped *Julius Caesar*. But the quality of the productions was not the only issue. Television as static medium induces passivity; like any other machine, it has to have a purpose. Purpose is a function of interpretation. When the purpose becomes mindless consumption, television has become a version of the invention of the mad scientist that turns on him and becomes his master.

I advocate an involvement of student and teacher in an examination of an art form—a production of Shakespeare—and an implication of student and teacher in history, his or her own—since individual subjectivity is a major factor in response to performance—and that of the moment at which a specific film or television version may have been created, since time and place determine what the result can be, as both product and interpretation. Instead of merely seating students in front of the tube, we can unashamedly make what appears there the focus of our study. If we help students to understand the media, we empower them.

We teach what we enjoy, what we feel comfortable doing. The trick is to empower ourselves. This power then can become available to students. One option is to have students pick an aspect of a play—a character or scene—and contrast that element as it occurs in different productions. As they work, students notice differences and begin to describe them. Their writing takes a leap toward maturity, an inevitable consequence of their suddenly strengthened powers of observation. If they present their contrasting versions on cassette to the class—a good approach in a small seminar—the class itself contributes to the process of perception, so that a "corporate mind" is energized, as opposed to the single student struggling at the eleventh hour with a paper he or she is not interested in, based on a topic only dimly defined at best or selected from a list of the instructor's devising and therefore in no way enlisting a student's commitment.

Since some of the chapters in this part are self-contained, they do not require the thrust of an ongoing thesis for their comprehension. Self-containment does, however, require some reiteration of basic points, that is, ways of discerning and phrasing what is observed.

REFERENCES

Baker, Russell. 1996. "Man and Product." *New York Times,* 9 July, A19.

Coles, Jane. 1992. "Teaching Shakespeare." *English and Media* (Autumn).

Collick, John. 1989. *Shakespeare, Cinema, and Society.* Manchester: Manchester University Press.

Cook, Hardy M. 1994. "Table of Contents." *Shakespeare Newsletter* 44, no. 4, 223, 77.

Cox, Dan. 1996. "H'wood Going Over-Bard in Quest for Will Power." *Variety*, 22–28 January, 1, 115.

Davies, Anthony. 1988. *Filming Shakespeare's Plays.* Cambridge: Cambridge University Press.

Gibbons, Brian. 1993. *Shakespeare and Multiplicity.* Cambridge: Cambridge University Press.

Gibson, Rex, ed. 1993. *Shakespeare and Schools*, 2.

Hale, David. 1995. "*Henry V:* 5.2." *Shakespeare and the Classroom* 3, no. 1, 21–23.

Hall, Peter. 1969. "Shakespeare's *Dream.*" *Times*, 26 January.

Hearst, Stephen. 1978. "It Ain't Necessarily So." *New Review* 5, no. 1, 3–13.

Jorgens, Jack. 1977. *Shakespeare on Film.* Bloomington: Indiana University Press.

Kantorowitz, Ernst. 1941. *The King's Two Bodies.* Princeton: Princeton University Press.

King, Rosalind. 1993. "Teaching Shakespeare." *Times Literary Supplement*, 3 September.

Kozintsev, Grigori. 1966. *Shakespeare: Time and Conscience.* London: Dobson.

Lau, Edie. 1994. "Parents Part of Teaching Team." *Portland Press Herald*, 4 October, 1A.

LoMonico, Michael. 1994. "Teaching Shakespeare with Video." In *Shakespeare Set Free.* New York: Washington Square Press.

McMurtry, Jo. 1994. *Shakespeare Films in the Classroom: A Descriptive Guide.* Hamden, Conn.: Archon.

Newlin, Louisa Foulke, and Mary Winslow Poole. 1995. "*Othello.*" In *Shakespeare Set Free.* New York: Washington Square Press.

Renino, Christopher. 1993. "*Macbeth.*" In *Shakespeare Set Free.* New York: Washington Square Press.

Reynolds, Peter. 1991. In *Shakespeare in the Changing Curriculum*, edited by Lesley Aers and Nigel Wheale. London: Routledge.

Robinson, Paul. 1978. "TV Can't Educate." *New Republic*, 5–12 August.

Schwartz, Evan I. 1995. "The Changing Minds of Children: Growing Up in a Context-free Reality." *Omni*, January, 28.

Slover, George. 1990. "Video Versus Voice: Teaching Students and Teachers Shakespeare." *Nebraska English Journal* (Spring/Summer).

Tashman, Billie. 1994. "Sorry Ernie—TV Isn't Teaching." *New York Times*, 12 November, 21.

Wood, James. 1993. "Teaching Shakespeare." *TLS*, 23 April.

1

Background

THE MEDIA AND THE MESSAGE

Film and television are different media, emerging from different heritages that define what they are. Film comes from the silent film and still relies more on image than on sound or the spoken word. TV comes from radio and can include more language than film. TV also requires language to augment the inevitably small image. Film emerges from the photograph of the mid-nineteenth century and is therefore not limited to modernist premises (thematic coherence, for example) as TV tends to be. Film, particularly black-and-white film, can create a field of depth that TV cannot emulate. A television transmitter converts light rays into electric signals for modulation on a radio carrier wave or for transmission over wires. The receiver reconverts the signals into electron beams that bombard the fluorescent screen of a cathode ray tube, reproducing the original image. Film is a light-sensitive medium. Light shines through images that change infinitesimally from frame to frame and projects the moving image onto a screen. The cassette tends to erase differences, but film on cassette suffers, as do films made for TV, which must reduce themselves to the conceptual space that the medium provides. The cassette becomes television, with all of its disadvantages and none of the advantages of film.

A magnetic medium that bombards a cathode ray tube with electrons physically alters a light-sensitive medium in the process. More important is that the dimensions of film are greatly reduced on television. TV has a field of depth that reaches to the back of the picture tube. Furthermore, color flattens depth. Color TV must be a close-up medium. Film can use close-ups, of course, but can also employ deep-field shots, particularly in its black-and-white manifestation. Good examples are Olivier's *Hamlet* and Kurosawa's *Throne of Blood*. Even color film will mute its colors when it uses deep-field shots, as in the opening of Polanski's *Macbeth* or Olivier's Bosworth Field in *Richard III*. Television's advantage over film when it comes to a Shakespeare script is that TV is a more linguistic medium than film, requiring words to augment images low in sensory data. Film can still incorporate long stretches of silence, which television cannot tolerate. Of course, the title cards in silent films can be very intrusive and often represent an uneasy marriage of print media and image, and they are timed for slow readers.

These observations are necessary as a preliminary to any response to a Shakespearean script as performed in any medium. The space—stage (and type of stage, size of auditorium), film, television—defines what can occur within it. We must put the script against the space. *Julius Caesar*, for example, runs into massive problems with television, since the medium cannot handle large scenes. One reason that political conventions in the United States have become so dull is the necessity of packaging them for television. Contrast their scaled-down formats with, for example, Reifenstahl's film, *The Triumph of the Will*. It is not just that the outcomes of U.S. conventions are no longer in doubt—as was the 1940 Republican convention in its presidential choice or the crucial 1944 Democratic convention in its vice-presidential candidate—but television does demand the happy ending, and everything about a convention is designed with that end in mind.

Television is virtually unreadable. Its camera formats are entirely predictable, even including a mandatory shot of the interviewer listening to the person being interviewed to indicate that the program involves more than just a talking head. Television is easily readable in one sense. It mission is to sell products. Caryn James asks, "How much does television reflect reality and how much does it create reality?" (1996, H27). As a subartistic medium, television and reality exchange their formats, each conditioning the other until they have become indistinguishable. The marketplace is virtually ubiquitous in each environment. In film, we respond to what the camera is doing and can usually describe its activity. On television, the camera is a much less visible intermediary. We believe we are looking at whatever the camera is showing. The camera work is predictable and hard to describe because of its pursuit of a formula that incorporates limited points of view. What happens to a Shakespeare script when it confronts television is a question to be asked—and answered in various ways from the many examples available.

Here are some questions to ask students: For what space was this production designed? What are the difficulties that this script encounters in this space? If television cannot deal with scope and depth, film cannot include all that language. Immediately, then, another question becomes, for film, How is the script edited? Words in film are greatly subordinate to what we see. "Dialogue? We had faces!" says Norma Desmond of silent films in *Sunset*

Boulevard. Another question is, What specifically, does the filmmaker sub-stitute for the language? Or, How does the filmmaker support the language with imagery? Look at the radically steep steps in the Mankiewicz *Julius Caesar*, which create long and ominous shadows and show Antony against the sealike mob as if he were a kind of a malign creator.

We see the Olivier *Henry V* because of the Branagh. Olivier's fixed cam-era suggests a defined view of history. His long shots provide the big picture. Branagh's seemingly random montage technique suggests the chaos of a bat-tle whose only certainty seems to be the cutpurse wending among the corpses. We see zeitgeist at work, of course, and history. A film made just be-fore D-Day 1944 (though not released until October) will show a different war than one made after the Vietnam and Falklands wars. Certainly our own view of war is not the same as it would have been had we been of the Allied side in 1944 looking at Olivier's film. Notice, however, that Branagh alludes to the Olivier film during the battle with a close-up of a horse that Olivier also uses as a synecdoche for the battle.

Students see the script through production. They see it as a script, full of options and decisions that must be made. The genius of the Shakespeare script is that it was designed to be interpreted—not just presented—by Shakespeare's company, and it still is. The potential meanings are there, awaiting our own times and understandings to show us what the meanings are. The best scene in the 1995 Stratford (Canada) *Macbeth*, for example, might have been the one in which Lady Macduff fought so furiously for her children, eliciting an enthusiastic response from the audience. But that scene is not just a function of our wish that Nicole had fought against O. J. in his documented beatings of her. It is there—"the poor wren, / The most diminu-tive of birds, will fight, / Her young ones in her nest, against the owl." The production made the line a context for the scene that follows it.

Students who are shown two or three different versions of the same mo-ment in a given script can see some of the options in that moment and how the decision has been conditioned by the medium in which the production is occurring. A good choice is to have them pick a spot they are interested in and, if the class format permits, show the versions to the class and lead a dis-cussion. (My success here has been with first-year college seminars of about twelve to fifteen students, but the format works with advanced placement classes in high school.) Students should look at the plays as scripts—sites for performative response—as opposed to books—just another something to be read. Reading is a preliminary activity— necessary but not an end in itself.

THE CONCEPT OF SCRIPT

The plays are meant to be produced, not just read, but reading is an impor-tant precondition to a production, particularly for a director and the actors. A good production should make sense to a spectator, whether that person has read the play or not, but a knowledge of the play and the possibilities inherent in the script is useful before one encounters a production in any medium. The script is designed as a set of choices for actors, not as something to be delivered in some standard or accepted way. The joy of watching a production is in the observation of the ways in which the many options in any script are confronted. A number of plays—*Macbeth, Romeo and Juliet*, and *A Midsummer Night's Dream*, for example—have televised stage versions available, making for vivid generic contrasts between them and conventional studio productions. Even a televised stage production can communicate some of the excitement attendant on being within the same space as the actors.

The word on the page—the so-called text of Shakespeare—is incomplete. The word awaits incarnation: the voices of actors, the response of spectators. Philip Edwards once said that "the nearer we get to the stage, the further we get from Shakespeare" (1968, 4). Shakespeare for him is a vast platonic storehouse of universals best not diminished by taking on the manifestation of specific forms. And Shakespeare does partake of something akin to universality. His works are inarticulate only where the minarets of Islam shadow the sidewalks, but that universality is expressed only, I would argue, in manifold specific ways, in the near infinity of choices available to actors as they decide how to perform a script and in the ways in which a script can be interpreted in the most local of terms. Actors choose in the light of their understanding of the words, an understanding that incorporates a sense of the moment in which the words will be understood by an audience. In other words, universality does not encompass infinity; it is made up of infinite numbers of possibilities that are a function not just of words on the page but also of the moment in which those words are spoken. Shakespeare may be ubiquitous but also local. The movement of whatever history may be adds to the number of possibilities. The meanings are there (Thompson 1988, 81). They await the historical circumstances that will make them clear. In 1972, John Barton brought *Richard II* to Brooklyn, into a society experiencing Watergate. Richard Pascoe and Ian Richardson alternated every other night in the two main roles, but there was a third Richard among them. Houseman and Mankiewicz intended that their 1953 *Julius Caesar* remind people of the Führer at Nuremberg or Mussolini gesturing from his balcony, but the film derived response from what Sam Crowl calls the contemporary "hysteria about supposed subversives" (Davies & Wells 1994, 149). The intention of directors is often confuted by the powerful pressures of the zeitgeist into which the production is thrust. The concept of an atemporal production of Shakespeare is just that—a concept available only when there is no production to refute it. My generalization applies to ontogeny as well. Some years ago, I took my nine-year-old daughter to a performance of *A Midsummer Night's Dream*. She liked the production, all right, but remarked that "Puck's cartwheels were terrible."

That is an extreme example of history's function on the inherited script, but we can discern history in the script as it is performed at any given moment. Looking at performance, like reading criticism, is an archaeological expedition in which we may learn something about Shakespeare and also about the historical moment that is producing that version of Shakespeare. Thus we do learn about Shakespeare. He is of all time only as his plays reflect the form and pressure of an age.

Consider the over fifty years of film and television versions of the rejection of Falstaff at the end of *Henry IV, Part II*. This is a fairly straightforward moment. Hal has learned how to handle Falstaff from Falstaff, from the many times the prince has been bested by Falstaff. At the end, Falstaff runs headlong into the trap Hal has been setting from the first. It is not Hal, of course, but Henry V who denies Falstaff language—"Reply not to me with a fool-born jest." "May not young men die as well as old?"—Is that what Falstaff is about to say, predicting the "Small time" the new king has ahead of *him*? Without language with which to create a countering scenario, another world, Falstaff has had it, and so the king can measure Falstaff's grave as he measured Hotspur's: for Hotspur, "two paces of the vilest earth"; for Falstaff, "the grave doth gape . . . thrice wider than for other men."

Notice the differences in the treatments of film and television. We get personalized interpretations: Olivier's Falstaff is forced to listen over and over again to the king's rejecting voice, until death turns off the speaker. England is at war, in 1414 as in 1944, and there is no more room for Falstaff in 1414 than there is for Lord Haha in 1944. In the Olivier film, the rejection has already occurred (as it has in the Shakespeare canon). Falstaff is a temporary survivor of the riotous career of someone called Hal, but Hal has renamed himself. The BBC-TV version (1980) creates a small parenthesis out of the rejection—a delay along the king's triumphal route. While television must whittle the scene down, Henry's speech in the play is a public pronouncement meant to be rebroadcast throughout his kingdom as a central component of the sudden reformation he has planned and of which the bishops talk at the beginning of the next play. It is to be taken as a warning to the misleaders and the misled of Henry's kingdom. In the BBC version, the rejection tends to be personal, not political. TV lacks the width and the depth to suggest the larger dimension, though this production, with its ground-level camera, does give a good sense of a crowd forming and breaking up, even as Falstaff's certain hopes are fragmented. Pennington, in the Bogdanov version (1989), hates to be rejecting Falstaff, but one must ask, Why? The rejection represents a first public triumph in the new king's reign.

Branagh, in his 1989 film, suggests that big public scenes are no longer the fashion. He embeds a flashback to Falstaff in his film as Burgundy burbles on about war and peace. The psyche of the English king spaces out for the moment, after all that tension, and places the words themselves in the tavern, which is not the site the script provides. Within this regress, Falstaff intuits Henry's words from his facial expression. The sequence represents an exploration of what historicists call interiority. Welles's Falstaff (1965) breaks through the many barriers, military and ceremonial, hedging the king and into the cathedral. There he is! Hal! "I speak to thee my heart!" "I know you all," Hal had said. "I know thee not, old man," Henry says. At the end, Falstaff smiles, as if to say, I taught you well, didn't I? And Henry V strides away into history.

Olivier's use of the rejection is a kind of afterthought, intentionally set into the film to suggest the single-mindedness of Henry's war effort. Falstaff dies alone, hearing those words, trying to get his own word in, and falling back in silence. Welles's rejection scene is the triumphant conclusion of a sequence of events. One is a small moment in Henry's career: his first public speech as king. We go with Henry off to France. The second is a final moment in Falstaff's career, as Falstaff staggers off in the opposite direction of history. The same segment of script can be used to make very different points without in any way misrepresenting the script, which offers those and many other interpretations.

The important matter for teachers is not what the scene means—it means variously—but how it means on the media represented here. To televise a stage play is to be unfair to the production by "depriving the audience of an opportunity to participate in a collaborative construction of meaning" (Holderness 1986, 69). But interestingly, televised stage plays often work well on television; they can provide a sense of participation and the need to suspend disbelief. The latter necessity is seldom a component of television (Saturday morning kids' shows and presidential news conferences excepted). But I would point to Papp's *King Lear*, Epstein's *A Midsummer Night's Dream*, and a number of productions from Stratford, Ontario, as successful translations of live performance to television. Television itself can be a difficult medium for Shakespeare. Its lack of dimension in a physical sense often results in failures of emotional and intellectual depth. And our expectation conditions the result. We expect nothing, and, as the TV people say, we are getting what we want.

But have a look at the BBC-TV *Richard II*, which does well with that difficult script. A camera that can close up on individual performances has John Gielgud, Wendy Hiller, Charles Gray, Clifford Rose, Jon Finch, and Derek Jacobi to observe, and it is microacting of remarkable skill and considerable power. The production gives a sense of history on a medium where drama—the soap opera—occurs within a constant present.

Film has the field of depth and the close-up capacity that Shakespeare's scripts demand. Black-and-white film, as in Cukor's *Romeo and Juliet*, Olivier's *Hamlet*, Mankiewicz's *Julius Caesar*, and Welles's *Chimes at Midnight*, has an ability to create deep fields that color does not. Color tends to flatten depth. But film—any film—functions with the image, not the word. Shakespeare's language creates the scene. "The deep of night has crept upon our talk," says Brutus, but it is really only late afternoon on Bankside in 1600. Night is a fiction that results from our imaginative collaboration with the actors. Film can do with the camera all that the words in the script do, and, perhaps to prove the point about the image and about film's incompatibility with the spoken word, we need only to show that many more silent films were made of Shakespeare before 1927, when the Babe hit 60, Lindy flew to Paris, and Al Jolson sang "Blue Skies" in *The Jazz Singer*, than since. "At its most effective," says Wolf Rilla, film dialogue "is based on an essential inarticulacy" (1973, 89), but Shakespeare's characters are seldom inarticulate.

I stress the conceptual space to which the script is moved because this is a vital and too often unrecognized component of using film and television in teaching. We can get the students to compare and contrast and to take remarkable leaps forward in the specificity of their writing as they notice details, but the medium conditions the message; that is, the space defines what can occur within it. With the conflation of all meaning onto the cassette, it becomes more necessary to make distinctions than less. When a teacher, for example, says that the Polanski version of the Scottish play, *Macbeth*, is the best for the execution of Cawdor, the teacher ignores the fact that Polanski's film presents what is narrated by Malcolm in the script. Polanski's film adds the execution—one of his grisly impositions upon a bloody-enough script—as he does a naked Lady Macbeth, and a Donalbain at the end going off to that coven of weird ones to seek their support for his own ambition, Donalbain's anticipating the disbanding of the National Endowment for the Arts. These are the filmmaker's concepts, and we have to debate them within the context of his or her collaboration with the inherited script, not as if they came with the script. The Thames TV version, with Ian McKellen and Judi Dench, occurs in radical close-up with a lot of unconventional lighting, but it is a television production that emerges from a live studio production. For better or for worse, it gives the report of Cawdor's execution as scripted. If we use video in our classrooms, we owe it to students to assist them in the process of "reading video instead of watching television" (Hale 1995, 21). Suffice it that video does not emerge as a time-saver for those who teach Shakespeare, but it issues its own challenges and offers further chances to learn about Shakespeare in production. If the issue of education is the growth of the teacher, here is an area where we have plenty of growing to do.

ACTUAL AND CONCEPTUAL SPACE

Space cannot be discussed "in space." It needs a filling in. Here I use as my points of reference a variety of snippets from film and television, all commercially available. The approach will suggest how a modest library of cassettes can be examined as media. They are:

Emil Jannings, *Othello* (1922)
    Emil Jannings/Ika Lenkeffy/Lya de Putti
    (Othello strangles Desdemona)

Max Reinhardt and William Dieterle, *Dream* (1935)
    Rooney/Cagney/Joe E. Brown
    (Bottom transformed)

George Cukor, *Romeo and Juliet* (1936)
    Howard/Shearer
    (Romeo enters the Capulet gardens)

Joseph L. Mankiewicz, *Julius Caesar* (1953)
    Mason/Brando
    (parts of each funeral oration)

Trevor Nunn, *Antony and Cleopatra* (1972)
    Richard Johnson/Janet Suzman
    (the opening)

David Giles, *Richard II* (1978)
    Jon Finch (Bolingbroke)
    David Swift (Northumberland)
    Charles Gray (York)
    (Bolingbroke condemns Bushy and Green)

Jonathan Miller, *King Lear* (1982)
    Gillian Barge (Goneril)
    Penelope Wilton (Regan)
    Michael Kitchen (Edmund)
    (Goneril and Regan conspire after the division of the kingdom)

Grigori Kozintsev, *Lear* (1970)
    Yuri Jarvet (Lear)
    Valentina Shandrikova (Cordelia)
    Regimentas Adomaitis (Edmund)
    (Edmund orders Lear and Cordelia to prison)

Peter Brook, *Lear* (1971)
    Paul Scofield (Lear)
    Anne-lise Gabold (Cordelia)
    Ian Hogg (Edmund)
    (Edmund orders Lear and Cordelia to prison)

Lawrence Olivier, *Henry V* (Agincourt)

Kenneth Branagh, *Henry V* (Agincourt)

Orson Welles, *Chimes at Midnight*
    Welles (Falstaff)
    Keith Baxter (King Henry V)
    (the rejection of Falstaff)

We live in the postmodernist era of multiple responses, an era at enmity with what are called totalizing myths. For Shakespeare, that is a good thing. Most critical theories can find a home in Shakespeare. The question is no longer, What does the play mean? It has never been that in production. The question has been, What do we find here on which to base our production? In other words, How does the script create meanings? A script is a set of incomplete signals—words on a page—awaiting interrogation by the imaginations of actors and spectators within a theater. Different conceptual spaces—film and television, obviously—impose challenges for the script. How does it create meanings in a black-and-white silent film? A color film? A magnetic tape making images on a cathode ray tube? A cassette? I will offer some examples and a few answers to these questions. A space-time continuum exists here, of course. Space has changed in time, from Shakespeare's open stage to the proscenium formats after the Restoration, to the gaslit, limelit, and electrically illuminated stages of the nineteenth century, to silent film, sound film, color film, television, color television, and the all-embracing but not necessarily satisfactory environment of the cassette. As conceptual spaces change in time, our own sense of the performative moment changes, and that is to say nothing of the ways in which historical circumstances shape our interpretation of a given script.

By defining the space, we define what can occur within it. In the 1922 silent *Othello*, language gets in the way of action. Those title cards should give poor Desdemona plenty of time to get out of there. Language always gets in the way of action, but invariably on film, which demands a moving image. We understand why the early filmmakers liked a scene that remains the staple of films even today: the chase scene, with its uninterrupted sequences and opportunity for cross-cutting from chaser to chasee and back again, its insistence on the invention of sudden obstacles and close calls. And it may be, as Jim Andreas (1994) has suggested to me, that the "Elizabethan flow of action, unimpeded as it is by acts or scenes, anticipated and perhaps helped to precipitate the concept of cinematic montage."

With the advent of sound, fewer Shakespeare films were made than previously. Sound films were expensive and, again, the language gets in the way. John Collick makes this point in discussing Olivier's *Henry V*:

On the one hand the intricate visuals of the film need little of the text to complement their implicit reiteration of the spectacular tradition and the mythology of British wartime culture. On the other hand, Olivier and the producers of the movie definitely perceive the text as the idealized source of meaning and so the speeches are delivered with the precise and measured enunciation of a BBC radio broadcast. (1989, 50)

The sequences in two great early sound films—Bottom's translation in the Reinhardt-Dieterle *A Midsummer Night's Dream* (1935) and Romeo's entrance into the Capulet orchard in the Cukor *Romeo and Juliet* (1936)—are not silent, but they depend on the image. That is not to say that the films were not controversial. Samuel Crowl, for example, objects to Bottom's awareness of his transformation in that reverse narcissism when Bottom sees his face in the pond: "Bottom's beauty is his obliviousness; his absolute lack of self-consciousness is his most stunning quality. The film's translation of Bottom is ass-backwards" (1992, 66). And certainly the *Romeo and Juliet* has been cursed forever by its casting of a thirty-six-year-old Juliet (Norma Shearer) and a forty-two-year-old Romeo (Leslie Howard). The 1953 *Julius Caesar* places the orations against a clifflike set of steps that suggests how far power seems to be from the person in the street and that pulls the long shadows of history from the speakers. In front is the crowd. James Mason's Brutus handles it all quite well, quite rationally, even absorbing into his agenda the crowd's gasp as Antony enters with the corpse of Caesar on the word *death*. But even if we do not know the play, we know the crowd has not heard enough as Brutus exits by himself, and we see Antony closer to the crowd that he will invite even closer as he devolves them to a mob.

Film can create special effects. Mickey Rooney can become a hound. In the deep field of a film, a donkey can be scared off by a fraternity brother. A moonlit night with an ornamental pool becomes at once real and surreal as the camera tracks beside Romeo. Monumental Rome is suddenly inhabited by people and by our imaginations as well. Notice that these are all black-and-white films. Black-and-white creates depth and forces us to fill in the colors—if we so desire. The point can be illustrated by looking at Olivier's *Hamlet*, shot in a deep-field format and featuring a long-range love scene between Hamlet and Ophelia.

The television selections are in color. The *Antony and Cleopatra* swims in a golden haze. It does not matter that the eye is stopped by the first color it contacts. Television is not trying for depth of field. The depth that the screen allows is literally a couple of feet, as opposed to the cinema screen, which angles back through the Sears tire-patching facility to the J. C. Penney shoe department. But notice the microacting that television can provide. Richard Johnson gives a public speech about Rome's dissolution; the politician revels in the undercutting of his own position. He tries to figure Cleopatra out: "Last night you did desire it." But she has changed her mind and keeps insisting that Antony hear the messengers. The actors work superbly at role reversals. The great public man must grovel. The courtesan exposes his irresponsibility and manipulates her audience into opposing him. She exposes the powerlessness of the great man.

York (Charles Gray) responds to the brutal executions of Bushy and Green as Bolingbroke (Jon Finch) talks of a kinder, gentler policy toward the soon-to-be-deposed queen. A film director might have wanted to show the executions, as Branagh did with Bardolph in the film of *Henry V*, but on television, David Giles permits what is happening just off camera and what is being said on camera to create a zone for our response—what used to be called irony.

The competition between Goneril (Gillian Barge) and Regan (Penelope Wilton) is beautifully delineated. They have always been rivals, it seems, perhaps once for their father's affection, in what seems to have been a motherless household, but now gloating, each in turn, about who must endure his visits in the months to come. The older sister here is the more physically controlling and the more insistent. The subtexts reflect the place of each sister in the birth order hierarchy. The scene is a rack shot, with Edmund out of focus until the end. They notice him, and he inclines slightly. The sisters look at him speculatively and at each other. The future triangle is predicted. Edmund looks at the map, specifically at Gloucestershire. Television carefully done (as it seldom is) can give us language, subtlety, and relationship. It has no long distance and little middle distance, but when close-up is the right medium, it can be effective. One reason that it so seldom is is that we expect so little of it. Our expectation is part of what can occur in any given medium.

Television tends to domesticate its content—that is, to accommodate to our space, our domestic space. That is a limitation when it comes to Shakespeare, but a skillful director can give us the bigger scenes—those at court, for example—by giving us a sense of the speakers and of the reactions of the listeners, through close-ups, two- and three-person shots, and a quick glimpse of the larger space in which the conflict is occurring. On television, if a scene does occur in a space larger than a kitchen—early television plays were "kitchen table dramas"—the larger area is suggested rather than shown in detail.

The scope of the Kozintzev *King Lear*, for example, is enormous. It was filmed originally in a 70-mm format, and I recall being overwhelmed by the film when I first saw it in that format. The sequence I have selected shows Cordelia and Lear being captured; the soldiers are suddenly confused when a king and a queen turn up in the line of those surrendering. It is not just that Lear is oblivious to the danger his daughter is in and perhaps reimposes the agenda of the opening upon her, but that Edmund cannot understand what he is seeing. Lear and Cordelia "walk," says Kozintsev, "past the ranks of men armed to the teeth—like conquerors. This is the beginning of Edmund's defeat" (1972, 199). Edmund stares. Don't they know they have lost? His sudden vehemence is motivated against the subversive thesis that Lear expresses. Men are as the time is, Edmund insists. Still puzzled, Edmund goes into combat with Edgar, and gets nailed.

Kozintsev shows how one scene is at once powerfully itself and the motivation for an entire sequence of action. Brook drains the same praxis of positive meaning. A bucket with a hangman's noose sits behind Lear and Cordelia. The bucket can do nothing against the fire, but the noose will take care of Cordelia. Lear talks of firebrands but ignores the fire that is there. He says that he and Cordelia will not be separated. They are. Edmund, momentarily in power, reacts in a rage as he incarcerates those he perceives to be his enemies. He has no motive, unless the paranoia that accompanies unearned or ill-earned power is a motive. The camera moves as if it is hand held by a combat camera person at ground level—a camera person who feels that Lear is important even if the camera cannot get his face in the center of the frame. The camera work contrasts, for example, with Kozintsev's beautifully composed crane shots. We are not, in the Brook film, detached from what is happening but close to it, implicated in it, in the manner of Artaud's theater of cruelty. At the same time, however, the intentional awkwardness of technique alienates us; it calls attention to itself and our attention to what Anthony Davies calls the "film's failure to achieve the orchestrated fluidity of conventional cinematic expression" (1988, 148). We can hardly indulge in any sentimentality. There is nothing redemptive here. It is brutal, documentary, and Edmund will get his quickly enough for no particular reason in a cosmos that does not respond to our hopes for its reflection of our own sense of justice.

Brook sets out, says Davies, to "strive to disturb an audience in the same way that his insight into the play disturbs him" (1988, 149). We are not given a coherent or stable point of view here (contrast, for example, Olivier's use of camera in *Henry V*). It is conventional, often fixed, suggesting a normative view of history that Brook rejects in his version of *King Lear*. The Brook and Kozintzev films, made at the same time in the early 1970s, create a wonderful context for the exploration of contrast and for the asking of the question, What are the options when a filmmaker decides to translate a Shakespeare script to a medium for which Shakespeare did not write? And are those options the same as they would be in the late 1990s?

We see the Olivier *Henry V* better through the lens of the Branagh version. Olivier's film is stylized—a Henry V goes to Disneyland—and we expect that although his Agincourt has mud—as history suggests it did, we will not linger long in the mire. The French charge in an elegant tracking shot; a low-angle shot shows Henry's decisive arm about to drop; ultimately Henry squares off in hand-to-hand combat against Charles de la Breth, the constable of France. It is, Jack Jorgens suggests, "a detached overview" of the battle (1977, 131). Branagh shows a grimy English force looking at the French charge as if it is a tidal wave. The English archers do not send their arrows off like so many miniature Spitfires but seemingly willy-nilly, into friend and foe alike, the odds suggesting that they are much more likely to find a Frenchman than one of their own. Perhaps to suggest the randomness of battle, we watch one hapless soldier die twice, an arrow in his back each time. Pickpockets ply the muck and are themselves dispatched.

Branagh provides a brief allusion to Olivier. The latter had shown the grimacing mouth of a horse; Branagh shows a horse's frightened eye. Branagh moves to slow motion—an alienating device that insists on a fiction and a technique that suggests a nightmare—specifically, the Somme in 1917. Each film is a vivid rendering of a king and the history he dominates at a moment in history. Olivier's "personality is already complete at the start" (Donaldson 1991, 65). Branagh is finding out who he is, as the film sequences suggest. Olivier's film is framed; it begins at the Globe and ends there, as we discover that all that we have seen had been controlled by the conventions of theater with perhaps a bit of improvisation as the actor-king woos Katherine. Branagh's film conveys a more provisional tone, appropriate to the discoveries his character is making about himself as man and king. Olivier had to find a space free of the wreckage of Henkels and Dorniers in which to film. D-Day, another invasion of France, was about to begin. Branagh's version effortlessly absorbs attitudes shaped by Vietnam. It may even be that, as one critic has charged, Branagh's Henry is "a literary Ollie North who has deliberately shredded vital documents provided by the text. [He is] at the heart of an establishment coverup" (Fitter 1991, 260). Regardless of how we interpret them, each film is a kind of history lesson—the history being our own past fifty years, plus a couple.

Finally, in perhaps the greatest moment in filmed Shakespeare, Welles's Falstaff smiles at King Henry, whom Falstaff has mistaken for an oxymoron known as "King Hal." What does Welles's smile say? The film shows Falstaff breaking through rank after rank of guards and attendants, all the layers of symbolic and actual power around a king. That includes the liturgical music, which Welles uses as a function of film as opposed to just a reinforcement of meanings, which is how lesser filmmakers, insecure in their camera work, tend to use their horns and violins. Finally, nothing stands between Falstaff and the new king except Hal's intention from the first: "I know you all"—the "you" signaling familiarity—to "I know thee not"—the "thee" conveying contempt. Falstaff begins to counter but is cut off, and without language, he is powerless. His smile is that of the teacher who recognizes how well his student has learned the lesson. This powerful scene shows that the new king has learned how to translate an obscene disturbance into the high point of his coronation, a public lecture to his kingdom. He learned how to do that from Falstaff. We learn what the scene is all about from the maker of the film.

Although television was developed before World War II, it is a postwar phenomenon. Programming, its spread from very regional to national and satellite formats, and the development of color are all products of the years from 1948 to 1960. Is television trapped in modernist criteria of thematic unity, coherence, and structure? Possibly, which means that the medium is intrinsically limited. Certainly it has no field of depth technically, and, it follows, it must be a close-up and shallow medium with very conventional camera techniques. Even with the advent of larger screens, it has no field of depth intellectually or emotionally. It is a literal medium, meaning that plays in which women disguise themselves as men or in which twins are supposedly mistaken for each other are extremely difficult to perform. These ancient stage conventions do not convert to modernism.

Television is to some extent a product of our expectations—CBS once believed that it could bring culture through its networks but brought the National Football League instead—and it never stood for more than entertainment. Its one transcendent moment was John F. Kennedy's funeral. It is not accidental that the wars reported on television are small wars, regional and guerrilla, or that sound bites and rapid montage reporting are its modes of transmitting information. It was "radio with a picture," but the picture took away, absorbed the imaginative completing of radio that we provided, whether listening to Don Dunphy broadcast the fights of Joe Louis, or Mr. and Mrs. North, or Captain Midnight. Film, which began in a premodern era that incorporated radical changes, like the addition of sound (a difficult transition), enjoys a deep field that makes it far more flexible than television; it is light sensitive and is not trapped in specific modernist categories. The automobile, which can be improved in all kinds of ways, is a good example of a modern agent. The addition of air bags merely points at the intrinsic limitations of the automobile.

It may be that television will remain trapped in its own banality, for the reasons that Peter Brook (1968) gives—that it emerged at a moment of stasis at which it is frozen:

The cinema degenerated because, like many a great empire, it stood still: it repeated its rituals identically again and again—but time passed and the meaning went out of them. Then television arrived at the very instant when the dramatic clichés of the cinema were being dished up for the nine millionth time. It began showing old movies—and rotten movie-like plays—and enabled audiences to judge them in a completely new way. In the cinema the darkness, the vast screen, the loud music, the soft carpets added unquestionably to the hypnosis. On television the clichés were naked: the viewer is independent, he is walking around his room, he hasn't paid (which makes it easier to switch off), he can voice his disapproval out loud without being sssshed. Furthermore, he is forced to judge, and to judge fast. He switches on the set and immediately judges from the face that he sees (a) whether it's an actor or someone "real"; (b) whether he's nice or not, good or bad, what his class or background, etc., are; (c) when it's a fictional scene, he draws on his experience of dramatic clichés to guess at the part of the story he has missed (because, of course, he can't sit round the program twice, as he used to do at the movies). The smallest gesture identifies the villain, the adulteress, and so on. The essential fact is that he has learned—from necessity—to observe, to judge for himself. (27)

But this unknown citizen makes only the judgments dictated by the conventions with which he has been inundated. The insidiousness of television is that it is not merely itself, which is more than enough, but that the shallow psychology of perception that it has engendered has become the expectation of most spectators at any live event, sporting or dramatic. Too often the practitioners of drama have surrendered to these expectations. Perhaps the most valuable contribution of the new historicism will turn out to be that it forces us to judge for ourselves by insisting that as individuals we discern the flow of history as it moves *us*—not as it may move others, or cultures, or countries.

REFERENCES

Andreas, James. 1994. Comment. Clemson Shakespeare Festival. March.

Brook, Peter. 1968. *The Empty Space*. London: McGibbons and Key.

Collick, John. 1989. *Shakespeare, Cinema, and Society*. Manchester: Manchester University Press.

Crowl, Samuel. 1992. *Shakespeare Observed*. Athens: Ohio University Press.

Davies, Anthony. 1988. *Filming Shakespeare's Plays*. Cambridge: Cambridge University Press.

Davies, Anthony, and Stanley Wells, eds. 1994. *Shakespeare and the Moving Image: The Plays on Film and Television*. Cambridge: Cambridge University Press.

Donaldson, Peter. 1991. "Taking on Shakespeare: Branagh's *Henry V*." *Shakespeare Quarterly* 42, no. 1, 60–71.

Edwards, Philip. 1968. *Shakespeare and the Confines of Art*. London: Methuen.

Fitter, Chris. 1991. "A Tale of Two Branaghs: *Henry V*, Ideology, and the Mekong Agincourt." In *Shakespeare Left and Right*, edited by Ivo Kamps. London: Routledge.

Holderness, Graham. 1986. "Radical Potentiality and Institutional Closure." In *Shakespeare on Television*, edited by James C. Bulman and H. R. Coursen. Hanover, N.H.: University Press of New England.

Hale, David. 1995. "Touching with Film and Television." *Shakespeare and the Classroom* 3, no. 1 (Spring): 21–23.

James, Caryn. 1996. "Television, the Medium that Defies Sharp Focus." *New York Times*, 7 July, H25, H27.

Jorgens, Jack. 1977. *Shakespeare on Film*. Bloomington: Indiana University Press.

Kozintsev, Grigori. 1972. "*Hamlet* and *King Lear*: Stage and Film." In *Shakespeare 1971*, edited by Clifford Leach and J.M.R. Margeson. Toronto: Toronto University Press.

Rilla, Wolf. 1973. *The Writer and the Screen*. London: Macmillan.

Thompson, Ann. 1988. *King Lear*. Atlantic Highlands, N.J.: Humanities Press International.

2

Energizing Weaker Productions: *The Tempest*

When no television version of a particular script is good, it helps to ask why. It also helps to sort out elements that do work on television and to ask why. Negative examples are often more useful than positive.

None of the three available television versions of *The Tempest*—the 1960 Schaefer, with Maurice Evans; the BBC production of 1980, directed by John Gorrie, with Michael Hordern; or the 1983 Bard, directed by William Woodman, with Efrem Zimbalist, Jr.—is particularly successful. The reasons lie not only in the productions but in the nature of the medium. Television is not a good vehicle for this script. As Caryn James suggests in a recent review of a PBS analysis of television (1996, H25), television shows real people snarling at each other over their pizza. It has evolved from its early days as "kitchen table drama" to a depiction of the frustrations and crude solipsisms of the lower middle class that occur in the same zone. *The Tempest*, with its magician, prince and princess, dynastic conspiracies, monster and its spirit, and possible examination of the deep shadow that colonialism casts, is not likely to extend a medium that trivializes and domesticates its trivial and domestic material. Add to that the structural limits of television, which are also imaginative limits—lack of physical depth tends to mean lack of artistic depth—and there is no fit between script and medium.

The Schaefer production is pleasant but lightweight. Jack Gould notes that the play "poses a severe traffic problem" for the small screen and that close-ups are not helpful in a play that "requires [the] fanciful, not [the] factual" (1960, 63). Television lacks the magnitude for the play's larger effects, even as its capacity for intimacy proves no advantage. Close-ups invite psychological interpretations perhaps less appropriate to this script than for others. Prospero's soliloquies and major speeches, for example, tend to be grand announcements or pronouncements.

The farcical byplay among Caliban, Stephano, and Trinculo, abetted here by an Ariel voluntarily concealed in a tree as opposed to imprisoned, is well framed for television. Ariel must seem to be hidden, of course, since television is a realistic medium that does not ask us to suspend our disbelief. The Bard version, which is a televised stage play, keeps Ariel in full view of us. We are asked to assume his invisibility to Trinculo and Stephano.

Here is a scene (3.2) where contrasting versions will be useful in class. The generic question is a good one to ask. We are to some extent conditioned to farce by TV, "I Love Lucy" being one of the supreme examples. Its scope is small, requiring only three characters, and therefore the predictable camera work can occur without our noticing it. The close-up, two-shot, and reaction shot are inevitable here. We are granted superior knowledge in that we know Ariel is there. We need comprehend only the situation—that is, that neither of the other characters can see Ariel. No imaginative work is involved, or any thinking. Even those who complain about the difficulties of Shakespeare's language can probably translate "Thou liest!" into, "You are lying!" We can probably infer that no harm will come to anyone. It is a practical joke. The context tells us that Trinculo is in no real danger and that Stephano is posing as tyrant. Scale and degree of difficulty are calibrated precisely to those limited things that television can do.

Well charted by the actors are the wine-induced descents into the stereotypes of paranoia, megalomania, and compulsiveness. Tom Poston's vulnerable Trinculo, Ronald Radd's queasy and cowardly Stephano, and Richard Burton's sonorous Caliban—with finlike ears, armadillo shoulders, and a brush of tail—work well together. All are "obviously having a good time" (Vaughan 1984, 3).

The play is shaped, shortened, and simplified for commercial television and its presumed audience. The opening storm is brief (one minute), narrated, and unconvincing. We are introduced to characters who roll and rock "near a mysterious and uninhabited island." Two of the inhabitants, Prospero and Ariel, talk about the storm before Miranda makes her plea and Prospero brings her up to date. Prospero's narrative is accompanied by a crystal ball in which the disembodied characters of the story swim. The Caliban-Stephano-Trinculo meeting precedes the Antonio-Sebastian conspiracy, a transposition intended to permit Burton and the others to hold the audience.

Antonio is a potbellied villain, Sebastian a fop in peach, pink, and pearls, and Claribel gone. Sebastian does not realize that he is heir of Naples until Antonio points it out to him. The "living drollery" are squat and dancing rocks. No banquet appears or, it follows, disappears. Ariel does appear and gets one of his wings tangled in a bush. The wedding masque is miniaturized and lasts for one minute. Prospero's "No more!" expresses disapproval, not just dismissal.

Maurice Evans's Prospero is of the crinkly "father-knows-best" model. The role suits the actor's tendency toward recitation. Roddy McDowell's Ariel has stiff, sticklike spangles gleaming from his head, as if he has just slid from the frost-baked earth. Ariel admires Lee Remick's dewy Miranda and wishes he were human. Having an experiential sense of what punishment is, he pities Caliban. McDowell makes one hilarious entrance from above, to Stephano and Trinculo. Released too soon, he plummets to the floor and seems lucky to escape a broken leg. Another moment one misses in today's more sophisticated productions occurs in the last scene, when Alonso's ornate collar brushes a camera lens.

The production accepts Margaret Webster's suggestion and ends with the "Revels" speech. Evans moves forward as the camera dollies back. The rest of the characters grow indistinct on a diminishing promontory. This is a good production for 1960, but except for the Caliban underplot and a few moments in the Antonio-Sebastian conspiracy, the effect is bland.

The BBC version is not as bad as critics claim: "Everything goes wrong here" (Charney 1980, 290), "Horrendous . . . a lead-footed production" (Smith 1980, 4), and "Stiff, aimed at the archives, and one can certainly see it gathering a lot of dust there in the years to come" (Reynolds 1980, 9). Certainly the critics have something to complain about, as would students were we to sit them down in front of this production and then put ourselves in the false position of trying to defend it.

The opening scene is filmed, as opposed to taped, yet it presents no sense of emergency. Masts and sheets appear under the opening credits, but the rain falls straight down, as if the ship were safely moored in a windless harbor. Film, if carefully scaled, works on television, but BBC wastes four minutes and forty seconds of film here. As in the other productions, most of the words are inaudible, so that the Conradian contrast between sea and land and the point that "authority" and "the name of king" are useless in the face of "these roarers" are lost. To lose the lines in any medium is invariably a mistake.

The production tends to fall between stage, which can incorporate long speeches, and film, which demands visual equivalents for the language and uses the camera as an aspect of the art form. Even in an oral medium like television, Prospero's expositions are tedious, though Pippa Guard does what she can as listener. She delivers the "Abhorred slave" speech, as Folio says she should, and surprises and frightens Prospero. Having seen Hordern in Clifford Williams's tame 1978 Royal Shakespeare Company production, I thought that a muted Prospero might work on television, a medium that rewards underplaying. "What has been very interesting," Hordern says, "is that instead of trying to reach the back of the gallery with your most innermost thoughts, you have only to cover the distance between you and the

camera, which may be only 18 inches away" (Fenwick 1980, 26). The result
is the irascible schoolmaster model. His stupid students are right in front of
him. When he is not angry, Hordern delivers a "droningly grandfatherish"
Mr. Badger (Charney 1980, 290), slightly warmed by the mild affection he
feels for his daughter.

Caliban's is the complaint of the aborigine, who, having instructed the
colonist on the local environment, is consigned to its slums. None of the television productions touches on the ideological implications that recent materialist critics discern in the script (Barker and Hulme 1985; Breight 1990;
Brown 1985). This Caliban (Warren Clarke) is a shaggy, pot-bellied bum
awaiting introduction to his first six-pack. Clarke's Caliban contrasts with
David Dixon's frail Ariel, with his boy-soprano voice. Each contrasts with
Christopher Guard's tall, dark, and virile Ferdinand.

Director Gorrie's concentration on body types runs into disaster with the
group of virtually naked men who, prancing to the lascivious pleasings of a
pipe, form the "living drollery" of the banquet scene (3.3). It is, as Cecil
Smith says, "quite embarrassing in a professional production" (1980, 4, 8).
Almost as embarrassing is the masque, meant to resemble a Morris dance
(Fenwick 1980, 22). It is remarkably awkward. Spirits step on other spirits'
lines, spirits cast heavy shadows, and those naked boys return as pale sickle-
men bent on having an orgy with nymphs peeled from a Victorian mural.

For all the lapses in taste that make students laugh and teachers cringe, the
production sometimes places characters effectively within the frame. Television's dimensions prevent much movement within its space, but relationship
and emphasis can be established with placement. As Miranda and Ferdinand
exchange the sight of first love, Prospero, camera right, tells us that he must
prevent "too light winning" (1.2.451). Antonio and Sebastian plot in a two-
shot that frames Alonso and party, the target of the conspiracy. Trinculo's
lines about Caliban (in 2.2.141 73) are delivered as sour asides, a technique
that grants the jester surprising interiority. The main plot and subplot conspiracies are splendidly orchestrated. Nigel Hawthorne's Stephano is particularly good as he tries to concentrate through his stupor on Caliban's plot to
kill Prospero. Clarke's "Be not afeard" is excellent. He expresses a sense of
selfhood symbiotically interfused with his island. One senses the source of
his grievance against Prospero. Since the banquet disappears beneath Ariel's
enclosing wings, Prospero's "A grace it had devouring" has a visual an-
tecedent. At the end, Miranda's "How beauteous mankind is" is directed at
Antonio. It is a wonderfully ironic instant, neatly setting up Prospero's bitter, " 'Tis new to thee."

The Bard production begins as Prospero's head dreams up the storm. Or
are we to take the entire play as Prospero's dream (as *Shrew*, with the induction, can be viewed as Sly's fantasy of male supremacy)? This production
is set on a Globe-like stage, with Tudor facades on the sides, a long balcony
between, and an inner stage underneath the balcony. The ship is the balcony,

a placement that gives the storm an oddly linear quality accentuated by the two long streamers of blue, pulled up and down by spirits, that simulate wind and wave. One problem with having Prospero in charge from the outset is that the storm lacks even a theatrical sense of danger, though the sound effects drown the lines. Another is that Prospero's calming of Miranda is irrelevantly ex post facto.

Zimbalist is a naturalistic television actor, notable as an FBI officer in a long-running series of the 1970s. Perhaps as a carryover from his role, he is mildly ingratiating—the public servant pretending to be concerned for the public. Instead of the modulation that can occur at the beginning of act 5, a softening into an insight informed by its compassionate equivalent, Zimbalist's Prospero is blandly consistent. J. E. Taylor's Miranda is not helped by having her hair pulled back to sharpen her severe bone structure. Prospero's luxuriant mane would have looked better on Taylor. William Hootkins plays Caliban with sullen and understated precision. The scene between Caliban, Stephano, Trinculo, and Ariel (3.2) is excellent. Ariel is in full view, but we are asked to accept his invisibility. A lithe dancer, Duane Black, as Ariel would have been excellent in live performance. In fact, the entire production would have picked up a useful energy had it been played in front of a live audience.

The Tudor facade keeps forcing us to unsuspend the disbelief that the stagelike setting and the front-on camera work encourage. Its presence also blurs the nature-nurture, savage-civilized tension in the script. Our own imaginations are seldom pulled into the transaction, partly because Woodman does not vary the lighting. The lack of contrasting visual tones makes the production duller than it needs to be. Woodman does have an event occur off-camera now and then. The banquet is replaced by skulls, but we are looking at Prospero when the substitution occurs. Thus issues that could be a problem on a stage are not a problem here. Still, the production does not work out a consistent compromise between the premises of stage and television camera. The production could itself be more imaginatively conceived, as when the living drollery become the dog-faced creatures that chase Caliban and confederates. This "doubling" gives us a brief glimpse of the plasticity of Prospero's and Shakespeare's "bare island."

A *Page to Stage* cassette, produced by the Stratford, Ontario, Festival, is based on John Hirsch's 1982 production. Narrator Nicholas Pennell tells us that the script "distills the imagery of [Shakespeare's] life work." That, I believe, is accurate, though I think that the author means themes, not imagery. Is it helpful, however, to ask, as Pennell does, whether "Prospero's desire for revenge motivates him towards positive action because he is an innately good person"? Is it accurate to claim that at the end of the play, "justice prevails and the natural order is restored"? That seems Gonzalo-like—too all embracing and, as far as a production is concerned, smothering as well.

From what we see of the production, one of its high points is Pennell's Stephano, "a masterly miniature," Ralph Berry says, with the "brutality of sentiment" of Iago (1983, 96). From the brief glimpse we get, it seems that Pennell is creating a parody of Ian McKellen's superb Macbeth.

Caliban (Miles Potter), however, is incredibly grotesque, a creature incapable, one must assume, of copulating with a human, a gray and weed-bearded thing covered with rocks and shells, having emerged, it seems, from the bottom of a tidal pool.

The production employs the multitiered Stratford main stage splendidly. The storm finds the Boatswain on the upper stage, wrestling with a huge wheel. Antonio enters from a trap in the main platform below. The audience confronts a full-scale storm, one that television permits us to appreciate, if not experience. We do, though, lose some of the lines. The masque represents an actual wedding, with Miranda in white gown and Juno presiding from the upper stage. Here physical levels become conceptual planes. A quasi-Shakespearean stage can create a sense of the script's integration as a design for a specific space. Most modern stages cannot do this, and television seldom tries. Jane Howell uses a unit playground set for her brilliant *Henry VI* sequence for the BBC, and Desmond Davis, in his excellent BBC *Measure for Measure*, deployed the same set with a different paint job for his convent and brothel.

The weaknesses of the Stratford *Tempest* would seem to reside in Sharry Flett's Miranda, who sought not for Ferdinand but for Congreve or Sheridan, and, chiefly, in Len Cariou's Prospero. His "Revels" speech is read in a panic, an acceptable interpretation even if it runs against the poetry. Here it was badly overdone. Cariou's delivery is often singsongy, as if he has been told to "go for the music," but it is disinterested and oddly stressed ("As you from *crimes* would pardoned be," as opposed to parking tickets). He gives his fellow actors nothing on stage even as he carries on an unrequited love affair with the audience. Berry says that "all that emerged was that Prospero was in a foul mood . . . For Miranda to say 'Never till this day / Saw I him touch'd with anger so distemper'd' suggested that she hadn't been paying attention: he was like that all the time" (1983, 95).

Regardless of the production, the tape has the great virtue of showing how the Stratford stage can make visual, and thus imaginative, sense of this complicated script.

Television has a linear movement and lacks the frame that held a metaphoric cosmos in front of Shakespeare's audience within the "great globe itself." Television can incorporate splendid spots of time, but the good moments are not integrated into a sense of the whole. No frame exists within which to include the large and the small, the soliloquy and the spectacle, and to relate them to each other. With postmodernism now in control of production, television's inadequacies should be strengths, since any mishmash of styles now passes as production. Unfortunately (or fortunately) BBC either exhausted the possibilities of or discouraged further television productions of Shakespeare. Only the occasional televised stage play occurs anymore.

Television is also limited in its ability to produce special effects. The twisters in *The Wizard of Oz* and the final cataclysm in *Forbidden Planet,* products of the great MGM special effects expert Arnold Gillespie, do not work well in miniature. Schaefer's special effects in his *Tempest* are better than they were for his 1954 *Macbeth.* In that early color production, Banquo's head bounced through the Banquet Scene like a runaway, bright-orange bowling ball. The effects in *The Tempest* are almost as silly, particularly for a latter-day audience that knows that television does try to do such things. At one point, Prospero tries to waft Ariel from his arm, but the timing is off, and it looks as if Prospero is trying to shoo a clever and irritating insect. Except for an Ariel who leaps into space and vaporizes, Gorrie eschews special effects. "We felt, " says his producer, Cedric Messina, "it wasn't fair to the play to do too much. If you make an electronic night's dream, you are asking for trouble" (Fenwick 1980, 17). That is a wise decision, but it leaves Gorrie with his heavy Doré set and the blank wash of studio land, not a "real place where magic things happen" (Fenwick 1980, 17). Television style, with its emphasis on reality, is not a site for the strange or miraculous.

"Magic" on television is, to borrow a phrase from Robert Frost, "a diminished thing," where "Star Trek's" Kirk and Scotty "beam up," where the explosion of a tiny spacecraft cannot threaten domestic space from twenty-one diagonal inches as it can when it shatters on a large screen in a darkened cinema. Television is a fourth-wall medium that asks little of us. Color does much of the imagining for us. The stage asks us to disbelieve. Film forces us to believe in the twister tugging at Dorothy as she struggles with that storm door, or in the biplanes buzzing around King Kong as he straddles a pre-TV Empire State Building with Fay Wray in his paw, or in the flames behind Rhett and Scarlett as they flee Atlanta (and part of the old *King Kong* set adds to the conflagration). Film has the width and depth within which to create its effects. Television tends to psychologize the supernatural, rendering it "natural," and it renders special effects "questionable, even laughable" (Dessen 1986, 8; Coursen 1989). Thus directors who attempt to translate the otherworldly or the supernatural in Shakespeare to television are likely to be defeated as they try to calibrate that material to a resistant medium.

The animated version of *The Tempest* (1992), edited by Leon Garfield, directed by Stanislav Sololov, and designed by Elena Livanova, is a good précis of this very short script. The background is narrated by Martin Jarvis, thus eliminating the need for Prospero's long exposition. The wedding masque is also cut. It is a good story for animation—in this instance, puppets. "On a misty, forgotten island [lives] Prospero the mighty enchanter." Ariel is an androgynous sprite, feminized by the voice of Ellen Hoard. Caliban is a squat monster who scuttles around like a crab. He has no grievance, it seems, but he is a threat, at one point attempting to wrest Prospero's magic staff away. The island features splendid music by the Mosfilm Symphony, directed by Vladimir Rylov, and, in addition to Ariel's observant scouting, Easter Island faces that look on and report directly to Prospero's cell. Ariel makes an impressive harpy, and viewers also notice a unicorn munching the foliage. A lot of famous lines are there, though not the one about "strange bedfellows" or Ariel's promise of "clear life ensuing." As in other cartoons, all the characters are reduced to stereotype. At the end, Caliban capers happily on the yellow sands as the king's ship sails away, and Prospero breaks his staff and dumps the pieces and his book into the drink.

This version makes for an excellent introduction to the play for younger students and a good assignment for more experienced students, the basic question being, What does the animated version tell about the script, and what does it not?

The Tempest has produced four interesting offshoots. I do not recommend Peter Greenaway's *Prospero's Books* for use in the teaching of *The Tempest*. It adds nothing to our understanding of the play. It does nothing with Caliban and ends with the most stultifyingly conventional closure possible. It also includes a twelve-minute parody of Home Shopping Network and incorporates long and pointless tracking shots, and its imposition of high-definition television on film undermines its claim to be film. The definition of a television picture does not affect content, does not make a Warhol a Rembrandt or a Rockwell a Raphael. Greenaway aims at the perfection of a cliché, and one has to call that a stupid effort for all of the sophistication of the surface. The books themselves are often interesting, but are totally irrelevant to *The Tempest* and thus to the narrative. The books do not interact with the story. Something escaping from one of those books and getting into the film might have been interesting. I have dealt with *Prospero's Books* elsewhere (1992, 163–76) and have tracked down many of Greenaway's allusions to suggest their irrelevance to any purpose other than to demonstrate his intellectual superiority and the abysmal ignorance of anyone seeing his film.

Douglas Lanier, in "Drowning the Book: *Prospero's Books* and the textual Shakespeare," defends the film from a postmodernist stance. Lanier's argument is complicated, but it goes to the heart of the purposes of this book, so I will deal with it here in some detail. Lanier argues that "Shakespeare can take the stage only insofar as the actors are not made to stand before the judgement of his book" (188). I do not think anyone is arguing otherwise today, except when an actor is robbed of the book, as Terrence Rafferty rightly claims Laurence Fishburne was in the recent *Othello*: "What [director] Parker sacrifices is the volcanic flow of language that conveys the hero's pride, confusion and anguish, and without it Othello is nothing" (1995, 127). Furthermore, as Laurie Osborne argues in the Bulman anthology (1996), Lanier's argument that "modern performances of Shakespeare [are seen as] supplemental, fleeting theatrical variations, of varying authenticity on a prior, originary book" (188) is increasingly not the case. One reason is that, as Lanier says, citing Stephen Orgel, we may be recognizing at last "that Shakespeare anticipated and approved both textual and performative variations" (190). Whether Orgel is right in his hypothesis that "Shakespeare habitually began with more than he needed" (1988, 7), options have always existed: the Q1 placement of Hamlet's "To be or not to be," earlier than in Q2 or Folio, Quarto's trial of Goneril and Regan in the hovel, almost invariably incorporated into Folio-based productions, the Hecate material in *Macbeth*, which is usually cut. The nature of film as medium insists that much of the language itself be excised. As Lanier says, "The cinema has more readily taken up the challenge of textual authority than the theatre, perhaps because filming Shakespeare entails more consciously translating the work from one medium (and cultural register) to another" (191). The issue of translation also involves expectation, a segment of Aristotle's fourth cause, that is, response to the work of art. We tend to expect more of the language in a stage production than in a film. We may object to the editing of a script for stage or film, but we accept the fact of editing, particularly for film.

Lanier's argument serves what he perceives the need to "(re)graft [Shakespeare] on to performative media or textual documents (re)conceived as performance scores or unique artifacts," so that "he and the cultural capital he represents can be uncoupled from the decline of the book in an increasingly post-literate society" (191). But Shakespeare as book is really an ex post facto development. True, quartos were published during his lifetime, and the 1623 Folio appeared shortly after his death, but it was the publishing explosion of the eighteenth century that made Shakespeare into text. The plays, as we know, were being radically translated into Restoration and eighteenth-century paradigms and performance spaces. At any rate, *Prospero's Books* is an odd choice of example of Shakespeare's being uncoupled from the book. Whatever Shakespeare may be, he is chained to *Greenaway*'s books in the film.

Lanier cites the prompter in Olivier's film of *Henry V*, a caricature of Shakespeare, to demonstrate the "textual ideal that casts its shadow over the performance we are seeing" (192). But the film escapes from its early moments in a model London and replica Globe Theatre and becomes a film, perhaps best exemplified by the long tracking shot of the French charge at Agincourt, an event neither depicted nor described in the text. At the end, we return suddenly to Henry V-Burbage-Olivier next to his boy-actor Katherine, but the film meanwhile has moved far from both its textual and theatrical premises. The prompter's shadow is cast only over the opening stage performance. His erasure emphasizes the performance of the actor playing Henry. That actor may begin as Burbage, but he quickly becomes Olivier. Furthermore, since the film was produced during World War II, just before another invasion of France, it is better examined as a piece of propaganda than of textual authority. A cultural materialist argument, of course, would say that the entire project served the dominant ideology for which the story of the patriot king is canonical. If so, the text is manipulated toward a dominant cultural authority, as in the cutting from the film of the cutting of the throats of the French prisoners, a topic recently discussed in the context of Douglas Hughes's 1996 production in New York City (see Weschler 1996 and, on Olivier's erasure of the episode, Patterson 1994).

"In *Prospero's Books* Greenaway recasts *The Tempest* within a filmic vocabulary that constantly acknowledges its competition with Shakespearean textuality while remaining faithful . . . to the play's received text" (194). What we *see* is Prospero (Gielgud) writing the text quite literally with a quill pen. As Lanier says, "The written text [is] kept obsessively before the viewer" (195). This is to deny film its own identity and its ability to escape from written word to the plasticity of image. The constant presence of the text cannot be said to be at once "faithful to it while dismantling its received monumentality and authority" (196). With Gielgud reading it? Greenaway is credited with doing a lot of clever things with books that come alive, but it is an old device. Some of us recall the many 1940s musicals that began with an etching of Olde New York that suddenly moved as a jolly policeman stole an apple from a fruit stand and a struggling but upright songwriter banged out a song on an ancient upright piano. Shakespeare's script is simply hijacked as a vehicle for Greenaway's self-proclaimed genius. *Prospero's Books* is not a good film. At times, it is not a film at all.

It may be that "by eschewing the characterology of the realist stage and cinema, Greenaway is free to treat the text as a collection of verbal images that he can defamiliarize by (re)literalizing them as arresting visual tableaux . . . static though visually sumptuous dumb shows that emblematize the text's imagery" (195). But these tableaux do not derive from the text and are far more static than sumptuous. The exception is the one Lanier makes the rule: "Gonzalo's famous set-speech outlining his ideal island commonweal, wo observe, is culled from the Book of Utopias. Through such allusions Greenaway makes visible *The Tempest*'s intertextuality, its status as a collection of discourses culled from a variety of prior sources rather than a unified freestanding artwork" (197). Perhaps, but Gonzalo's discourse refutes itself, as Antonio and Sebastian deftly show, and the play surrounding the discourse hardly supports any vision of utopia. The play forms a disjunctive analogy to this example of intertextuality, a point that Greenaway's ingenuity fails to discern. The Alphabetical Inventory of the Dead is not a source of *The Tempest*. "The Book of Revenge," another of this Prospero's books, is one that Shakespeare's character has read and long since discarded. That Prospero has not yet experienced his rejection of the revenge thesis emotionally is probably true, but Greenaway does not permit Gielgud to chart that progress.

"The *act* of writing and imagining," Lanier says, "is false to the very bodily processes that bring it into being [and therefore the bodies of *Prospero's Books*] are patently *not* in the service of thematics, a fact that explains why many have labeled the production's nudity gratuitous" (199–200). In other words, the many naked bodies parading around Prospero's palace were meant to show the irrelevance of writing and imagining even as the film is being simultaneously written and imagined. The bodies are just there, naked, as in a locker room. Meanwhile the text of *The Tempest* itself is saved from drowning at the end by

the barbaric man-fish Caliban, here a wry surrogate for the *enfant terrible* director himself . . . a desecrater of books who nevertheless saves them from oblivion. . . . In the end, Greenaway's film is itself destined to become a cinematic "text" to be "read" according to interpretive protocols of close reading with many of the same assumptions about "textual" monumentality. (202)

The film, then, serves the tenets of a creed outworn: the new criticism. For all of its facile inventiveness and its claim to be on the edge of the future, it is deeply anachronistic conceptually and trapped in time insofar as it deploys the modernist medium of TV.

But his film does not serve the old mythology, nor does any other film, in spite of Lanier's assertion that "video and film have encouraged us to assimilate . . . performances to the condition of texts, stable artifacts, rather than contingent, unstable, ephemeral experiences" (203). Olivier's *Henry V* must be seen in its historical context. Olivier's Othello mimics stereotypic black mannerisms consciously before an enthralled Venetian senate in a performance that is likely to be read as racist more than a quarter-century later. Brook's *Lear* emerges from his despair about the Vietnam War, but it also captures vividly the element of existential despair in the script and thus is not confined in its Kottian premises—*Lear* is a script framed for existentialist approaches—even though it is helpful to understand them as generative force behind the film. It is also helpful to contrast the minimalist Brook film with the 70-mm Kozintsev version, hugely panoramic and inclusive, where Brook's camera is intentionally exclusive and often decentered. But Kozintsev's film is of its time in its sense of the tide of the proletariat beneath the parapets of absolute power and in its sheer size. Twenty-five years later, the film might well have been scaled to the cassette. The 1936 *Romeo and Juliet*, with the famously superannuated Howard and Shearer, can be viewed and even enjoyed against the zeitgeist of 1936: its songs, its films, and its Great Depression (see my response 1996). What Lanier calls a "technological revolution—the VCR— . . . subtly reestablishing . . . a new monolithic and stable 'text'—the ideal performance, recorded on tape, edited and reshaped in post-production, available for re-viewing" (203–4) is itself, in its specific manifestations, subject to history and the product of a past that recedes rapidly, and as rapidly dates its productions. I doubt that "the 'videotext' [will] encourage us to elide the very historicity and materiality we have sought to recover with the return to performance" (204). If anything, the videotext, implicated as it is in technology, presents itself as a historicized commodity almost immediately, particularly in that warning from the FBI. It is true, of course, that we can restudy a production on cassette as we cannot with a stage production, unless the stage production itself is available on tape. But then it is no longer a stage production, having been removed from the space and the dimensions in which it occurred.

While reading this essay, I agreed that the concept of character may be a socially determined construct but I kept asking, It is still something an actor must work with, isn't it? Derek Jacobi suggests how in discussing the role of Hamlet: "The personality of the actor playing the role . . . is the determining factor. You don't actually have to play the character, you play the situation in which Hamlet finds himself and your own personality, your own outlook, takes over" (Ungar 1980, 19). I have a strong sense that something like what Jacobi describes is what Shakespeare had in mind when he wrote the part. He had actors in mind. They complete the script by interacting with it. They must do that within any of the conceptual spaces to which Shakespeare is translated.

However the plays came into being—it seems that no one wrote them or, if written down, the writing was without intention—they were not shaped under postmodernist premises. Although Richard Levin demolished thematic approaches to the plays almost two decades ago (1979), a director probably still should seek some unifying principle within a script in a collaborative effort with an assumed playwright, who like Hooker's host, coexists at the moment of reception. This principle is particularly true in film, where weaknesses are often thematic, as in the 1995 *Othello*, which exchanges images and bodies for the few clarifying lines that would have helped us understand why in the film, as opposed to the *ur*story, some of these events are occurring. Multiple signification is not the same as nonsignification.

I am not dealing here with the Jarman version (1980), which is not commercially available. It was made, says John Collick, "in the context of various transgressive movements within 1970s sub-culture," including punk rock, and it "often deliberately challenges orthodox perceptions of Shakespeare" (1989, 103). Of it, eminent critic Samuel Crowl says, "The film is decidedly Jarman's recreation of the text in his own, highly individualized cinematic style . . . more Jarman's *Tempest* than Shakespeare's." Crowl finds

Elizabeth Welch's wonderful rendition of Harold Arlen's *Stormy Weather* . . . inspired. Its refrain of "Keeps rainin' all the time" became a wonderful modern equivalent for Festes's corrective to *Twelfth Night*'s mid-summer madness: "the rain it raineth every day." This moment worked because it created a witty resonance with all those other moments in the comedies where, in the midst of the festive celebration of love and romance, Shakespeare carefully places reminders that holiday is not every day. (1980, 7)

Russell Jackson says of the film that "the world we enter is not so much an island whose magical properties are drawn on by a magus, as the realm of a magus who has withdrawn into a house which his magic has since made special" (1994, 107–8). Vincent Canby, however, calls the film "very nearly unbearable" and Welch's song "a bravura effect gone feeble" (1980, C20).

While Pauline Kael calls Fred Wilcox's *Forbidden Planet* (1956) "the best of the science fiction interstellar productions of the 50s" (videocassette cover), more sophisticated students today find its depiction of A.D. 2300 amusing. Ariel is Robby the Robot, a character whom the *New Yorker* says "has a quiet dignity about him" (12 May 1956). Altaira (Anne Francis), the Miranda counterpart, loses her virginity symbolically. Her symbiotic relationship with her environment fades as her contact with the space visitors grows. She is here a product of "the male gaze" (Mulvey 1985, 57). Perhaps the film's most interesting theme is its suggestion that the person who attempts to control nature represses in nature powerful and destructive forces, here known as id. The extension of Freudian or, for that matter, Jungian psychodynamics from individual psychic to planetary dimensions gives the film an unexpectedly strong and convincingly apocalyptic ending. "It makes King Kong look like an organ grinder's monkey," says *Time* (9 April 1956). Merrell Knighten suggests that the Prospero analogue, Dr. Morbius (Walter Pidgeon), "has made his Caliban"; it is himself, of course, who "in his initiation into forbidden knowledge" becomes "this thing of darkness" (1994, 36–37). Knighten suggests Marlowe's *Dr. Faustus* as a possible further source of the film: "Precisely in the manner of his cautionary model Faustus, Morbius rejects his Id-beast too late and dies at its hands" (37).

Paul Mazursky's *Tempest* (1982) is a slow and underwritten contrast between the world of Manhattan upper-crust careerists and that of a sexless Aegean island, which does have some horny inhabitants. It has its king, duke, jester, islander, mariners, prince, and princess, the last played luminously by Molly Ringwald in her screen debut. Students will respond to her line, "We're studying *Macbeth* in school. It's unbelievably boring!" Allusions to the source abound. "It's a paradise here! You're learning things here you'd never learn anywhere else," says John Cassavetes, the Prospero figure, to Ringwald. "I was boss here before you showed up," says Raul Julia, Kalibanos, to Cassavetes. "I'm a monkey, just like you," says Cassavetes to Kalibanos. "Anyway, I'm a virgin," says Ringwald to Freddie (Sam Robards). We are asked to believe that Cassavetes achieves magical powers through celibacy, which, in turn, is the product of a mild and unconvincing midlife crisis out of Gail Sheehy's *Passages*, as critic Richard Combs notes (1983, 179). Lucianne Buchanan plays Dolores, a hilarious and apparent afterthought of the screenwriters, and the film ends with a vocal from the great Dinah Washington.

These offshoots are not in a class with Kurosawa's *Throne of Blood*, but each will chase the student back to the original, and each argues, however marginally, Shakespeare's continued power to generate further imaginative efforts. *Forbidden Planet* invites futuristic conceptions of other scripts, while *Tempest* raises the issue of translating Shakespeare into a contemporary mode.

These make good assignments, since they point out the limitations of adaptations of the inherited scripts. Any production, of course, is a translation.

To involve students in the issues of translating Shakespeare to film or television is to get them to ask some good questions: What are the difficulties of this script as television? As film? To what extent do one's expectations of a light-sensitive or a magnetic medium condition what can occur there? How does zeitgeist affect the work and our response to it? At the risk of sounding like T. S. Eliot, I suggest that each new production alters our perception of all previous productions. Kenneth Branagh's 1989 *Henry V* permitted us to see Olivier's 1944 version as we had never done before. Another *Measure for Measure* would permit us to look anew at Desmond Davis's very good 1980 television production, the only version of that script available. Since a film or television version is fixed in time, we learn about that time, as it deals with Shakespeare and about our own as we respond to an artifact from the past. We thus move out of the biased formulations, either positive or pejorative, that are likely to produce a too-immediate reaction and into the zone where we can create contexts for evaluation.

Perhaps the greatest contribution of film and video to learning is that the productions insist that students notice detail. If the student selects a short segment from three *Tempests*, for example, she or he has no choice but to enter into a detailed analysis. We contribute to a student's growth when we move the student from the swamp of generalities to the friction of specifics.

REFERENCES

Barker, Francis, and Peter Hulme. 1985. "Nymphs and Reapers Heavily Vanish." In *Alternative Shakespeare*, edited by John Drakakis. London: Methuen.

Berry, Ralph. 1983. "Stratford Festival Canada, 1982." *Shakespeare Quarterly* 34, no. 1, 95–98.

Breight, Curt. 1990. "Treason Doth Never Prosper." *Shakespeare Quarterly* 41, no. 1, 1–28.

Brown, Paul. 1985. "This Thing of Darkness I Acknowledge Mine." In *Political Shakespeare*, edited by Jonathan Dollimore and Alan Sinfield. Manchester: Manchester University Press.

Bulman, James, ed. 1996. *Shakespeare, Theory, and Performance*. London: Routledge.

Canby, Vincent. 1980. "Jarman's *Tempest*." *New York Times*, 22 September, C20.

Charney, Maurice. 1980. "Shakespeare Anglophilia." *Shakespeare Quarterly* 31, no. 2, 287–92.

Collick, John. 1989. *Shakespeare, Cinema, and Society*. Manchester: Manchester University Press.

Combs, Richard. 1983. "Mid-Life Crisis *Tempest*." *TLS*, 25 February, 179.

Coursen, H. R. 1989. "Special Effects on Television." *Shakespeare on Film Newsletter* 14, no. 1, 8.

———. 1992. *Shakespearean Performance as Interpretation*. Newark: University of Delaware Press.

————. 1996. *Shakespeare in Production: Whose History?* Athens: Ohio University Press.

Crowl, Samuel. 1980. "Stormy Weather: A New *Tempest* on Film." *Shakespeare on Film Newsletter* 5, no. 1, 1, 5, 7.

Dessen, Alan. 1986. "The Supernatural on Television." *Shakespeare on Film Newsletter* 11, no. 1, 1, 8.

Fenwick, Henry. 1980. "The Production." In *The Tempest*. London: BBC.

Gould, Jack. 1960. "Review." *New York Times*, 4 February, 63.

Jackson, Russell. 1994. "Shakespeare's Comedies on Film." In *Shakespeare and the Moving Image*, edited by Anthony Davies and Stanley Wells. Cambridge: Cambridge University Press.

James, Caryn. 1996. "Television, the Medium That Defies Sharp Focus." *New York Times*, 7 July, H25, H27.

Knighten, Merrell. 1994. "The Triple Paternity of *Forbidden Planet*." *Shakespeare Bulletin* 12, no. 3, 36–37.

Lanier, Douglas. 1996. "Drowning the Book: *Prospero's Books* and the Textual Shakespeare." In *Shakespeare, Theory, and Performance*, edited by James Bulman. London: Routledge.

Levin, Richard. 1979. *New Readings vs. Old Plays: Recent Trends in the Reinterpretation of Renaissance Drama*. Chicago: University of Chicago Press.

Mulvey, Laura. 1985. "Visual Pleasure and Narrative Cinema." In *Film Theory and Criticism*, ed. Gerald Mast and Marshall Cohen. New York: Oxford University Press.

Orgel, Stephen. 1988. "The Authentic Shakespeare." *Representations* 21, 5–25.

Patterson, Annabel. 1994. "Teaching *Henry V*." In *Teaching Shakespeare: Critics in the Classroom*, edited by Bruce McIver and Ruth Stevenson. Cranbury, N.J.: Associated University Presses.

Rafferty, Terrence. 1995. "Fidelity and Infidelity." *New Yorker*, 18 December, 124–27.

"Review of *Forbidden Planet*." *New Yorker*, 12 May 1956.

"Review of *Forbidden Planet*." *Time*, 9 April 1956.

Reynolds, Stanley. 1980. "*The Tempest*." *Times*, 28 February, 9.

Smith, Cecil. 1980. "Review." *Los Angeles Times*, 7 May, 4, 8.

Ungar, Arthur. 1980. "Derek Jacobi: A Special Kind of Hamlet." *Christian Science Monitor*, 7 November, 19.

Vaughan, Virginia. 1984. "The Forgotten Television *Tempest*." *Shakespeare on Film Newsletter*, 9, no. 1, 3.

Weschler, Lawrence. 1996. "Take No Prisoners." *New Yorker*, 17 June, 50–59.

3

Student Writing: Contexts and Vocabulary

The basic assignment is that a student pick out two or three versions of the same scene or character and describe the differences, with reference to what the text seems to say. A student will notice that the Caldwell television version of Banquo's assassination shows a character from the castle, stage left, to whom Banquo says, "It will be rain tonight," in the friendly way of people talking about the weather. I have never seen that interpretation before or since, but it makes sense on a stage where movement across stage is necessary to depict movement. The apparently friendly person stage left blocks Banquo from his destination and reiterates the motif of deceptiveness that we notice earlier as Duncan remarks the "pleasant seat" of Inverness.

In looking at contrasting scenes, students will notice detail, describe it, discover that their prose is suddenly more mature, and will be pleased. If they then go on to talk about their preferences among the versions available, their evaluations will be based on an accounting for the medium in which production occurs, a sense of what the script offers for a specific moment in the play, and a precise observation of what a particular production does with that moment. In a recent production of the Scottish play, Banquo said, "If you can *look* into the seeds of time." I prefer a more skeptical, "If you *can* look into the seeds of time," in keeping with Banquo's attitude toward the Weird Sisters, less credulous than Macbeth's. That makes the first three syllables an anapest and is the kind of choice to which we alert our students in making performance materials available and to which they alert us once they hone their powers of observation.

I am by no means ruling out the performance techniques advocated by Michael Kelly, Rex Gibson and *Shakespeare Set Free*. I am suggesting that the use of film and television versions has more than just a reinforcing function. *Shakespeare Set Free* offers a naive and uninformed sense of how these materials should be deployed. A use of film and TV shows students how the script works and does not work and educates them to how the media work. That goal is not incidental. *Shakespeare Set Free* talks of students' being "true veterans" of film and television, as if they knew something about what they experience. Some do, of course, but questions about the media in which they are immersed will often draw a blank stare. Some students, having seen several versions of a scene, will want to do their version live with colleagues.

Showing only one version of a script is not a good idea. A film can have a normative effect on a student. The Polanski film shows the murder of Duncan. That is a decision dictated by film, one assumes, but it is not in the script. Polanski substitutes a bear baiting for the ironic reminders of Communion that the Banquet Scene provides. Polanski places us in a wholly violent world, predicted by that dagger the sisters buried in the first scene, with few reminders of a more humane weal. We lose the contrast that the Thames (Trevor Nunn) version gives us, where the liturgical music plays under Macbeth's simultaneous passing of the loving cup and interrogation of the murderer of his friend, Banquo. The latter contrast is what the scene shows. Trevor Nunn believed that it was available in 1979. Can a postmodern audience still grasp the distinction and parallel inherent in "We'll drink a measure the table round" and "There's blood upon thy face"? I am not a fan of the Polanski film, but the moment in which Macbeth's severed head observes the celebration of his overthrow is worth the price of admission. Polanski borrows it from Camus's essay (1951) on the guillotine. Some students will be interested in looking at a literary source for a brilliant few seconds of film.

The approach via film and TV means that we befriend the medium rather than merely rail against its pervasiveness. We make of the cathode ray tube a site for response and interrogation for that currently most popular of activities, interactivity. Under this agenda, the technology becomes part of a learning process. The problem becomes a solution.

Students understand the script as script (as opposed to a book to be read) through production. They glimpse the options and the decisions that actors and directors must make. The genius of the Shakespeare script is that it was designed to be interpreted, not just presented, by Shakespeare's company, and it still is. The potential meanings are there, awaiting our own times and understandings to show us what the meanings are.

Once they see more than one version of a script, students will also understand that production is interpretation. As John Freed says of the Tony Richardson film of *Hamlet*, the teacher can emphasize "the highlighting, albeit by exclusion, of some of Shakespeare's most troublesome choices—the ones that have to be incorporated eventually into a student's understanding of what Shakespeare, as distinct from Richardson, is all about" (1977, 7). We have to sort the translation from the inherited material. Any production forces us back to the script, or, in the case of *Hamlet*, the scripts, to explore the choices not made by that production but still potential within the latent page.

I am not an advocate of disseminating topics for possible papers. That process places limits on the richness of the script, reducing it to mere pedagogy, and, crucially, it tends to define a student's response to the script. Assignments grow from what interests a student. With three versions of the same play available, students will have no difficulty in finding something to write about. The teacher's job will usually be to get the student to limit the topic.

Potential topics are manifold. Examining three versions of Hermia's dream (2.2.151–62) allows students to look into modern psychological theories and to assess their applicability to Shakespeare. Contrasting the Agincourt sequences in the Olivier and Branagh versions of *Henry V* gives students an opportunity to deal with very different camera techniques and to evaluate the effect of different zeitgeists on the films' content. Looking at the relationship between Lord and Lady Capulet in different productions of *Romeo and Juliet* can show students that actors and directors can develop subtexts for performance that are not written into the script. The "going off to prison" scene in *King Lear* (5.3) can be read toward the feminist point of view, in that Lear seems there to reimpose the agenda interrupted by his tantrum in act 1—that is, to set his "rest / On [Cordelia's] kind nursery." Or, in *Macbeth*, how much power does a director cede to the Weird Sisters? The opening of the Polanski film suggests that they dictate destiny. Is that an option that the script supports? In what ways is the role of Lady Macbeth as depicted in act 1, scene 7 consistent with or in conflict with feminist theories? When only one good version of a play is available—the 1953 *Julius Caesar*, for example—a student can historicize the production by looking at the conventions and techniques of filmmaking the time—at its historical moment (McCarthyism, in this instance) and the critical response the production received. We learn a lot when we discover what other films a Shakespeare film was compared to in order to contextualize it for a contemporary audience. When a student brings a topic forward, we, as teachers, must be ready to help the student shape his or her response. Even a weak production, like the Burge *Julius Caesar*, can be used to contrast its treatment of a scene with another.

The teacher should make sure that more than one version of a play is available to students. Some plays—*A Midsummer Night's Dream* and *Macbeth*, for example—have films, television versions, and televised versions of live performances on cassette and thus present plenty of options, including a contrast between the media within which the script is interrogated. Different versions of the same script show a student that no right interpretation exists, but that the script itself is a site for options and decisions. Any production, then, becomes an interpretation, and any interpretation is conditioned by the medium. The one-on-one debates between Brutus and Portia, Caesar and Calpurnia, are made for television. Different treatments of the same character—a minor character or a major character in a small segment of action—and an analysis of different design concepts applied to the same script also make for excellent avenues for student response.

The orations in the Forum defeat the one television version of *Julius Caesar* available (BBC). The effort to suggest a crowd merely suggests a studio, a low budget, an inadequate medium. The scene is scaled to film. The Mankiewicz is in black and white, which may be a better medium for this script than color, because of its documentary quality and because color flattens depth. But a contrast between Antony's oration in each film makes an immediately valuable assignment. In the Burge, Antony's "You gentle Romans" is a cynical comment on the citizens' discarding of Caesar. In the Burge, some of the conspirators hang around to listen to Antony and then shift away in fear. And in the Burge, the camera is placed to show the mob exiting, with Antony in the distance, above a multitude of bobbing heads and a babble of rage. These three points and others contrast with the Mankiewicz film and give very different conceptions of Antony (Heston and Brando) and very different approaches to how a crowd becomes a mob. An analysis of what we see when we hear the words will help a student understand how a scene is created for film. That process includes editing out some of the language in favor of the imagery that a director captures. In film, images often replace the language of the script. That tendency is less prevalent on television, where image alone seldom carries complete meaning.

One topic that will engage some students is that of style of production. This involves them in understanding how an aesthetic stance conditions, perhaps even controls, performance.

Michele Willems defines three different conceptions of production for the BBC-TV Shakespeare series: the naturalistic, the pictorial, and the stylized. The first dominated the early years of the BBC series as produced by Cedric Messina. The second characterized the Miller and Moshinsky productions, and the third typified the Jane Howell versions of the *First Henriad* and *The Winter's Tale*. Willems finds the last, "where the visual element is used as functional or suggestive preferable to one in which it is referential ['naturalistic'] or decorative ['pictorial']" (1987, 100).

The naturalistic approach tends to resemble the Hollywood period pieces of the 1930s and 1940s, laden with costumes and furniture but light on anything but cliché villains and lovers. The complexity of Shakespeare's exploration of politics in the *Second Henriad*, for example, tends toward simplistic close-ups of character. The effort to depict battles falls between film's sweep and depth and Shakespeare's technique of keeping the battle just out of sight while the stage becomes a zone into which survivors stagger, across which retreats and pursuits are conducted, or in which two combatants go hand to hand. Mark Crispin Miller delivers an accurate indictment of the naturalistic approach as it was applied to the *Richard II–Henry V* cycle:

These adaptations are desperately "Shakespearean" and entirely meaningless, turning the plays into empty antiquarian spectacles.

Their emphasis, in other words, is the opposite of Shakespeare's. The actors at the Globe performed on an empty stage, expecting their audience to listen with imagination. . . . Shakespeare's language was evocative enough to make backdrops and props redundant. In order to let that language do its work, the best directors of Shakespearean film and television—Olivier, Brook, Welles, Kozintsev, Hall—have tried to stylize their productions. Each has avoided historical literalism, using his medium not to bolster vulgar notions of the past but to convey a certain set of meanings derived from personal study of the text. "Shakespeare's plays," on the other hand, reflects the corporate approach, hiring lots of "experts," spending too much money, and making something deadly out of something good. Each play is just another useless product, meant for quick consumption. . . .

Struggling to create the proper aura, the BBC has blown a wad on later medieval bric-a-brac: hogsheads, crossbows, goblets, scrolls—everything but ye kitchen sink. These irrelevant items clutter irrelevant sets—all those dungeons and taverns and banquet halls which Shakespeare only mentions but which the BBC has meticulously reconstructed. Such "realism" is supposed to lend these shows an atmosphere at once authentic and colorful, but it only distracts us from the verse, and has the further ill effect of implying a certain condescension, both to the plays and to the past. This literalism becomes hilarious when the action moves "outdoors," that is, onto a studio set covered with fake knolls and plastic trees. While the film studio can present a credible illusion of the natural world, the nails and plaster are always obvious on television. (Using the real thing is no less of an error, as [the 1979 version of] *As You Like It*, set disconcertingly amid actual woods, made very clear.) This fact of video adds a touch of humor to the BBC's battle scenes, in which small groups of uneasy men try to roughhouse on fields of Astroturf. (1980, 46–61)

That is not to say that these productions are unmitigatedly disastrous. Some fine moments come through, as when the heartbroken duke of York and the courageous bishop of Carlisle are brought into a relationship by the camera that the script does not suggest, there is a series of dissolves through which Richard II's long prison soliloquy meanders, and the opening of *Henry V*, where Canterbury and Ely posture at prayer while discussing politics. This conflict between pose and agenda might have been repeated in the production but is instead, like so much else in this sequence, just an isolated moment.

The pictorial approach—what I would call the "painterly"—creates beautiful pictures. The emphasis is on color, tonality, and composition, as in Miller's use of Vermeer for his *Shrew* and Veronese for his *Antony and Cleopatra*. Dramatic issues are buried somewhere beneath the pictures. A play is not a painting. What we get is surface. This tendency is augmented by Miller's insistence on "normalizing" his characters, so that Kate becomes domesticated within a Puritan household, Antony is a middling-good rugby player ten yards from his last scrum with a provincial club, and Othello is a King Hussein. Such a reduction might seem to be dictated by the medium; it in fact represents a surrender in advance to the medium. I and others have discussed the pictorial approach at length (1992). One of the values of these productions is that they force us back to the scripts, not only for their range of possible interpretations but also for their potentially televisual values. These productions, then, reinforce the continuum between production as manifestation of the text and the text as print, where it retains its enormous potentiality.

What Willems calls the "stylized," I would rename the "theatrical." In this category we find productions televised in front of live audiences, often with the audience in view. Some of these suffer from the weaknesses that can plague any stage production, but many seem to pick up energy from the fact of an audience and at least imitate the concept of suspension of disbelief. Not only does the energy of the audience transmit itself to the television viewer, but some of the excesses of the stage that suffer from a close-up technique—projection and gesture, for example—can work within a frame that simulates the presence of theater. Bad acting is bad acting anywhere, of course, and television is merciless with acting that might just get by on stage. Some of the live productions that have appeared on television are the energetic American Conservatory Theatre's *Shrew*, Papp's *King Lear* and *A Midsummer Night's Dream*, a number of productions from Stratford, Canada, Sarah Caldwell's *Macbeth*, and Trevor Nunn's *Comedy of Errors*. A variation of this technique, where the camera observes a stage and all angles are as if from a spectator's position, are the Bard productions of, for example, *Macbeth, Antony and Cleopatra*, and *The Tempest*, the BBC's *The Winter's Tale*, and the Renaissance Theatre's *Twelfth Night*. The absence of an audience can create the feeling of an empty theater. Although rehearsals scarcely off-book can be very exciting, as the actors make discoveries among themselves, the effect of an empty theater tends to deaden these productions, as does the static stance from which we watch. One production of this type that is effective, however, is the Bard version of *Othello*, with William Marshall and Ron Moody.

Another variation of the theatrical mode is the production redesigned for TV after appearing on stage. Some of Derek Jacobi's characterization of Hamlet—his donning of a skull mask before the play scene, for example—derives from his Old Vic stage performance. The excellent RSC *Macbeth* and *Antony and Cleopatra*, perhaps the two best television versions of Shakespeare ever, emerge from a stage history, as do the recent RSC *Othello*, Miller's *Merchant of Venice* with Olivier, and the Kline *Hamlet*. Such productions partake of all that the actors have learned and worked out in front of live audiences. Not only are they not underrehearsed, as some of the BBC-TV versions were, but the actors' familiarity with the roles permits them relax into the lower-key style demanded by TV. In the instances of the *Macbeth* and *Antony and Cleopatra*, director Trevor Nunn creates a minimal context in which superb acting—that of Judi Dench, Ian McKellen, Janet Suzman, and Richard Johnson can work. The *Antony and Cleopatra* contrasts the black and white of Rome, with its metallic surfaces, harsh angles, hard columns, and purposeful movement, with the languid pace of molten Egypt, swept by slow fans and Cleopatra's eyelashes. Egypt is a place of pillows on which to lean and lie and filmy curtains that open onto more curtains as Cleopatra enticingly reveals this or that fraction of her infinite variety. The style is consistent with a play that encompasses two worlds and their radically divergent worldviews and the scale of television. Why the BBC did not "go to school" with this production baffles me. The Nunn *Macbeth* comes from the studio-like dimensions of the Other Place and the Warehouse. On television it uses stark contrasts and tight framing to create a claustrophobic intensity.

Another successful approach within the theatrical model is the set that works like a stage. In Desmond Davis's *Measure for Measure*, for example, the brothel and the convent are the same set with different paint, so that the linear movement of television tape permits us to experience the same set as emblem of both purity and the licentiousness that overly zealous purity may repress. Given its theatrical premises, this production employs a technique that would have seemed like a continuity glitch in other "perfected" TV productions. The sound of a previous scene continues into the next scene or the image of the previous scene overlays the sound of a new scene. This interplay of sound and picture is a televisual equivalent of the simultaneous exit and entrance of the Shakespearean stage. In Peter Brook's 1953 *King Lear*, with Orson Welles, Lear, having dragged the dead Cordelia in, slumps onto the throne from which he had commanded the opening sequence. Cordelia lies on the steps where she had knelt earlier to be auctioned off to France or Burgundy. As the frame expands, we see the pedestals on which Lear's daughters had stood so long before, prize dolls in the king's collection. Brook does not pursue Albany's order to "Produce the bodies," one that permits the final tableau to mirror in death the opening scene, so deceptively vibrant with life and new beginnings and which gives us a gestalten glimpse of all that has happened between those moments. The "staging" of the final scene, however, reminds us that the silence and emptiness of the ending are directly attributable to the fulsomeness of the opening. The link between beginning and ending is the continuing silence of Cordelia, as Lear leans forward for a word from her. At the end, he gets nothing. Earlier, Cordelia's asides had been voice-overs, with Cordelia occasionally mouthing the words. She speaks her "Nothing, my lord," making it remarkably powerful and permitting it to carry over into the silence of the finale.

More successful than her unit set and geometric shapes for *The Winter's Tale* is Jane Howell's stage set for the *First Henriad*—a unit set with ramps, doors, balconies, curtained areas, and a central space that word and lighting can translate into throne room, street, or battlefield. As she says,

Some sets you find in your head, some sets are in books. I knew this one was in the street. I did not know what it was. Then one day I was out in a car, and suddenly I saw the top of an adventure playground which had been crudely painted in medieval colours by the kids. It was lovely. I was in such a hurry that I couldn't stop, but I knew I had solved it. It was some strange area in which you could play, in which you could pretend, which is an equivalent of Shakespeare's stage. (quoted in Willems 1987)

Howell's set becomes a place for exploration, a space in which the relatively unknown dimensions of these plays can be charted, and it works superbly, as critics note: "The paradox was that of television accommodating a self-consciously staged production, rougher and more pantomimic than anything to be found in the theatre itself" (Ackroyd 1983); "the production and setting managed to contain both the kindergarten babyishness and the noble savagery of the work" (Jones 1983). Another device that Howell deploys in her refusal to yield to television's normative "realism" is the use of doubling: David Burke as Gloucester and Dick the Butcher and Antony Brown as Whitmore and Iden, for example.

While television tends to hide its techniques the better to sell us something, Shakespeare on television demands that we pay attention to technique. Watching Shakespeare on television may not be like watching Shakespeare, but it is not like watching television either.

One of the possible fallacies of any discussion of Shakespeare and television is the assumption that television is subject to rational evaluation, that is, that it conveys meanings in ways that can be described in language. We are lulled into such an assumption by the predictable pattern of the camera—close-up, two-shot, reaction shot—a rhythm employed even in newsmaker interviews. The consistency and straightforwardness of the camera does not necessarily convey the same attributes to the content. We are meant to believe so, but, as David Marc says, "Television is American dada, Charles Dickens on LSD, the greatest parody of European culture since *The Dunciad* . . . Art or not art? This is largely a lexographical quibble for the culturally insecure. Interesting? Only the hopelessly genteel could find such a phantasmagoria flat" (1984, 35). Some aspect of revelation—Christ or anti-Christ?—must be at hand. Certainly Marc makes the conventional critiques of, for example, "the new fall lineup on NBC" wonderfully irrelevant as delivered by those who take TV on its own terms.

Marc may also make a discussion of Shakespeare on television irrelevant, unless the discussion accounts for the parodic nature of the medium itself, consciously realized in shows like "Monty Python's Flying Circus" and "Black Adder." Can the potentially subversive underscript of the script emerge from television, or does TV subvert depth so that serious Shake-speare on television becomes a parody of theater? Jane Howell manages the fit superbly in her *II Henry VI*, a script whose phantasmagoria suits TV, if a director lets the play's parody of politics emerge via a stylization that some directors claim cannot work on television. A director must account for and overcome the potentially generic and tonal distortions that the medium itself is likely to impose on serious drama.

The number of possible topics when productions are contrasted against each other approaches infinity. Students who define a moment in the script and deal with it in two or three versions will create an essay that is organized, perceptive, and detailed. They will write better if they chose the moment that they want to examine. *Julius Caesar* is often the first Shakespeare play that students encounter, and it can be deadly. It will be if teachers assign the BBC version and plop students down in front of it, veterans though they be. But when different versions are available, the script becomes an energy sys-tem that demonstrates its variables and, most important, produces some-thing that insists on student response. Some students will want to write about how they would direct a given scene. In a seminar, students can bring tapes into class as part of their presentation to their classmates.

Here is a simple project that a student might select: *Contrast two versions of the Yorick sequence, as rendered by Olivier in his film and McKellen in the 1970 television version.*

Olivier the performer never lets us forget that he is an actor playing a role, greatly playing a role, of course, chuckling ever so slightly as some dirt falls from Yorick's skull. The dirt reminds us of the sand falling in an hourglass and is a metonymy for the lawyer's fine pate full of fine dirt, a line cut in the film. Olivier does not make the mistake of the amateur actor of knowing what comes next, but he is always in control, and at the end, he sits in the throne in a production without a Fortinbras. McKellen permits his charac-ter to go out of control, totally fascinated by the skull and its stink. Can we imagine Olivier probing the skull with a finger, sniffing that finger, then thrusting the grisly object at a Horatio who is clearly not enjoying this pause and whose own gorge may be rising? We get two very different acting styles, each right for the actor and his conception of the role and for the moment in which the play is being sent outward into its zeitgeist: the late 1940s in one instance and the early 1970s in the other.

The Yorick sequence elicits other questions. The design of the scene brings Hamlet from disquisitions about death to increasingly specific confronta-tions with it: to Yorick, whom he knew and loved, to Ophelia, whom he knew and loved, and into contact with the men who will kill him and he them, Claudius and Laertes. The sequence permits the historian of ideas to talk about Yorick as the culmination of the *memento mori* tradition, made remarkably available here by dint of its being rendered in a theater by a character the audience would, in all probability, have identified with. Why is Ophelia buried in Yorick's grave? She has been a jester, of course—a speaker of truth in song and rhyme—and may represent "the feminine," as it has been argued Yorick did to the very young Hamlet.

Some students really are knowledgeable about the media that dominate our culture. Excerpts from different media—film, which emerges from the silent screen, where images alternated with the print of title cards; television, which stems from radio and absorbs more of the spoken word than does film; and stage, with its recent movement out from under the proscenium arch—can engage students in the important questions attendant on the conceptual spaces in which the plays are produced. Space defines what can occur within it. In the Yorick contrast, some students will notice that Olivier's deep-field, black-and-white photography allows for considerable depth, while the McKellen color version for television is much more a close-up approach to the play. It should be obvious that teaching with taped performance materials complements the approach whereby students deploy themselves in available spaces to make the moves that the scenes seem to dictate. The two approaches inform each other. It is a good idea to have students look at a professional production on tape after they themselves have mastered a scene in their own way. They will probably prefer their own way and be able to defend it cogently.

Assume, for example, that a student is dealing with Hamlet's interrogation of Yorick's skull in the Olivier, Richardson, and Zeffirelli films. Behind a compare-and-contrast assignment are questions like these:

- What is the structure of the scene: from the Gravedigger's demonstration that Ophelia killed herself in self-defense, to Hamlet's discovery that a specific skull is Yorick's, to the approach of "maimed rites" for someone Hamlet suddenly learns is Ophelia?

- Has Hamlet undergone a change of heart as a result of his sea voyage, as is often claimed for him?

- Is the apostrophe to Yorick a tight two-shot, or does the camera acknowledge Horatio and the Gravedigger?

- Is Hamlet's speech to Yorick read as a summary statement about the past or delivered as a set of discoveries?

- What is the relationship of the speech to the rest of the play? ("Alas, poor ghost!" —"Alas, poor Yorick!")

- Does the scene suggest any continuity of ideas between the medieval *memento mori* tradition and our own era? (cf. Jessica Mitford's *American Way of Death* 1963).

- What does each version show about Hamlet's relationship to the Gravedigger, Horatio, and Yorick? Theirs to him?

- How is each version edited? Olivier does not say "his fine pate filled with fine dirt," but dirt does drop out of the skull. What visual equivalents of language do the other versions show? (The Kozintsev film provides a rotting jester's cap for Yorick.)

- Why is Ophelia buried in Yorick's grave? (Some sense of the function of the fool may help with this question.)

If we contrast two versions of a line by Fortinbras, one in which Robert Coleby (in the 1970 Hallmark production) says, "Take up the bodies," and another in which Don Reilly (in the 1990 Kline production for PBS) says, "Take up the body," we can make some points about texts and the options they present. One is clearing an open stage of bodies, even on television. The other is, perhaps, using a single body that would have proved "most royal had *he* been put on" the throne as part of a combination funeral-coronation, similar to the one that Claudius conducted much earlier. Fortinbras, knowing that he has the voice (or vote) of the man who was briefly King Hamlet II, will use that fragment of body politic to consolidate his own "rights of memory in this kingdom." The choice between Q2's *bodies* and Folio's *body* is not a quibble. The decision as to singular or plural tells us whether, in choosing the singular—meaning Hamlet's body—Fortinbras is thinking of his own plurality as king. The moment in contrasting performances permits us to talk about textual variations, to introduce the concept of the king's two bodies, and to ask students to defend their own choices on this and other notorious textual alternatives, like the "Judean-Indian" crux in *Othello* (5.2.401).

One aspect of production that invariably summons student ingenuity is the analysis of framing in the scripts and in production. Frames are difficult for television—they are stage conventions—but have been successfully constructed, as in Rodney Bennett's production of *Hamlet* for BBC. The play-within-the-play motif, as in *Love's Labour's Lost, A Midsummer Night's Dream, Hamlet*, and *The Tempest*, a framing story like that of Egeon in *The Comedy of Errors*, the use of a chorus as in *Romeo and Juliet* and *Henry V* or of an epilogue, an actual frame like that of *The Taming of the Shrew*, a staged scene like that of the statue in *The Winter's Tale*, and other "insets," as Francis Berry calls them (1965), pose challenges for the director of a shallow medium like television and make an excellent topic for student observation and report.

The frame—whether a formal play, a presentational device, or a scene in which one or more characters stage something for others—involves different levels of awareness. Almost never do we as an audience not share the largest circumference of knowledge—the Statue Scene in *The Winter's Tale* being the exception. Some unreconstructed structuralists still find it valuable to talk of the plays as if they were designed to mediate audience response. *The Taming of the Shrew* is a notorious case in point and possibly deserves attention as a site in itself as opposed to a document in a problematized inter-textual contextualization.

The recent Alexander production at Stratford-on-Avon, for example, has a group of young aristocrats of the 1990s play a trick on a drunken lower-class Sly. The play within is done in Elizabethan dress by a down-at-the-jowl company that enlists the aristocrats to play smaller roles. Petruchio actually slaps the Honorable Constantia Durham, a dainty rogue in porcelain, who is playing one of Petruchio's servants. At one point Sly offers candy to a "starving" Kate. Are we to see him as compassionate or as unable to sepa-rate art from life? Alexander's framing raises all kinds of questions about class, status, history and its ongoing hierarchies, art versus life, and "keep-ing in character." Lady Eustacia Meredith, called on to play the Widow, has done the part in school and tosses her script away. She sneers at Kate's final speech but is eager to pursue a theatrical career, to play Kate (to borrow a phrase from Barbara Hodgdon), even if she herself as real person remains a radical feminist.

Framing distances us from the fiction, gives us space in which to evaluate our response and determine our reality. It keeps us, as Brecht would wish, from identifying with the characters. A frame reminds us that we are not looking at reality. Minimum framing, like the plastic around the tube or the proscenium arch, creates a fourth wall and makes a pretense of presenting reality. One of the problems for Shakespeare on television is that he wrote plays for a more flexible, open format.

Shakespeare's stage would have kept Sly in view, at least until his inter-ruption at the end of scene 1. Then, says George Hibbard in his excellent in-troduction to the play, "he is quietly dropped" (1968, 15). But how? Or does he disappear? At the end of the 1981 production at Stratford, Canada, the lord threw a purse to the actor who had played Baptista in the inner play as Sly was being carried out. He awoke later to play out part of the "A Shrew" ending. If that ending is used, we may infer that the inner play has been Sly's dream of male superiority. The joke is on Sly, however, as he re-peats Hortensio's belief (5.5.77–79) that Petruchio's "taming" formula is in-stantly transferable.

At the end of the elegant Stratford, Canada, production of 1990, which was also televised, Colm Feore, who had doubled as Sly and Petruchio, was discovered just waking up—as Sly—as the wedding party exited. His dream had come from his brief confrontation, before passing out, with Goldie Sem-ple, who had been the hostess and was alchemized into Kate in his dream. He had had a rare vision of sybaritic pleasure and opulence. He exited somberly, without a word.

If a production provides the induction, or part of it, without the "A Shrew" closure, it may be that the play within has become Petruchio and Kate's game, as they play stereotypic roles for Padua's consumption and their own enjoyment. The Road to Padua Scene in which Petruchio and Kate bewilder Vincentio becomes the first scene of their play—their fictionaliz-ing of reality. Director Richard Sewell, playing Sly, had himself yanked into the line of servants awaiting Petruchio as he approaches his country house.

Sly was later observed waiting on tables at the final banquet. Sewell erased one plane of fiction by absorbing it into the play.

Shrew without a frame can become a wild, slapstick farce, like the American Conservatory Theater production, with Marc Singer and Ferdi Ostler, which has the great benefit of having been televised before a live audience, or it can become a realistic and somber "Puritan" version, like Jonathan Miller's for BBC. In the latter we are meant to take Kate's submission speech at face value and submit without a quiver to the communal singing of Psalm 128:

> Blessed is everie one that feareth the Lord
> and walketh in his wayes.
> When thou eatest the labours of thine hands,
> thou shalt be blessed, and it shalbe wel with thee.
> Thy wife shalbe as the fruteful vine on the sides
> of thine house, and thy children like the olive plants
> round about thy table.
> Lo, surely thus shal the man be blessed,
> that feareth the Lord.
> The Lord out of Zion shal blesse thee and thou shalt se
> the welth of Jerusalem all the dayes of thy life.
> Yea, thou shalt se thy childrens children,
> and peace upon Israel.

In the "Moonlighting" variation, which appeared on ABC on 25 November 1986, the inner play becomes a projection of the boy forced upstairs by his mother, away from the TV, to do his homework. "Shrew," then, incorporates his zeitgeist: "music," kung fu, "controlling" women, and what Jack Oruch calls "a feminist revision of [Shakespeare's] plot" (1987, 7). The frame ends when the boy's mother tells him he has not missed anything. "It wasn't very good tonight," she says, and the standard "Moonlighting" credits roll. In the film version of *Kiss Me, Kate! Shrew* becomes the play within. The final scene of the film, in which Lilli Vanessi reconciles with Fred, is the final scene of the film's *Shrew*, played out in front of a "theater" audience innocent of the backstage struggle to which we have been privy. Here, the frame collapses into the inner play and is resolved therein, through Lilli's adoring looks and whispers and Fred's gradual comprehension. We witness the interplay of the "real" people from cameras placed upstage. Thus Petruchio's "Kiss me, Kate!" and her compliance become the physical signal that resolves two stories: the one being played for the "spectators" of *Shrew* and the one that has been played for the auditors of the film. At the end of the three-dimensional film, Fred and Lilli, Petruchio and Kate, are thrust at us for a "curtain call." The stage version of the musical insists that we—the only audience—sort out the analogy between *Shrew* and "Kate." The stage version also insists that we respond at the end to curtain calls made by actors playing characters playing characters in an old play by Shakespeare.[1]

Students can also examine the relationship between the title cards in the 1966 reissue of the Mary Pickford–Douglas Fairbanks *Shrew*, the first talking version of Shakespeare (1929), in which Pickford remembers the troubles that she and Doug were having during the filming, and the Kate-Petruchio story, which includes Kate overhearing Petruchio's, "Now have I politicly begun my reign" speech and her eclipsing wink to Bianca at the end. To historicize the Richard Burton–Elizabeth Taylor version of the mid-1960s is also to provide the frame that zeitgeist and biography inevitably lend to any production of Shakespeare. Zeffirelli's allusion to the frame is a cage holding a "Drunkard," at which Lucentio (Michael York) glances on entering the gates of Padua (see my discussion of framing, 1992).

To prove that television need not eliminate the frame for the sake of simplifying content, the animated version includes both halves of the frame. A bloat Sly is tossed out of the tavern, picked up by the lord and his retainers, who exchange him for a boar they are bringing back from the hunt. Sly awakens in a luxurious chamber, replete with Tintorettos, and is presented with "The Taming of the Shrew" from a proscenium stage. At the end, the lord and the stage manager applaud while standing in a perspectival commedia dell'arte stage, which had been the room where Sly awakened and watched the play. We look at them from the stage as we make the transition back to the sleeping Sly. Knowing now "how to tame a shrew," he reenters the tavern and is immediately tossed out again. This version plays neatly with the script's own playing with art and life, perception and reality, and gets a surprising amount of the inherited script into its half-hour without strain. The only problem is the idiotic introduction by Robin Williams, who says that "Kate makes Tonya Harding look like Gidget." The interior story owes a lot to the Zeffirelli film. The elegant puppet format is a great relief after the dreary literalism of the Miller production for BBC.

Various critical approaches can be applied by students as they examine a production. I give several examples in Part II of this book. Is it helpful to historicize a production—to place, for example, the two versions of *Henry V* in their historical moment? Does thematic criticism still work in a postmodernist era? What is postmodernism? Does feminist criticism inform our response to production? Is psychological criticism useful in the analysis of production? Does deconstruction help in responding to production? The answer is invariably yes, but the affirmative requires an understanding of the paradigms and qualifications that make some of them applicable to an experience of the script as script—that is, as a text that is meant to be performed, not merely read and responded to as a piece of literature or as a document within a flow of documents.

Here are brief descriptions of some basic approaches to examining Shakespeare:

The *new critical*—what Peter Donaldson calls an "aesthetic of opposition and tension within organic unity" (1990, xiii)—involves the reading of a play as a poem, as a unified whole, and as a product of an author's intention. This is an outmoded approach. Critics no longer believe that they can read any work effectively if equipped with the right vocabulary (irony, paradox, ambiguity). Nevertheless, this approach can still be useful in reading the text as a prelude to editing it for performance. Assuming that a director wishes his production to achieve some sort of coherence, he or she may discern themes and rhythms in the text that were to be retained in the speaking of it on stage. We "read" a film somewhat as a new critic, paying close attention to signals in the film, but using a different vocabulary from the new critics and an awareness that the work of art occurs in history, which the new critics tended to ignore. They read atemporally.

The *generic critic* tells us what usually happens in the world of a given type of play—what can happen and what cannot in comedy, tragedy, or romance. If death occurs, as in *The Winter's Tale*, a long expiation is necessary for the guilty party, in this case, Leontes, who is responsible for two deaths in the play and an apparent third. Although the world of the romance may threaten, yet is it kind. Reconciliation occurs after apparent loss. Shakespeare is not strictly formulaic; in fact, he spoofs formulas though Polonius in *Hamlet*. The question, What kind of a play is this? is a good starting place for the interrogation of a particular script. Some of the plays that combine generic assumptions are called "problem plays."

The *feminist critic* forces us to look at women in the plays—at how relationships are conducted, at marginalized characters, at sexuality as it circulates in both literature and culture, and at gender issues. It insists that we examine point of view, including our own.

New historicism insists that we see play in context and ask what ideological assumptions underlie the literature and how the literature interrogates official doctrine and assumptions of Elizabethan and Jacobean culture. The approach may uncover some original and originating contexts that help us understand the script. It is necessary to historicize production, that is, to see it as a product of its moment, not as a facet of some universal truth. Some feminist criticism is new historicist in that it examines early modern cultural practice.

Cultural materialism, a British, left-wing approach, sees literature as either complying with or subverting dominant ideologies. The cultural materialist would reject the "romantic reading" of Shakespeare, one in which authority and aristocratic love matches are validated as "what the play means." A typical cultural materialist reading would go like this:

There are still attempts from within Anglo-American culture to create a world-wide cultural hegemony based on the orthodoxy of New Criticism. The targeting of an international market by Time/Life, Morgan Guaranty and the BBC is symptomatic of this. . . . The BBC Shakespeares, with their glib re-assertion of the mythology of the universal bard, contribute to the continuing suppression of radical and interventionist readings of the plays. (Collick 1989, 194–95)

The cultural materialist helps us see the shadow cast by apparent political success, as in the current debate about Henry V's killing of prisoners at Agincourt, an episode erased from Olivier and Branagh films.

Psychological criticism focuses on the characters as if they were subject to modern psychological theories like those of Freud, Jung, Adler, Horney and others. This can be a fallacy in that it is anachronistic and can deal with the characters as if they were real, as opposed to constructs in a fiction. The characters do at times correspond to Elizabethan psychology, or humor theory, of which the melancholic, phlegmatic, choleric, or sanguine were the four major types. This approach often crosses over into feminist criticism. The psychological approach is useful not only in probing the motives of characters but in understanding our response to them and to the complex worlds in which they act, interact, and suffer.

Post-modernism insists on multiple signification (a work of literature has no single or fixed meaning), fragmentation (a work of literature lacks unity), and a rejection of the "author function." The work is independent of any licensing authority and of what he or she may have meant or intended. This is a disintegrative (or deconstructive) approach that obliterates the perceived rigidities of previous methodologies. It is a version of the oedipal rhythm that Harold Bloom finds in literature: One must kill the father before one becomes king. What will be raised on the razed ground in Shakespeare's case is already clear: performance as the criterion of "meaning" and an increased emphasis on understanding and phrasing what we mean by performance and how we respond to it.[2]

An ability to describe what the camera does is vital to a description of how film works. This is much less true of the more limited camera work of most television productions, where the camera's mediation is meant to be unobtrusive, the better to reveal the "reality" that TV purports to show.

TV tends to use a three-camera format: close-up (which can be of speaker or a reaction shot), two-shot (two people in frame, usually a medium shot, that is, from the waist up), and over-the-shoulder shot. Variations exist—for example, a three-shot, with one person in the foreground and two behind. This format works well for one-on-one confrontations but has difficulty accommodating big scenes. Television's inabilities to provide a big picture or any artistry in technique are in some ways consistent with the fragmented vision of postmodernism—and may have contributed to our current unwillingness to accept "totalizing mythologies," "artistic unity," or even "meaning." Television as author of postmodernism is an arguable thesis.

Film can use the three-camera format and tends to do so in films made for television, which are scaled to the medium.

A shot that TV and film share is the rack shot, where one part of the frame is out of focus and the other in focus. This is a way of controlling point of view.

Here are descriptions of some frequently used film shots:

Pan. The camera is fixed but turns to follow action or to view a scene. A *swish-pan* is a rapid sweep in which objects blur. If camera pans up or down, the shot can be called a *tilt.*

Tracking. The camera moves on a track paralleling the action, as in the French charge in Olivier's *Henry V.*

High angle. The camera looks down on subject (it can be judgmental, like the shots at the beginning of Olivier's *Lear*). If the camera is on a boom, this is called a *boom shot.*

Low angle. The camera looks up at subject (the subject can be "commanding," for example, Olivier as he waits to signal his archers in *Henry V*).

Straight shot. The camera is at the subject's level. Contrast Branagh with Olivier as Agincourt begins.

Zoom-in. The camera closes up rapidly on subject.

Here are some of the frequently used transitions from shot to shot:

Cut, straight cut. One shot is added to another.

Montage. In this series of straight cuts, the whole exceeds the sum of its parts.

Cross-cut. Different scenes, often occurring at the same time, are connected (cf. the cavalry charging toward a threatened wagon train). This technique was perfected by D. W. Griffith.

Dissolve. One image fades out while a superimposed image fades in. Usually it means that the first context brings about the second. It can be used to suggest time's passage, as in the brilliant sequence of Richard's soliloquy in the BBC-TV *Richard II.*

Match-cut. A character exits one space and enters another.

Reverse shot. A character is pointing at someone looking at the character and the next shot shows the person looking. If characters are talking, the reverse shot can also be a reaction shot.

The approach via film and television means that we befriend the media rather than merely rail against their pervasiveness. We make of the cathode ray tube a site for response and interrogation, for that currently most popular of activities, interactivity.

NOTES

1. Barbara Hodgdon, in "Katherina Bound; or, Play(K)ating the Strictures of Everyday Life." *PMLA* 107 (1992): 538–53, launches a devastating attack on the voyeuristic approach to the script, particularly in *Kiss Me, Kate!*

2. See Terrence Hawkes, "Shakespeare and the New Critical Approaches," in *The Cambridge Companion to Shakespeare Studies*, edited by Stanley Well, 287–302. Cambridge: Cambridge University Press, 1986.

REFERENCES

Ackroyd, Peter. 1983. *"I Henry VI."* *Times*, 7 January.

Berry, Francis. 1965. *The Shakespearean Inset*. London: Routledge and Kegan Paul.

Camus, Albert. 1951. "Reflections of the Guillotine." In *Resistance, Rebellion, and Death*. New York: Knopf.

Collick, John. 1989. *Shakespeare, Cinema, and Society*. Manchester: Manchester University Press.

Coursen, H. R. 1992. *Shakespearean Performance as Interpretation*. Newark: University of Delaware Press.

Donaldson, Peter. 1990. *Shakespearean Films/Shakespearean Directors*. Boston: Unwin Hyman.

Freed, John. 1977. "A Marriage of Directions." *Shakespeare on Film Newsletter* 1, no. 2, 7.

Hibbard, George, ed. 1968. *The Taming of the Shrew*. Harmondsworth, U.K.: Penguin.

James, Caryn. 1996. "Television, the Medium That Defies Sharp Focus." *New York Times*, 7 July, H25, H27.

Jones, D.A.N. 1983. *"I Henry VI."* *Listener*, 6 January.

Marc, David. 1984. "Understanding Television." *Atlantic*, August, 33–44.

Miller, Mark Crispin. 1980. "The Shakespeare Plays." *Nation*, 12 July, 46–61.

Mitford, Jessica. 1963. *The American Way of Death*. New York: Simon & Schuster.

O'Brien, Peggy, ed. 1993. *Shakespeare Set Free*. New York: Washington Square Press.

Oruch, Jack. 1987. "Shakespeare for the Millions." *Shakespeare on Film Newsletter* 11, no. 2, 7.

Willems, Michele. 1987. "Reflections on the BBC Series." *Shakespeare Survey* 39, 91–102.

4

Some Extra-Shakespearean Contexts

A further field that students enjoy exploring and writing about is Shakespeare in contemporary culture. The ability of whatever Shakespeare is to generate meanings becomes a way for students to find meanings in much of what they see and hear.

In *Star Trek VI: The Undiscovered Country*, for example, Kirk and McCoy are sentenced to the lithium mines on the Penal Asteroid of Ruapectae—"The Aliens' Graveyard." Martia, a fellow captive, offers to help them escape beyond the security shield so that they can be beamed up to their home ship. She is a Comaloid, or shapechanger, who shifts to a young girl to get rid of her leg irons. When she becomes Martia again, Kirk questions whether she really is as she seems. "I thought I would assume a pleasing shape," she says. The line is Hamlet's, of course—"The devil hath power to assume a pleasing shape"—and represents an extension of Shakespeare's treatment of appearance versus reality into the fortieth century. When Kirk sees through her plot to betray him and McCoy, she becomes Kirk. "I can't believe I *kissed* you!" says Kirk. "It was probably your lifelong ambition," says his alter ego in a neat allusion to his narcissism. Fortunately for the real Kirk, the Ruapectaen constabulary vaporize his hapless imitator, and Kirk and McCoy are beamed up in the nick of time.

The film is full of lines from Shakespeare, most delivered by Captain Chang (Shakespearean actor Christopher Plummer). Martia's line from *Hamlet*, as the prince ponders the Ghost ("The devil hath power to assume a pleasing shape"), links up neatly with the space narrative. Hamlet believes that the Ghost may be misleading, him, as Martia obviously is attempting to betray Kirk and McCoy. The theme in Shakespeare is not confined to *Hamlet* but comes up in *Macbeth*, where the Weird Sisters offer "things that do sound so fair," and "honest trifles" to "betray . . . in deepest consequence." In the *Star Trek* variation, the allusion deepens the dramatic moment and suggests that Shakespearean motifs inhabit even the edge of the fortieth century, at least as imagined by the creators of *Star Trek*.

In the *LA Story* offshoot, Steve Martin leads Victoria Tennant into a cemetery where lie Benny Goodman and Rocky Marciano—and Shakespeare, who "wrote Hamlet, Part 8—the Revenge," in Los Angeles. An earth mover exits a grave, scattering a flock of pigeons and sending Rick Moranis into the hole to do some final touching up. Moranis asks whether they want to know how long it takes a body to rot. "Boy, do we!" Martin responds. The person to be buried "used to be a woman," Moranis says upon questioning, "but now she's dead." "Finally—a funny gravedigger," says Martin.

Moranis forces his insights into rotting upon Martin and Tennant, claiming that "some of those Beverly Hills women, they'll last twelve years." "How come?" Martin asks. Their skin is "polished like a bloody shoe," says Moranis, and "them extra parts they're not biodegradable." Moranis tosses up the skull of the Great Blunderman. "Not so great now, is he?"

Martin picks it up. "I knew him. A funny guy. He taught me magic."

"A fellow of infinite jest," says Tennant.

"That's it!" says Moranis, as if hearing something he has long tried to remember.

"He hath borne me on his back a thousand times," she continues, pulling the lines from her English schoolgirl's memory.

"She knows. She's got it!" cries Moranis, as if hearing fragments out of some vestigial ancestral memory—the voice of the archetype.

"Where be your gibes now, your flashes of merriment that would put the table on a roar?" she asks. To the sound of "Close Encounters" music, Martin realizes he is in love.

An elfin wind brushes across the graveyard. The gravedigger, who is either from Liverpool or learned to talk from listening to Beatles records, looks on. Finally, when it is established that each of the would-be lovers is seeing someone else, Moranis asks, "Can I have your friend's head back?" Martin, who did not realize that he was still holding it, tosses it back.

"Come back and see me," says Moranis. "They all do!" Addressing the skull, he says, "Don't they!"

This sequence suggests that the awareness of death is a spur to love. Neither masters nor mistresses can afford to be coy. The lines from *Hamlet*, heritage of the memorizing that the British schoolgirl had done years before, seem to be recognized on some level by Moranis, who is our alter ego during this brief episode. Martin is merely falling in love, his character—effectively enough—not knowing why. While some amusing moments do occur in the film, this is the only sequence in which it reaches for any sense of depth—of connectedness with the web of meanings beyond the ways of a particular city. For the most part the film is just another warning to stay away from L.A.

I wonder what people who do not know of *Hamlet* would have made of the scene. Would it convey the sense of the linkage between love and death as stressed by Shakespeare, Keats, and Rollo May? It may be that the Zeffirelli *Hamlet* gives some filmgoers a grasp of the take-off in *LA Story*. If so, fine, since it argues that parody is still possible since the work parodied is still alive to be recognized.

In the much-maligned *Last Action Hero*, Danny (Austin O'Brien) leaves a movie theater, having been promised a midnight preview of the new Jack Slater film. He arrives in class as the teacher (Joan Plowright) describes Hamlet as the "first action hero." She introduces Olivier as someone the class might have seen in Polaroid commercials or *Clash of the Titans*. She shows a clip in which Claudius's line, "O bosom black as death!" draws giggles and snorts from the class. Olivier comes up behind and begins his soliloquy.

"Don't talk," Danny snarls, "just do it!"

Danny imagines Arnold Schwarzenegger as Jack Slater as Hamlet. Hamlet lights a cigar.

"Hey, Claudius. You killed my father. Big mistake!"

Hamlet flings Claudius up through a stained glass window. A reverse angle shot shows Claudius, heels kicking at heaven, trailing debris as he plunges into the atmosphere. Hamlet ponders the skull of Yorick. As a voice-over says, "Something is rotten in Denmark, and Hamlet is taking out the trash," Hamlet flings the skull and knocks out a soldier.

Polonius, a Felix Alymer look-alike, appears from the folds of a curtain and says, "Stay thy hand, fair prince."

"Who says I'm fair?" Hamlet asks, oozing some rounds from a hand-held automatic weapon. Hamlet wanders through the castle, killing soldiers left and right, and mounts a horse.

"No one is going to tell this sweet prince good-night," says the voice-over.

Hamlet mutters, "To be or not to be," lights his cigar, says "Not to be," and rides away as the castle explodes behind him.

Schwarzenegger is remarkably faithful to the visual tonalities of the Olivier film, which is black and white, shot in a deep field that required a lot of light and created a chiaroscuro effect.

Danny's is a fantasy of one fictional hero for another. Hamlet is translated into the medium of Hollywood violence. Danny is pulled into a Slater film by means of a magic ticket that once belonged to Houdini. The film moves between levels of fiction. Los Angeles is the world of film, where Danny keeps trying to convince Slater that they are in a film. Danny asks Slater to read a word that is verboten in a PG-13 film. New York is "reality," where

Danny warns, "This isn't a film"; automobiles do not blow up like faked test crashes, and Slater's hand hurts as he punches out windows. We even get a brief "identical twin" sequence where the real Schwarzenegger and the fictional Slater come face to face.

The film is an effort to tell Schwarzenegger fans that his films are fantasies. The young filmgoer is meant to identify with Danny and thus experience a sense of artistic detachment. *Hamlet* is a splendid allusion because its hero is constantly baffled by appearances. But Brecht is beyond the audience that violence has spawned, and the critics have been conditioned to respond only to convention, stereotype, and surface. "I think people thought it was going to be a typical Arnold movie," says O'Brien (AP, 10 February 1994). As columnist Mike Royko says of the film, "It is too good for [Schwarzenegger's] fans. . . . Anything that confuses and frustrates modern teenagers can't be all bad" (12 July 1993).

Maria Crawford and the Center for Shakespeare Studies, Southern Oregon College, Ashland, have put together a tape, *Pop Culture 'Hamlets'* used in discussions with visiting high school students. Selections include snippets from *Dead Poet's Society*, "Star Trek," "Addams Family," "Gilligan's Island," *The Last Action Hero*, "Saturday Night Live," *LA Story*, *Red, Hot, and Blue*, and "Animaniacs." These are mostly parodies: Robin Williams holding the skull and saying, "We have a malpractice suit here," O'Brien imagining Schwartzenegger as a very lethal Hamlet, Martin saying, "Finally—a funny gravedigger," Betty Hutton doing one of her frantic routines, and Spielberg's talking animals simultaneously performing and subverting the Yorick speech. They show that Shakespeare is still circulating in popular culture, making meanings not necessarily controlled or condoned by those who would use Shakespeare as a prop to dominant ideologies—unless it be that oxymoron known as popular culture. The parodies, often performed by well known figures, probably defuse Shakespearephobia and perhaps suggest that the plays themselves can be enjoyable as well. "We *use* [the plays]" says Terry Hawkes, "to generate meaning. In the twentieth century, Shakespeare's plays have become one of the central agencies through which our culture performs this operation. That is what they do, that is how they work, and that is what they are for. Shakespeare doesn't mean; *we* mean *by* Shakespeare" (1993).[1]

Another possible use of television in the teaching of Shakespeare is the trial format for dealing with the issues of a given play (cf. Boynton and Carducci 1993). Here an issue is defined. The class is formed into the components of a trial: judge, jury, defendants, witnesses, defense and prosecution teams. Topics are manifold: Bolingbroke's defense of his premature return from banishment to England, Othello's defense of his killing of Desdemona, Caliban's suit against Prospero for damages and recovery of property, Angelo's culpability in *Measure for Measure*, and so forth. The trial, with its intrinsic dramatic form, formatted setting, stereotypical characters, and opportunities for reaction shots, has long been a standard subject for film and television, from Fritz Lang's *Rage* to Perry Mason and "The Defenders." The recent rise of "Court TV," and its televising of the trials of Pamela Smart, William Smith, and the Menendez brothers among others, provides a possible format for a camcorder here, and the recent trial of Hamlet, held in an elegant room at the Supreme Court, could serve as a model.

The tape of "The Trial of Hamlet" will reward careful study and comment. Associate Justice Anthony M. Kennedy, who presides, defines the case against Hamlet around a narrow issue: Was Hamlet, at the time of his killing of Polonius, capable of understanding the criminality of his conduct or of conforming his conduct to the requirements of the law?

Hamlet has been allowed to survive Laertes's apparently fatal thrust, but "all questions of his accession to the throne of Denmark have been held in abeyance" until his criminal responsibility has been established. If he is found to be insane at the time of his killing of Polonius, he will be committed to a mental institution. If the jury finds him sane, he is criminally responsible and will be tried for anything from involuntary manslaughter to first-degree murder. If the latter charge were to be brought, it would be based, one assumes, on Hamlet's soliloquy as he decides not to kill the apparently praying Claudius and on his belief that the person behind the arras is Claudius ("I took thee for thy better").

The jurors are the arbiters of fact, Kennedy suggests, the judge merely the interpreter of the law. The evidence is made up of the text of *Hamlet* (the conflated text, one assumes) and the testimony of expert witnesses. The facts in this instance are not contested: Hamlet did kill Polonius. The mental condition of the defendant at the time of the killing is the jury's only concern. The defense has the burden of proof to show that the preponderance of evidence demonstrates that Hamlet was not criminally responsible at the time he killed Polonius. That means "more probably than not," as opposed to "beyond a reasonable doubt."

The defense, represented by the expert testimony of Dr. Thomas Guttheil of Harvard Yard, is that Hamlet shows no emotion as he kills Polonius— "how now, a rat?"—or remorse afterward. Those who know Hamlet best all attest to his madness. He is "mad as the sea," his mother says. Furthermore, Hamlet hallucinates, as proved by his seeing the Ghost in Gertrude's closet, an apparition invisible and inaudible to her. Hamlet suffers from what was once called manic depression, and is now termed bipolar illness— in Hamlet's case, of the rapid cycling form. This is a disease of the mood in which the victim alternates between elation and depression. Its manic phase manifests itself in hypersexualty, babbling speech, episodes of inappropriate hostility, and a grandiose sense of mission. The depressive symptoms are suicidal anadonia, loss of pleasure, bad dreams, loss of contact with the environment, and loss of a sense of right and wrong. Results of this illness for Hamlet are his inability to understand that he has killed someone, meaning that he did not have the mental capacity to appreciate his criminality or did not have the ability to conform his conduct to the requirements of the law. If a policeman were standing next to him at the time he heard Polonius behind the arras, he would have behaved the same way. To fake mental illness, the defense argues, is for the mentally ill person to claim mastery over his illness. The secondary gain is that the faking achieves something for its practitioner. But Hamlet gains nothing from it, as proved by his inappropriate hostility to Ophelia. "To conclude that his conduct is sometimes inappropriate is like saying that his father died of an earache."

The prosecution argues that Hamlet's "antic disposition" is a defense against a king who has killed Hamlet's father, and against Polonius and Rosencrantz and Guildenstern and even Ophelia, who are spying on Hamlet. He is an intelligent man, constantly aware of the precariousness of his situation. His feigning does not show diminution but enhanced capacity. It is essential to his survival. What triggers his melancholia are actual events, and, according to Dr. Alan Stone, also of Harvard Yard, if someone did not respond as Hamlet has done, "we would have a madman on our hands." Hamlet *is* spied upon and is therefore not delusional. He *is* a prince and does not then embrace a grandiose vision ("O cursed spite, that ever I was born to set [the time] right"). That is his mission. As a student of philosophy, Hamlet is profound, not merely suicidal. Camus's statement on suicide would be a modern example of Hamlet's exploration of the consequences of human action, including "self-slaughter." Hamlet does experience a grief reaction, complicated by his mother's behavior. Madness means that a person is trapped within himself, as Ophelia is, but Hamlet devises a "reality check," the play within a play, and appoints an independent witness, in Horatio, who agrees with Hamlet's interpretation of Claudius's reaction to "The Murder of Gonzago." He shows a remarkable ability to control his impulses when he decides not to kill an apparently praying Claudius. As for those who claim that Hamlet is mad, Polonius is "mistaken and wrong headed," says Stone. Although Ophelia goes mad after her father is slain by someone close to her who goes unpunished for the crime, Hamlet, a victim of similar circumstances, does not go mad. It is a matter of contrast, not a parallel case.

The prosecution argues that to hold Hamlet responsible is to offer him his only chance at vindication, presumably at a trial at which he could be acquitted. The defense counters that Hamlet "is a sick boy who needs help." It is enjoyable to see lawyers do with *Hamlet* what literary critics have done for years—take the same evidence and draw from it diametrically different conclusions.

The verdict of the jury, which includes Associate Justice Ruth Bader Ginsburg, is that Hamlet is "criminally responsible" for killing Polonius. The jury recommends to the prosecution that it "investigate whether Hamlet should be held criminally responsible for the destruction of Ophelia." This recommendation represents a knotty assignment, as does the question of Ophelia's suicide. Is it suicide?

The prosecution's case could be strengthened in several ways. That Dr. Stone believes in ghosts does not mean that Hamlet is not hallucinating the Ghost in Gertrude's closet. If the written text, as opposed to the performed script, is the evidence, however, one must argue that the Ghost's lines, which are there in the text, constitute a remarkable feat of ventriloquism on Hamlet's part. He projects a voice out that returns from his hallucination only to him. "It is not possible," says the defense's witness, Dr. Guttheil, "for a hallucination to tell you something that you don't know. It's your mind." While it can be argued that the Ghost represents Hamlet's repressed anxiety about delay and empathy with his mother, the Ghost's words on the parapets and later in Gertrude's closet do exist on the authority of the text, not just on the basis of Hamlet's belief that he hears them.

In the 1980 John Barton production, Gertrude did see the Ghost but kept that to herself. Suffice it to say that a key argument of the defense—the hearing of voices is a classic symptom of manic depression—can be refuted on the basis of the evidence. Dr. Stone counters defense's claim that Hamlet accosts Gertrude "on her bed," but could have been more assertive. The bed, after all, does not appear until Gielgud's famous production of the 1930s. In the illustration in Rowe's 1709 edition, based on a staged *Hamlet*, the Ghost enters what is obviously a sitting room. On that point, Michael Kahn, under whose auspices this trial was conducted, might have been helpful. Furthermore, the prosecution could have adduced some "precedents": the protective "madness" of Junius Brutus and of characters like Hieronimo and Malevole. Furthermore, Hamlet does say of Polonius, "For this same lord, I do repent me," and it could be argued that Claudius knows Hamlet's behavior is "not like madness," but that the useful official view must be that "madness in great ones must not unwatch'd go." It may be, as Dover Wilson (1935) argues and as the Olivier film shows, that Hamlet knows that Claudius and Polonius are eavesdropping on his meeting with Ophelia and that that knowledge motivates his otherwise inappropriate hostility. Furthermore, if others at the play scene can hear his remarks to Ophelia, his "hypersexuality" can also be explained as part of his antic disposition, not a symptom of mental incapacity.

In the hubbub after Justice Kennedy gavels the trial to a close, the actor playing Hamlet can be heard telling Kennedy, "I had a great time." We notice, however, that he is not called to testify in his own defense.

Since this trial is very much an anachronism, applying recent psychiatric theory to an early seventeenth-century killing, it would have been helpful for someone to historicize the moment, giving a sense of how the law, as Justice Kennedy says, "was beginning to change when Shakespeare wrote." Early modern England was, in this instance as in so many others, a testing ground for the new or evolving concepts that so deeply inform these plays. It would have been helpful as well for someone to provide an outline of the "insanity defense," beginning with Henry de Bracton in the 1400s on the legal consequences of mental disorder, moving on to Lord Hale's "child of 14 test," and

Justice Tracy's "wild beast test," which stems from Bracton. Perhaps the first real insanity defense was in the Hadfield Case (1800), where Thomas Erskine put forward the concept of "delusion" as the "true character of insanity," and convinced the court. The McNaghten Rules, formulated in 1843, became the basis of subsequent jurisprudence. They say that "the party accused . . . was laboring under such a defect of reason, from disease of mind, as not to know the nature and quality of the act he was doing; or if he did know it, that he did not know he was doing what was wrong." The issue is the condition of the defendant at the time of the crime, and the debate has diverged; in the United States, "morality" has tended to be the definition of "wrong," while in Great Britain it has been "contrary to the law." Critics point out that the problem with the McNaghten Rules is that they stress the element of rationality and present an old-fashioned model of how mind and psyche function.

One of the first modern insanity defenses was that of Clarence Darrow in 1925. In defending Leopold and Loeb, Darrow argued that the young men had no grasp of right or wrong when they murdered Bobby Franks: "They killed him as they might kill a spider or a fly," Darrow said. In the United States the "irresistible impulse test" has emerged out of dissatisfaction with the McNaghten Rules. "Partial insanity" or "diminished responsibility" can affect the element of premeditation, a factor of great importance in capital cases. The topic is a good one for research for future law students or defendants in murder cases.[2]

The media dominate our lives and those of our students. We can deplore that fact or do our best to befriend it. The media, even if anticreative in themselves, can be part of the process of education.

NOTES

1. On using the offshoots in the classroom, see Robert F. Willson, "Bardic Bricolage: Tracing the Playtext in Hollywood Offshoot." *Shakespeare and the Classroom* 2, no. 1, 37–38.

2. For information on obtaining the tape, write to: C-Span Viewer Services, 400 North Capital Street, Suite 650, Washington, D.C. 20001, (202) 737-3220.

REFERENCES

Boynton, Vicki and Jane Carducci. 1993. "Angelo and the Mock Trial Experience in the College Classroom." *Shakespeare and the Classroom* 1, no. 2 (Autumn): 13.

Hawkes, Terrence. 1993. *Meaning by Shakespeare*. London: Routledge.

Royko, Mike. 1993. "Arnold's Fans." *Chicago Tribune*, 12 July.

Wilson, J. Dover. 1935. *What Happens in "Hamlet."* Cambridge: Cambridge University Press.

5

Basic Resources

A course in Shakespeare on film and television requires resources. I will suggest what exists on tape in print in support of such a course, but basically what is needed is a library of productions.

RECOMMENDED FILMS AND TV VERSIONS

Here is a list of recommended films and TV versions for the plays most frequently taught. None is recommended, however, without a student's having a grasp of how the medium itself frames and controls the content of the inherited script.

Julius Caesar

Joseph L. Mankiewicz (1953). Brando, Gielgud, Mason. A powerful black-and-white film with a documentary effect.

A Midsummer Night's Dream

Max Reinhardt/William Dieterle (1935). Wonderful special effects to Mendelssohn's overture. Cast members include Cagney, Rooney, Joe E. Brown, De Havilland, Dick Powell, and Victor Jory.

Peter Hall (1969). Royal Shakespeare Company. A rainy summer in Warwickshire. Intentionally disconcerting camera work. Diana Rigg as Helena, Barbara Jefford as Hippolyta, and Ian Holm as Puck.

BBC-TV (1980). Directed by Elija Moshinsky. With Helen Mirren as Titania. A painterly approach to the scenes.

Joseph Papp (1982). Tape of an actual production. Some awful big-city acting, but a fine Helena from Christine Baranski and a hilarious "Pyramus and Thisby."

Romeo and Juliet

George Cukor (1936). Shearer and Howard are too old by two decades, but the black-and-white shots are often splendid.

Franco Zeffirelli (1968). A film for the 1960s. Wonderful duel scene. Michael York as Tybalt. A "high Renaissance" patina.

Stratford, Ontario (1992). Megan Porter Follows. The acting is uneven in this televised stage production, but the Festival Stage shows to good advantage and provides a generic contrast with the film versions.

Hamlet

Lawrence Olivier (1948). Intense psychological study in black-and-white deep-field camera work. Jean Simmons cruises down the river.

Tony Richardson (1969). Nicol Williamson, Marianne Faithfull. A close-up color version of the Roundhouse stage production, with a typically eccentric performance by Williamson. Anthony Hopkins is Claudius and Gordon Jackson (Mr. 'oodsin of "Upstairs, Downstairs") is Horatio.

Rodney Bennett, BBC (1980). The most complete and longest of available versions. Derek Jacobi is superb. Patrick Stewart plays Claudius.

Franco Zeffirelli (1990). Vivid. Helena Bonham Carter's Ophelia is superb. Many of the other minor characters are brilliantly depicted. The Yorick scene is excellent.

Othello

Lawrence Olivier (1965). He parodies "black" style for the Venetian senate, an element in his performance easily misunderstood today. Maggie Smith is Desdemona, Frank Finlay is Iago, and Derek Jacobi is Cassio. Film based on a stage version.

Orson Welles (1952). Some powerful Eisensteinian black-and-white camera work.

Thames (1989). RSC production directed by Trevor Nunn originally at the Other Place. A splendid production with Ian McKellen (Iago), Willard Wight (Othello), Imogen Stubbs (Desdemona), and Zoe Wanamaker (Emilia).

Janet Suzman (1988). With tribesman John Kani as Othello. Uneven performances but powerful, as we watch Othello fight against Iago's insinuations. The stage production is uneasy with TV.

Bard (1985). William Marshall is often good as Othello. Ron Moody plays a cerebral Iago. Straight television tends to domesticate the script.

BBC (1981). What father-in-law could object to Anthony Hopkins's handsome Moor? With no racial subtext, Bob Hoskins has no place to go but into unmotivated sociopathology.

Oliver Parker (1995). Branagh and Fishburne. Better than what the critics said of it. See my analysis below and Samuel Crowl in *Shakespeare Bulletin* 14, no. 1 (1996): 41–42.

King Lear

Peter Brook (1969). Intentionally jagged camera work. A bleak and existential "night of the living dead" (as Pauline Kael called it). Paul Scofield is Lear, and Irene Worth is Goneril.

Grigori Kozintsev (1970). One of the great Shakespeare films, although 70-mm Sovscope loses a lot on cassette. Massive and moving.

BBC (1983). With Michael Hordern. Groupings of characters sometimes show relationships, sometimes resemble a football huddle. Set in the late seventeenth century.

Lawrence Olivier (1984), directed by Michael Elliot. Homage to Olivier. Set in Stonehengian Britain. Intrusive music. Overpraised.

Macbeth

Thames (1979). McKellen, Dench, Rees. Remake of Nunn's Other Place production. Unabashedly theatrical.

Roman Polanski (1970). Overly violent, but it has its moments.

BBC (1982). Nicol Williamson makes mincemeat of the poetry. Useful only in contrast to other productions.

Orson Welles (1948). Uneven; often unintentionally amusing. The three weird ones at the end, holding their crooks and gazing at the castle, look like three hockey players sitting out a long penalty.

Throne of Blood

(1957). Akira Kurosawa's brilliant translation of the theme of ambition to medieval Japan. It is worthwhile in its own right, regardless of its links to the Scottish play.

The *Henry V* Olivier-Branagh contrast also makes for a good segment for courses that can bring in nonrequired texts. The BBC-TV series was panned, but *Measure for Measure* (with Kate Nelligan), *Richard II* (Derek Jacobi, Jon Finch, Charles Gray), and *II Henry VI* are excellent examples of how the inherited scripts can be shaped to accommodate to television. Olivier's *Merchant of Venice* (with Joan Plowright) is another good television production, although the editing simplifies the script. The Branagh *Much Ado* is very popular with students, even if it is a somewhat sentimental, sun-drenched "Hollywood" reduction of the script. Perhaps the best television version of any play is Trevor Nunn's *Antony and Cleopatra* (with Janet Suzman, Richard Johnson, Patrick Stewart, and, in a very small role, Ben Kingsley).

The animated Shakespeares may be useful in giving younger students a visualized sense of the story. The problems attendant on half-hour condensations are massive and perhaps best expressed by the person who edited the scripts, Leon Garfield: "I tried to use the famous lines where I could, as long as [they] didn't get in the way of the narrative" *(New York Times,* 9 November 1992, C-16). What we get here is a competition between famous lines and narration. See Thomas Pendleton's judicious review in *Shakespeare Bulletin* (Fall 1992, 37, 40).

I asked a ten year old, Cindy Brown of Wiscasett, Maine, who had seen a good live production of *Romeo and Juliet* by Shakespeare and Company in 1992 and who had watched the Zeffirelli film version, to respond to the animated version:

I don't really like that *Romeo and Juliet* as much as I liked the play and the movie. I guess it's because it's too much like a cartoon and it doesn't have enough details in it. I can understand it's only a half-hour long but it could be an hour long so they don't have to make each part so short. I am enjoying the [Zeffirelli] movie. I've watched it twice. I like Juliet's nurse the most.

With their condensation and cartoon or puppet premises, these versions lean, perhaps inevitably, toward the stereotype. The confrontation outside the banquet room in act 1, scene 7 of *Macbeth* ends with his, "If we should fail?" and Lady Macbeth's, "We fail? But screw your courage to the sticking place and we'll not fail." The emphasis is on her vehement certainty, not on a Macbeth who is going ahead with the "terrible feat" even though he knows it is wrong in every context, from the hugely cosmic to the deeply personal. We get a grim and chiaroscuro *Hamlet*, with a touch of color from Ophelia, a hint of the out-of-doors that Olivier also provided for her, but Claudius looks like the debauched Henry VIII, as Pendleton notes, and is Hamlet's "bloat king," not the complex character that Patrick Stewart describes in his tape on Claudius (see below). The cartoon king has no actor working with his character to make a "mighty opposite" of him. The animated versions give us a version of "Directors' Theatre." The cassettes will be valuable, however, if carefully used. A good assignment would be to ask students who have already worked with a particular script to review these productions, looking at what story *is* told—What is *Twelfth Night*, for example, if Feste's "deconstructing" songs are eliminated?—and at how the medium conditions and controls the "message."

The comedies in which identities are changed or interchanged are hard to televise because a realistic medium, where we are not asked to suspend our disbelief, makes the Dromio-Antipholis dualities, the Sebastian-Viola confusion, or Rosalind's disguise as Ganymede difficult to accept. One solution is the televising of staged plays. Such productions can, if well done initially and then carefully redirected for television, give some sense of the energy of live theater as well as a good television version of the play.

Such a successful conflation of two media is the cassette of the Stratford, Ontario, *As You Like It*, produced in 1983, directed by John Hirsch, directed for television by Herb Roland, with Roberta Maxwell (Rosalind), Rosemary Dunsmore (Celia), Andrew Gilles (Orlando), and Nicholas Pennell (Jaques). This is easily the best *As You Like It* available on cassette and one of the best versions of any of the festive comedies on the market. It should extend our ability to teach the comedies, particularly in high schools where they are not often taught. It makes a useful contrast with the Edzard film, which I discuss below. It is available at $39.95 (Canadian; about $28.00 U.S.) from:

The Theatre Store
Stratford Festival
Stratford, Ontario, N5A 6V2 Canada
(519) 271-0055 (Ext. 22)

Many of these cassettes are inexpensive. The latest Writing Company catalog shows, for example, the Cukor and the Zeffirelli *Romeo and Juliet*s, the Olivier *Merchant*, the Branagh *Much Ado*, the Polanski and the Welles *Macbeth*s, the Zeffirelli and Richardson *Hamlet*s, the Nunn *Antony and Cleopatra*, and the Olivier and Branagh *Henry V*s, all available for under $20.00 each. The Olivier *Lear* is listed at $29.95 and the Welles *Othello* at $22.50. The BBC tapes cost $99.95, but the *Hamlet* provides 222 minutes on two cassettes. The *Othello*, also on two tapes, runs for 208 minutes. The catalog is available from:

The Writing Company
10200 Jefferson Boulevard
P.O. Box 802
Culver City, California 90232-0802

Several productions not listed in the Writing Company catalog, can be obtained from:

Films for the Humanities
P.O. Box 2053
Princeton, New Jersey 08543-2053

Films for the Humanities markets John Barton's excellent Playing Shakespeare series, which is a good bridge between the literary and the dramatic qualities of the scripts.

SUPPORT RESOURCES

The materials noted here are available on cassette and in print. They will serve as support for a course in Shakespeare on film and some of them for courses that ask students to perform. Later, I offer summaries of some of the recent critical work in the field of Shakespeare on film.

Patrick Stewart does an excellent job of defending Claudius in a tape from Barr Films, part of a series that also deals with Shylock, Rosalind and Celia, and Polonius. Arguing against the "wet-lipped, grape-peeling villain" characterization of Claudius, Stewart calls him "intelligent, perceptive, intuitive, caring, affectionate, diplomatic, brave, patient," though not "trustworthy." Hamlet is "moody, selfish, uncooperative, insolent, unfriendly, violent, rude,

antisocial, egocentric." Stewart admits that he is being "deliberately provocative" with his adjectives. Stewart suggests that Claudius's opening
speech (1.2) has been carefully prepared and erases the issue of "sister-wife"
by expressing the question lurking in his listeners' minds. Meanwhile,
Claudius incorporates the "distorting knowledge that he is a murderer."
Stewart talks of Claudius's reason for keeping Hamlet at Elsinore—because
of Gertrude's love for Hamlet and Claudius's love for her—and deals with
his choices as actor as Gertrude drinks the poisoned wine.

Stewart does not discuss Claudius's reaction to "Gonzago," which in the
BBC-TV version shows Stewart's Claudius calmly holding a torch up to the
hands hiding the face of Derek Jacobi's Hamlet in a conscious reversal of
Olivier's action with Basil Sydney in the 1949 film. Stewart gives us
Claudius's "Oh my offense is rank" soliloquy in a medium close-up, more
effectively than his 1980 BBC-TV Claudius, who rushed the soliloquy in
radical close-up. In each version, however, Stewart pauses before "and my
queen" in the line about crown and ambition to show that Gertrude, last on
the list, is the most important to him. In discussing Alec Clunes's Claudius,
for Peter Brook in 1955, Kenneth Tynan says, "It is objected that he white-
washes Claudius? He shows us a man who has tried and failed to rational-
ize his faults—and if that is whitewashing, it is how most of us spend our
lives. Under his influence, *Hamlet* is the tragedy not only of a prince but of
a whole doomed family" (*Tynan on Theatre* [London: Penguin, 1964]: 83.)

The twenty-six-minute tape (number V228 in the catalog) includes a
study guide inside the case and is available from:

Barr Films
12801 Schabarum Avenue
P.O. Box 7878
Irwindale California 91706-7878
(818) 338-7878

Tony Church and his students at the Denver Theatre Conservatory have
produced the first in a series of tapes about the performing arts, *Shakespeare's Language: Action and Character*. The approach emphasizes that
what one needs to know about the meaning of the lines is in the lines, so that
the emphasis of John Barton in his *Performing Shakespeare* is reiterated
here. That is not surprising, since Church worked under Barton's direction
at the Royal Shakespeare Company. The workshop format is similar to that
employed by Brian Cox and Janet Suzman on British television a few years
ago as they worked with students on tragedy and comedy. Church, however,
uses three interesting and useful approaches: He employs a "scansion machine," he breaks speeches down into separate "voices," and he sets up an
"idea tree" to show how a speech is developed.

In the first instance, Church deploys an elastic belt with unaccented and
accented syllables represented by coins (pennies and quarters). The belt can

stretch for slow lines—"In sooth, I know not why I am so sad"—and gives a good visual equivalent of how a line of blank verse sounds.

The second technique has the excellent young actors alternate in reading phrases. This approach gives the speeches—the opening Chorus to *Henry V* and Portia's "quality of mercy" speech—a texture and sense of development that makes the old words come anew to the ear. The technique shows that like many of the sonnets, Shakespeare's poetry contains doubt and debate, and is not just a smooth progress to a forgone conclusion. Conclusions are results, resolutions, or possibly rationalizations of irreconcilable issues. The approach is valid in itself as Adrian Noble demonstrated in the recent Royal Shakespeare *Henry IV, Part II*, by giving Rumor many voices.

Church's idea tree emerges from his claim that a dramatic speech is not "read down" but "read up," from the roots to the top of the tree. Along with the rising action, Church stresses key words, plus links, suspensions, and blockings between and of the phrases in a given speech. This is an organic approach that allies the living speech to the living actor.

The tape ends with Church reading the *Henry V* chorus with Elizabethan pronunciation. Church is one of the finest verse speakers in the theater today; this speech is a treat. This tape is well worth having, particularly since it shows students at work with the lines. This is a remarkably talented group of young people, and they are enjoying themselves. One wishes that the tape were longer and that this company was shown in performance. The tape also shows a teacher who has an enviable rapport with his students. It is an excellent model of an energetic and interactive classroom.

Shakespeare's Language anticipates further workshops, one closing in on the implications of this one, that is, to the options that a single line can present to an actor, and another opening out from this one, to ensemble acting, where multiple voices will come more to conflict than cooperation, but still be at the service of dramatic meaning.

This tape is highly recommended for senior high school and college classes of Shakespeare and of acting. It is available at $89.00 plus $3.00 shipping from:

Denver Center Media
1245 Champa Street
Denver, Colorado 80204
(303) 893–4000, ext. 2433

A very useful and recent cassette is *Great Performances*, featuring excerpts from four Royal Shakespeare Company productions of 1994–1995. The most valuable segment is that of the late Sir Robert Stephens's *King Lear*, in a performance at once nuanced and powerful. Also included is a segment of Adrian Noble's *A Midsummer Night's Dream*, which shows how effective the doubling of the artisans and the fairies can be in shading Bottom's dream à la *The Wizard of* Oz, Des Barrit's tour de force Welsh Malvolio, and Toby

Stephens's Coriolanus, effectively toned down from his ear-splitting version on stage at the Swan in Stratford-on-Avon.

This is available in U.S. format at £12.99 (about $20) from:

The Shakespeare Bookshop
Henley Street
Stratford-on-Avon CV 37 6QW
United Kingdom

BOOKS

The bibliography in this field is growing. That suggests that it is a valid scholarly field in itself and should provide some arguments for the acquisition of primary materials. Here are some of the many books available.

Kenneth Branagh, *Much Ado About Nothing*. New York: Norton, 1993. The screenplay of the popular Branagh film, with an introduction and notes, and photographs by Clive Coote. Useful to students studying the film.

James Bulman and H. R. Coursen, *Shakespeare on Television*. Hanover, N.H.: University Press of New England, 1988. Essays on the media, individual productions, and selections from reviews. Deals mostly with the BBC series. Also includes Sheldon Zitner's indispensable essay, "Wooden O's in Plastic Boxes."

James Bulman, ed., *Shakespeare. Theory, and Performance*. London: Routledge, 1995. A series of brilliant essays that often bring recent theory and production into useful juxtaposition.

James Bulman and J. R. Mulryne, eds., *Shakespeare in Performance*. Manchester: Manchester University Press. These individual editions often include film and television versions of the plays, along with examination of stage productions. The *Shrew* edition, for example, edited by Graham Holderness, includes full discussions of the Zeffirelli film (1966) and the Miller BBC-TV production (1980).

John Collick, *Shakespeare, Cinema, and Society*. Manchester: Manchester University Press, 1989. Provocative and challenging materialist readings of the history of Shakespeare on film and the films of Kozintsev and Kurosawa. A bracing corrective to conventional assimilations of films into unperceived cultural assumptions.

H. R. Coursen, *Shakespearean Performance as Interpretation*. Newark: Delaware University Press, 1992. Includes examinations of *Dream, Shrew*, and *Henry V* in film and on television.

———. *Watching Shakespeare on Television*. Madison, N.J.: Fairleigh Dickenson University Press, 1994. An examination of many issues, including the media, editing for television, and the historical factors that impinge on production.

———. *Shakespeare in Production: Whose History?* Athens: Ohio University Press, 1996. Includes chapters on the 1936 film of *Romeo and Juliet*, Branagh's film of *Much Ado About Nothing*, and *The Comedy of Errors* on television.

Samuel Crowl, *Shakespeare Observed*. Athens: Ohio University Press, 1992. Includes a useful analysis of Polanski's *Macbeth*, the 1935 *Dream*, Welles's and Hall's films, Bogdanov's *Wars of the Roses*, and Branagh's *Henry V*.

Anthony Davies, *Filming Shakespeare's Plays*. Cambridge: Cambridge University Press, 1988. Davies looks at the films of Olivier, Welles, Brook, and Kurosawa, with special emphasis on how cinematic space works in ways very different from theatrical—in inhibiting complex dialogue, for example.

Anthony Davies and Stanley Wells, eds., *Shakespeare and the Moving Image: The Plays on Film and Television*. Cambridge: Cambridge University Press, 1994. Cogent essays on film and television versions of the plays. Good on Kurosawa.

Peter Donaldson, *Shakespearean Films/Shakespearean Directors*. Boston: Unwin Hyman, 1990. A shrewd analysis that uses Freudian formulations in looking at directors (Olivier, Kurosawa, Welles, Liz White, Zeffirelli, and Jean-Luc Godard) and their films. Neatly shows how current critical modes become tools for the interrogation of film.

Charles W. Eckert, *Focus on Shakespearean Films*. Englewood Cliffs, N.J.: Prentice Hall, 1972. An invaluable collection of essays about and reviews of classic films, from the 1935 *Dream* to the 1966 *Chimes at Midnight*.

Henry Fenwick, *The BBC TV Shakespeare*. New York: Mayflower. Individual editions that contain literary introductions by John Wilders, essays on the productions by Fenwick, still photographs of each production, and the script as edited for production by Alan Shallcross. The books are invaluable for study of individual productions, particularly in raising issues of editing. Should the queen, for example, get the last word in the Garden Scene (3.4) in *Richard II*? She does in the BBC but not in the inherited script.

Leon Garfield, *The Animated Shakespeare*. New York: Knopf. Beautifully illustrated editions to accompany the cassettes. They purport to contain the text in the animated version, though sometimes they do not *(Macbeth,* for example). The stage directions tend to do too much narrating. They can be good introductions, with guidance.

Jack Jorgens, *Shakespeare on Film*. Bloomington: Indiana University Press, 1977, reissued in 1991 by University Press of America, Lanham, Md. The classic study of films up to the mid-1970s. Jorgens has a superb eye for what happens on the screen.

Bernice W. Kliman, *Hamlet: Film, Television, and Audio Performance*. Cranbury, N.J.: Associated University Presses, 1988. Meticulous and informative analyses of *Hamlet* on film and television from the early days to Ragnar Lyth's 1984 Swedish production.

James Lusardi and June Schlueter, *Reading Shakespeare in Performance: King Lear*. Cranbury, N.J.: Associated University Presses, 1991. Offers a useful analysis of how to "read" performance, with attention to the BBC and Granada productions.

Jo McMurtry. *Shakespeare Films in the Classroom: A Descriptive Guide*. Hamden, Conn.: Archon, 1994. Lists the available materials, provides cast lists and brief evaluations, and gives addresses of suppliers. Although it blurs distinctions between the media, it is indispensable for anyone using film and TV in teaching Shakespeare.

Kenneth S. Rothwell and Anabelle Henken Melzer, *Shakespeare on Screen*. New York: Neal-Schumann, 1990. A comprehensive and invaluable listing of the Shakespeare that has been done on film and television. Includes comments and reviews.

Michael Skovmand, ed., *Screen Shakespeare*. Aaarhus: Aaarhus University Press, 1994. Like Davies's book, a series of useful essays that examine past films and some recent offerings, like Branagh's *Henry V*, Stoppard's *Rosencrantz & Guildenstern*, and Greenaway's *Prospero's Books*.

Willems, Michele, *Shakespeare à la télévision*. Rouen: L'Université de Rouen, 1987. Valuable interviews (in English) with directors and actors of the BBC-TV series that highlight the strengths and the problems of televised Shakespeare.

Sharon Hamilton's *Shakespeare: A Teaching Guide* (J. Weston Walch [P.O. Box 658, Portland, Maine 04104]: 1993. $12.95) is the best book on teaching Shakespeare. Hamilton is a superb teacher, and unlike most other virtuosos, she shows how it is done.

The book suggests that high school students read cast lists out loud, pausing to discuss each seemingly related group of characters, and that students do dramatic readings of opening episodes. Thus do they launch themselves into the "story," which can still be compelling for high school readers. They also begin to recognize that the "setting occurred in the words of the actors and the imaginations of the spectators" (15) and that they are part of the imaginative process, a responsibility that television tends to erode. Hamilton goes on to discuss the quiz as a way of testing motive, language, and event, of making sure that students are not getting lost and of rewarding others, indeed of demonstrating to them their own command of the material. A quiz with five identifications in order from each act of a given play becomes a précis of the play and an excellent way for students to review for any final exam. The book describes pantomime exercises that suggest the subtext behind the words—emotions and opposite sides of the same character—Claudius, for example.

A more complex live sculpture represents a key moment in a play. Each student memorizes and presents to the class a soliloquy or a sonnet. The performance of a speech insists that the student understand each word. Students also act out short scenes (twenty to forty lines) in front of the class.

Hamilton describes five kinds of writing assignments: the critical essay emerging from a thesis statement; the invented diary, in which the student "becomes" a character in the play; the parody subgenre in which Shakespeare engaged; a critique from a videotape of Branagh's *Henry V*; and papers that ask a student to describe how he or she would direct a key episode from a play that the class has studied.

These several approaches, Hamilton says, allow Shakespeare to appeal to "jocks and poets, remedial readers and National Merit finalists, underachievers and perfectionists . . . but not all in the same ways or through the same means" (2). The way not to do it, she argues, is to try "to turn all of them into novice scholars" (3). That approach fails "to tap other talents that many students bring to class: an intuitive understanding of people, athletic grace and energy, spatial orientation, a sense of humor" (4). To accept students in this way also means "resisting the stance of the expert: not lecturing, but creating a class dialogue in which I, too, am a learner" (5). Like any other good teacher, she recognizes that "the course of a discussion depends on what students are seeing and asking" (16).

By means of transcriptions of actual class discussions and excerpts from student writing, we get inside this classroom and the processes that Hamilton sets in motion. These are exciting places to be. I have read no other book on teaching that more vividly recreates these events. Hamilton's experience with Shakespeare & Company, and Miriam Gilbert's National Endowment for the Humanities (NEH) Seminar shows the value of those programs. They have, in Hamilton's case, performed exactly as they are supposed to: They have introduced teachers to activities and approaches that then get reintroduced in other classrooms. Reading the play and listening to lectures, for example, could never produce the results that Hamilton lists as "common factors" in the successful scenes that her students direct and perform:

a willingness to experiment, a sense of which words were key, an ear for shifts in tone, a readiness to use other actors—live props—to bring out feelings. Most important, the speaker had to be willing to let go—to become rather than act the character, even if that meant forgetting lines. (55)

Few, if any, of these students will go on to act, but they will become a better audience, and when they go to a play, they will always appreciate "how much work and talent go into making it look effortless" (57).

Hamilton's outline for analysis of Branagh's *Henry V* is excellent, showing a clear understanding of the choices that go into making a film. Students do write "original criticism" (106) when asked to write about filmed Shakespeare. My reservations about this analysis are twofold. First, the film will be viewed on video. How does that change the experience? Branagh seems to have made *Henry V* with the video market in mind: a lot of close-ups and a montage sequence for Agincourt so that we infer the overall scene through synecdoche. Some simplifications (the confrontations of the Henry and Williams, and the Fluellen and Pistol confrontations after the battle are cut, although Williams is given a moment of recognition when Henry returns the glove to him and Pistol gets part of his farewell soliloquy) are dictated by film, of course, as are the several flashbacks that regular television would not incorporate. A student's time, one assumes, does not allow him or her to watch the Olivier film as well as the Branagh, but Hamilton could put more stress on comparing the Branagh with the Olivier. Given that context, students begin to notice detail, and their writing can mature seemingly overnight.

The Olivier, with its incorporating shots, long tracking shots, and the camera's tendency to boom out from Henry's speeches, does not fare as well on television as the Branagh. A consideration of the conceptual space within which production occurs will open students' eyes to other dimensions of criticism than those that pertain when one looks just at the work, whether text or production. Furthermore, zeitgeist is a vital, if often unperceived, component of production. The concept comes vividly alive when students contrast the World War II Olivier film with the post-Vietnam, post-Falklands Branagh version. The introduction of Shakespeare on cassette also provides an opportunity for introducing students to the vocabulary of film and camera, something a lot of students enjoy and that a few have mastered already. Here is an area where Hamilton's splendid treatise scarcely scratches the surface.

This book shows teachers how to get students to show themselves how much there is in this ominous thing called "Shakespeare," how much they can learn by uncovering some of those elements, and how much fun they can have from the experience.

An excellent companion book for Hamilton's is Robin J. Holt, *Scenes from Shakespeare: A Workbook for Actors*, McFarland (Box 611, Jefferson, N.C. 28640), reviewed in *Shakespeare and the Classroom* 2, no. 2 (Fall 1994): 90.

JOURNALS

Here are some of the journals that offer reviews and background material in the area of Shakespeare, film, and television.

Shakespeare and the Classroom (Ohio Northern University, Ada, Ohio 45810). Reviews work on film and television as well as all books relating to the teaching of Shakespeare. $8.00 a year for two issues.

Shakespeare Bulletin (Lafayette College, Easton, Pennsylvania 18042). Contains essays on productions and reviews of major productions in the United States, Canada, Great Britain, and elsewhere. It incorporates what used to be *Shakespeare on Film*. $15.00 a year for four issues.

An index to the sixteen years of *Shakespeare on Film Newsletter*, edited by Bernice Kliman and Kenneth Rothwell, prior to its 1992 incorporation into *Shakespeare Bulletin*, is available for $10.00. A complete run of *Shakespeare on Film Newsletter* is available for $90.00. Contact:

James Lusardi
Coeditor, *Shakespeare Bulletin*
English Department
Lafayette College
Easton, Pennsylvania 18042

I highly recommend the complete run, particularly for schools that use taped performance materials in teaching Shakespeare. *Shakespeare on Film Newsletter* features reviews of the BBC-TV Shakespeare series, of films like the Zeffirelli *Hamlet* and the Branagh *Henry V*, essays on Shakespeare off-shoots, revaluations of older productions on film and tape like the Papp-Antoon *Much Ado About Nothing* and the Burge *Julius Caesar*, reviews of books and teaching materials in the field of filmed and televised Shakespeare, and reports on the availability of hard-to-find productions. It is a basic starting place for research on filmed and televised Shakespeare and an essential resource for teachers and students.

6

Recent Critical Work
on Shakespeare on Film

With new Shakespeare films being made at a more rapid rate than at any other time since the advent of talking pictures, the critical and scholarly work in the field will increase markedly. Here is a summary of recent work, done just before the sudden increase in Shakespeare film production that occurred in 1995–1996.

The cover of *Screen Shakespeare*, edited by Michael Skovmand (Aarhus, Denmark: Aarhus University Press, 1994), shows a backlighted Kenneth Branagh entering Henry V's council chamber, casting a shadow on the stones in front of him. The shadow is the future; the stones are what remains when the future is done. It is an effective entrance to a collection of essays that extends our ways of looking at recent and older versions of Shakespeare on film.

Skovmand's introduction argues that the apparent similarity between Branagh and Zeffirelli

is a surface one. Zeffirelli's approach is largely *melodramatic*, with a distinctive sense of *texture* and *mise-en-scène*, but with little sense of an overall interpretative strategy. . . . Branagh, on the other hand, has a clearly worked out strategy of "adaptation." . . . His approach is that of finding the right cinematic *equivalent* of a primarily *theatrical* concept, in which the dynamics of character and verbal delivery are essential ingredients. (9, his emphasis)

In "The Filmic Tradition of *A Midsummer Night's Dream*: Reinhardt, Bergman, Hall and Allen," Steven Shelburne argues that

Woody Allen's *A Midsummer Night's Sex Comedy* (Orion 1982) marks an important departure from the tradition of Reinhardt and Hall even as, indeed because, it recycles their film versions of *A Midsummer Night's Dream* rather than relying on stage tradition. . . . But of course Allen's film is not, in any strict sense a "version" of Shakespeare's play. It is not really even an adaptation. . . . Allen seems to take Hall's advice to "throw away the text altogether . . . and develop the fable with all its atmosphere." . . . Allen makes his point with the spirit ball, an obvious metaphor for his own medium, which is itself a projection. Introducing this invention explicitly thematizes filmmaking in a context that demands attention to the past and the future of the art. Andrew speaks for Allen and his camera when he says of the spirit ball, "I want that thing to emit light rays and capture the future and the past." (17, 22–22)

Bernice W. Kliman, in "Welles's *Macbeth*, a Textual Parable," deals with "the complex interactions and artistic struggles that shape a production" (25). The memos between Welles and his producer, Richard Alan Wilson, "sketch the sociology of collaborative filmmaking," while the two "scripts record the traces of that interaction" (26). Welles typically tinkered constantly with his scenario: "The image of Seyton hanging from the bell rope was late, as was Lady Macbeth's suicidal leap into an endless crevasse, a special effect that cost $53.36 when redone for the rerelease" (28).

In "The 'Bloody Business' of Roman Polanski's *Macbeth*: A Case Study of the Dynamics of Modern Shakespeare Appropriation," Per Serritslvev Petersen argues that the film fails because "Polanski's appropriation is incomplete or half-hearted, leaving, for instance, an artistically incomplete unbridgeable gap between Shakespeare's supernaturalism and the modern director's naturalism. Had the process of appropriation been allowed to run its full course . . . Shakespeare's text might have suffered . . . a sea change into something rich and strange, that is an authentic Polanski movie" (52).

In reexamining Peter Brook's version of *King Lear* and the hostile critical reception that it received, Michael Mullin, in "Peter Brook's *King Lear*: A Reassessment," asks, "Who can say what the essence of this or any other Shakespeare play is? Many strive; when audiences respond, as they did to Brook's *Lear*, it behooves scholars and critics to examine what was done and to elucidate the means. Accordingly, we may know Shakespeare's play in its many forms still better" (62).

In "Visible Darkness: Shakespeare's *King Lear* and Kurosawa's *Ran*," Ib Johansen says that in Shakespeare's play, "all the wondrous events taking place in the fourth act . . . are later annulled by the disastrous sequence of happenings in the last act" (65). He continues:

In *Ran*, the characters in many scenes tend to be reduced to nothing by their impressive surroundings—by the wide-open, "sublime" spaces of the film. . . . Jan Kott's reading of *Ran* is in accordance with . . . his emphasis on the essentially *sterile* character of the landscapes in which human beings tend to find themselves in contemporary culture. . . . But Kurosawa's later films remind us that perhaps the warring universals—heaven and earth, dream and reality, childhood and old age, etc., etc.—may come together and even get on speaking terms with each other in a less destructive fashion. (81–83).

Susanne Fabricius suggests, in "The Face of Honour: On Kenneth Branagh's Screen Adaptation of *Henry V*," that, in contrast to Olivier's version, Branagh's

is in all meanings of the word a dark film—often with a single luminous spot or section in the picture, not to illuminate but to create contrast. . . . The play/film's description of the complex transformation of a young man from wanton drunkard to a responsible statesman, commander and spouse in Branagh's interpretation is in its psychological insight quite novel and ranges much further than that the mere telling of history. (95–97)

If Branagh does suggest this transformation, the film accepts the Hal mythology at face value, something the two *Henry IV* plays certainly do not do.

William E. Sheidley suggests, in "The Play(s) within the Film: Tom Stoppard's *Rosencrantz & Guildenstern Are Dead*," that the film "does not merely translate a work of theater into a work of cinema; rather, it embodies a meaningful interaction between its 'medium' and its 'content.' . . . Stoppard's film in fact 'contains' not only his own play but also Shakespeare's *Hamlet*, a good deal more of which is present than in the play" (99). To "prevent Shakespeare's play from crowding out his own and taking over the film, Stoppard repeatedly employs the technique of viewing its action through windows, gratings, and peepholes, or from behind doorways or arrasses. In this way he achieves in film the quality of remoteness and of being framed that marks stage action for the theater audience" (107–8).

Skovmand argues, in "Mel's Melodramatic Melancholy: Zeffirelli's *Hamlet*," that

the *structure*, i.e. the developmental dynamics of the play, are unclear [in the film] . . . we are presented with a character whose motives are not complex, but unclear, up against an uncle who is not sufficiently villainous to provide that motivation, and a Polonius who is somehow neither the bureaucratic mastermind nor the loquacious comic relief, but somewhere in between. *Power*, in other words, is diffusely conceived in Zeffirelli's Elsinore. So, as a consequence, is the frustration of *powerlessness* which is such an important ingredient of the central domain of the play: Hamlet's state of mind. (130, his emphasis)

In " 'Knowing I Lov'd My Books': Shakespeare, Greenaway, and the Prosperous Dialectics of Word and Image," Claus Schatz-Jacobsen says that *Prospero's Books* "is unique in its respect for the literality of Shakespeare's text, in the original sense of *literal* as pertaining to the letter" (133). The "Prospero-Shakespeare figure is the demiurge and master-magician of his projected universe. . . . This symbolic exchange of identities as between Prospero and Shakespeare is the stepping-stone for Greenaway's boldest conceit in *Prospero's Books,* that of letting Prospero-Gielgud speak all the roles, which turns the film quite literally into a 'reading' of the play" (136). He continues, "Greenaway liberates the potential meaning of *The Tempest* as a metafictional record of the play's own coming into being, even as, towards the end of his life and dramatic career, Shakespeare surveys the topography of his work" (145).

These cogent and well-written essays provide a vivid sense of how Shakespeare on film will be discussed as the millennium turns on its thousand-year hinge. This book is highly recommended.

For those who teach *Julius Caesar,* Jo McMurtry (University of Richmond) has an excellent article in *Shakespeare on Film Newsletter* (April 1992, 7) on using film and TV to teach the play. Her article looks at three versions of the assassination scene but not before offering two caveats: (1) "To plunge into violent, complex action . . . can disconcert one's audience," and (2) "repetition is a comic device. The sight of yet another bunch of assassins coming at Caesar may touch the audience's funnybone in a kind of Monty Python reflex." McMurtry uses the Mankiewicz and Burge films and the BBC-TV version of the play for a compare-and-contrast exercise, which she delineates in useful detail. In the Burge, for example, "Trebonius, who had missed the murder while drawing Antony out of the way, bloodies his hands with obvious reluctance. We can deduce a practical reason for Brutus' insistence on this ritual: now Trebonius cannot pretend he wasn't there." This is the kind of detail that we would not get from a thousand readings of the play.

There are two highly recommended articles in the Spring 1991 *Shakespeare Quarterly* (vol. 42, no. 1).

R. B. Parker compares and contrasts mise-en-scène in the Brook, Kozintsev, and Kurosawa films based on *King Lear.* The

scenery, props, and costumes are not merely aids or background but provide a semiology of their own that comments independently on the dramatic action. They function, in Kozintsev's words, "like the chorus of a Greek tragedy," and they impose themselves so powerfully at times that they effectively determine interpretation. . . . Brook's film is existentialist in outlook and frequently expressionist (or surrealist) in mode and presents a Nature that is savagely inimical to human life and values; Kozintsev's *Lear* has a much more ethical focus on the play's social and domestic planes, with Nature reflecting, rather than causing, man's inhumanities to man; while Kurosawa's emphasis is on the cyclical repetitiveness of human history with Nature as beautiful but benignly aloof from man's self-punishing folly. Brook's film is philosophical and pessimistic; Kozintsev's is ethical and tentatively optimistic; and Kurosawa's mixes a retributive view of history with Buddhism to produce an enigmatic effect that eludes both simplifications. (75)

Parker goes on, in detail and in depth, to fill in this outline, particularly in contrasting Brook's nihilistic vision with Kozintzev's historical approach and Kurosawa's seemingly intentional refutation of his predecessors. Parker is particularly helpful in showing how Buddhism and Noh inform *Ran* and why Japanese culture insists on a "male Cordelia" (Saburo). The article concludes that "Kurosawa's final image catches the complexity of Shakespeare's conclusion most fully, though, paradoxically, it is furthest from the text" (90). If a single article were all we had to accompany our teaching of these three great versions of *Lear*, Parker's would be the one to choose. It is essential reading for this script and its filmic renditions.

Peter Donaldson suggests that if Branagh's

Henry V is more politically aware, more deeply skeptical about wars of imperial conquest than Olivier's, it nevertheless presents the king as a great leader whose heroism depends, to a disturbing degree, on his capacity for self-suppression and whose personal growth is fostered by inward assent to the necessary evils of politics, war, and courtship. . . .

Olivier introduces his audience to the inner workings of Elizabethan theater, including a tour of its tiring-house and backstage, but does not include his own medium, that of film, in his account of the production of Shakespearean spectacle. Film retains its own, undemystified magic. . . . Taking Olivier's suppression of the medium of film as his own starting point, Branagh begins with a modern-dress, Brechtian prologue set in an empty film studio containing the props and sets actually to be used in the film. Even the camera is briefly shown. . . .

Branagh emphasizes effort, human agency, force. . . . Olivier's authority, in contrast, tends towards the charismatic and . . . is typically exercised through the *voice*, with the king positioned at the vanishing point of the image and the camera pulling back to reveal a widening space filled with attentive subjects or soldiers . . . for Olivier kingship is inescapably performative. (1990, 61, 62, 63, 65, his emphasis)

"Olivier's *Henry V*," he continues, "does not show the king in the process of development, does not show him growing, but rather shows him performing, acting out of a well established repertoire of skills and competencies. Branagh's *Henry V* is a *bildungsroman*, and its view of the king is deeply developmental" (68). At the end of the Olivier film, "Katherine's transformation into the boy actor of the final tableau fuses history and representation, the heroic legacy of Agincourt and the artistic legacy of Elizabethan theater, assimilating both to the wartime image of England as repository of humane culture and courage" (69). "Branagh explores dimensions of Shakespeare's play that Olivier's version left relatively untouched—the myth of the king who is also one of his people, whose early experiences provide an intimate link to ordinary life, the king who, though he inherits a crown, must earn his success like a son of the artisan or merchant class making a go of the family business" (71).

Donaldson's contrasts are precisely drawn and show that the same script, as interpreted at different moments in history by different directors, can provide the rabbit and the duck and the shape of zeitgeist that Norman Rabkin discusses in his famous article (*Shakespeare Quarterly* 23, no. 3 [Summer 1977]: 279–96). Rabkin and Donaldson are essential reading for this script and its two translations into film.

As You Like It: Audio Visual Shakespeare, edited by Cathy Grant for the British Universities Film and Video Council (1992), is a valuable compilation of what is available on film and on audio and videocassette in Great Britain. It begins with incisive essays by Rex Gibson, David Olive, and Raymond Ingram.

Gibson stresses the importance of a student's seeing "at least two video versions" of each play and cites the difficulty of doing so in the too many instances where only one production exists of, for example, *All's Well, Measure for Measure, Much Ado*, and *Winter's Tale*. The "consensus," Gibson emphasizes, "is *that critical viewing, not passive viewing, is essential.*" The use of video, Gibson says, calls for "a technical vocabulary [and] awareness of the advantages and disadvantages of video/film" as media for Shakespeare. He lists many of the perceived advantages and disadvantages, and suggests that literature, stage, and film and video versions "can be mutually reinforcing. All are social constructs embodying ideology and values."

Olive uses video to "enhance the teaching of Shakespeare in performance." Students confronted with the problems of presenting a scene learn from seeing "how the professionals have treated the same problems." Having grappled with the issue themselves, the "students are in a much better position to accept or disagree with a [professional] director's interpretation." In other words, they are becoming more professional, or at least more adult, as a result of the process, which proves to them "that there is no definitive interpretation of any play."

Ingram suggests that Shakespeare saw a play as "evanescent and mutable, the present, unrepeatable collaborative interaction of players and spectators at a live performance." Films deny that "present" and that interaction; they cannot create the tension between the "actuality" of live theater and the "fiction" of the play that "energizes the medium." Shakespeare aims "to educate audiences in the art of perception via complex displays of deception [and] makes the spectators willing contributors to their own deception." Film "is a product shorn of the engagement devices Shakespeare utilized and replaced by others devised by the screen-version's makers." Ingram offers critiques of the "engagement devices" employed by Olivier, Kozintsev, Bennett, and Zeffirelli in their versions of *Hamlet*; a useful chart contrasts the techniques and the general experience of live versus filmic and televisual productions. The book is available from British Universities Film/Video Council, 55 Greek Street, London W1V 5LR.

A useful essay appears in *Shakespeare and the Changing Curriculum*, edited by Leslie Aers and Nigel Wheale (London: Routledge, 1991). Peter Reynolds suggests the tyranny of the moving image:

> [In] Roman Polanski's film of *Macbeth* . . . the camera follow[s] Macbeth into Duncan's bedchamber and shows [the murder]. . . . Many a . . . student writing about the play . . . has been tripped up . . . into supposing that Polanski's text and Shakespeare's are the same thing. But of course the fault lies not in the film but in the way in which the film has been used to teach the play. Polanski's decision to add a scene only described by Shakespeare should have been highlighted and used as a basis for discussion. (190)

Why does the script have Lady Macbeth solus as Macbeth does "the deed"? Reynolds argues for using recorded performances "to demonstrate that there are no 'right' answers, and no such thing as a 'definitive' production" (190). The teacher poses "open questions that require an *active* not a passive response. . . . The experience of watching *and* listening to [productions] on film/video can motivate a student to return time and again to the printed text" (190). "To be able to read . . . visual texts with the same degree of attention that we give to their spoken equivalent we have to know not only what a particular image is trying to say, but also how it has been constructed and why" (196).

Reynolds offers an excellent analysis of the closure of the Olivier and Kozintsev *Hamlet*s. He also provides a telling insight on television's skill in "erasure":

> [The] recordings are made in such a way as to conceal the artificiality of the process of their genesis. Although that process is highly artificial and contrived, it is eventually transmitted not as art, but as life. Action that may have been recorded over a number of days or months, and shot out of sequence, will be edited as to ensure its eventual representation as a seamless whole. The means of producing this illusion—the lights, the cameras, the film crew—are likewise hidden. . . . Illusionism is . . . used to encourage an emotional identification and involvement with the action. (199)

An exception to much of Reynolds's acute description remains Jane Howell's work for BBC-TV, particularly her wonderful *II Henry VI*, which shows how "artistically conscious" or "metadramatic" premises can work for Shakespeare on television, as Reynolds notes (200). He suggests one of the reasons that Shakespeare on television seldom creates a sense of "artistic wholeness" or convincing closure: "the director's preoccupation with creating identification and sympathy with individuals, rather than inviting a more reflective consideration of the totality of the events in which the individuals are caught up" (200). "Shakespeare is part of a *changing* curriculum. . . . Increasingly his plays will be effectively studied not only as literature (or literature that walks on a stage), but also as films and videos—material of equal status and interest to the printed text, and no less full of interesting and relevant critical issues" (202).

Susan Leach's *Shakespeare in the Classroom* (Buckingham: Open University Press, 1992) has an interesting chapter, "Shakespeare and Video," which suggests that teachers of English in England surveyed in the 1970s "said that their main aim in introducing mass media into lessons was to point out the 'dangers' of the media and to provide pupils with a 'defence' " (62). There "remained," says Leach, "a strong antipathy toward television" (62). She cites Len Masterman:

There persists to this day [the early 1980s] a deeply-rooted distrust of the mass media, and particularly television, as prime agents of cultural debasement and decline. . . . The second constant theme in the shifting relationship between English teaching and the mass media concerns the reluctance of those teachers who have taken the media seriously to unload much of the critical baggage acquired during their literary training. . . . Television is not ersatz literature, and is not best understood through the application of aesthetic or moral criteria having their roots in literary or even film criticism. . . . It may not be best understood through the attempt to apply *any* kind of evaluative criteria. (62–63)

Television, it seems, is not meant to be "read."

One issue that Leach raises though Masterman's provocative analysis is that some conventionally trained teachers have resisted the need to develop a new and nonliterary vocabulary in order to discuss film, stage, and television. The *Cox Report on Media and Education* (1990) pursues Masterman's suggestion that television programs must "be read as cultural texts, iconic in character . . . and invit[ing] a comparison with other possible, but suppressed, codings" (64). The problem is that English teachers "lack the kind of critical base indicated in Masterman's statement" (64).

Leach usefully differentiates between the variants that emerge from the "relationship of a video recording to a television production, and of both to a Shakespeare play." These include live productions on tape and film, live productions recast for television production, films designed for showing in a cinema now on cassette, and films shown at cinema but actually designed for the lucrative cassette rental and purchase market. What, Leach asks, "are the relationships between these different versions of the plays, particularly those undergoing transformation from one medium to another? . . . What light can any critique of this process throw on the study of Shakespeare on video?" (65).

Leach suggests that teachers are using video versions of Shakespeare to enable students to learn the narrative sequences, to find "character" illuminated by seeing and hearing the words of the play physicalized, to give the text some "reality" and palpable existence, and so that students can visualize what up to then has existed in their imaginations. But this is to attempt to treat the televised text in the same way as the printed text has been treated . . . that the play is a discrete entity, complete and whole unto itself, and that by reading, studying and then seeing the video of it we can somehow grasp that inherent meaning and confirm the intentions of the playwright. (69)

Indeed, some of us have seen students hunched over a monitor, "watching" a BBC version with the printed text in front of them. Some students use the "fast forward" as a study guide—to get a "gestalt," an imitation of an imitation of an action. Leach reports one student with his back turned to a video that the rest of the class was watching. He was a Seventh Day Adventist, his teacher explained, who could not watch but could listen and could apparently develop those delay-tuned neurons in the auditory cortex that allow bats, for example, to image their prey amid the clutter of competing signals. Television is an outgrowth of radio and can often be listened to.

Leach outlines the shortcomings of the "cassette as adjunct to text" approach: it is a "disservice . . . to the printed text itself . . . to the television text; and to the students in the classroom" (70). What is reinforced is the "hegemonic nature of the cultural institutions in Great Britain, the powerful and successful means employed to disguise the constructed nature of television and other artifacts from the consumer" (70). The result is a "generalized acceptance of what is 'presented' as 'right and proper,' the way things are and should be" (70). Mark C. Miller gave a similar critique of Exxon and Morgan Guarantee's sponsorship of, for example, the BBC's *Henry V*, where the king was presented as a CEO who is also a fine chap, "a peach" *(Nation*, 12 July 1980, 46–61).

For students, the unexamined use of the video "implies that there is only one video [of the play they are studying], or that it makes no difference which one is seen among different versions, because they are all essentially 'the play' " (70). "If the video has been used . . . as an introduction to the play [it is] often regarded by students as a way of avoiding 'work' for a lesson. . . . The video is used purely as a visual stimulus. If the video is used after the text has been read it tends to become a realism conferring agent" (70), as in the example from Reynolds above, where the Polanski film insists that the play shows the murder of Duncan. As Leach says, "students . . . betray . . . their own subjection to the expectations of realism fostered by television, infinitely powerful in its conditioning of young viewers" (70).

Allison Graham offers some useful exercises in point of view to the students taking her Introduction to Film course. "Understanding *who* is telling the story is as essential in film analysis as it is in literary analysis." Graham asks her classes "to locate the position of the camera" and then uses examples from films in which "a man sees a woman for the first time." From the process, "the representation of race and class arises as an intrinsic aspect of film structure, rather than as an issue imposed on films by an instructor."

By thinking about the different kinds of work experiences and social perspectives not usually explored in Hollywood narratives, students can more easily see the way movies have defined not only the parameters of mainstream American life, but who Americans are defined as being in the first place. . . . Do other people come of age in this country? Of course, but not usually in the movies. Does coming of age occur outside suburbia? Of course, but not usually in the movies. . . . Who else can tell us stories? What stories have not been told yet? (*Center News* [Spring 1995]: 3, 10. Center for Research on Women, University of Memphis, Memphis, TN 38152)

Shakespeare and the Moving Image: The Plays on Film and Television, edited by Anthony Davies and Stanley Wells (Cambridge: Cambridge University Press, 1994) is a remake of *Shakespeare Studies* 39 (1986), repeating essays by E. Pearlman, Kenneth Rothwell, Neil Taylor, and Michele Willems, and a filmography by Graham Holderness and Christopher McCulloch, but omitting essays by Robert Hapgood (on *Chimes at Midnight*) and Lorne Buchman (on Welles's *Othello*). The last two essays are assumed to be subsumed by essays on the history plays, by Michael Manheim, and on *Othello*, by Anthony Davies. New essays by Peter Holland (on *King Lear* on film), Russell Jackson (on the comedies on film), Sam Crowl (on the Roman plays on film and television), Ace Pilkington (on Zeffirelli's Shakespeare films), Neil Taylor (on filmed *Hamlet*s), and Hapgood (on Kurosawa's adaptations of Shakespeare) complete the book.

The comprehensiveness and intelligence of the essays make this probably the best book on the subject of filmed Shakespeare available. Jorgens's classic study stops at 1977, and recent books by Davies, Buchman, Peter Donaldson, and John Collick, although useful, are restricted by thesis and range of material covered.

The book, however, has some flaws (as any other anthology would). It claims to be updated from 1986, and indeed Davies's introduction incorporates important materials, both performance and critical, introduced since then, as do several of the essays. The filmography, however, stops at 1988, with Branagh's *Henry V*, and thus does not include his *Much Ado*, Edzard's *As You Like It*, or Zeffirelli's *Hamlet*, although each of those productions is dealt with at length in the book that follows. The Kline *Hamlet* (1990), a televised adaptation of his stage version, is mentioned in a note on page 194, given a date of 1986 (stage production), and attributed to "Liviu Ciuler." Other items, like the three-camera version of Eyre's 1992 *Richard III*, obviously are too recent to be included. The filmography also appears to include at least two archival tapes—records made by a single camera sited on the balcony—and is thus either inconsistent in its selection process or woefully incomplete, in that archival tapes are available at the Shakespeare Centre, Stratford, for RSC productions from the early 1980s onward, and at Stratford, Canada, for its recent productions. Neil Taylor's "Two Types of Television Shakespeare" is reprinted verbatim from the 1986 *Shakespeare Studies*. Its most recent citation is from 1985. Moreover, a lot of relevant material from *Shakespeare on Film Newsletter* and the editions of *Literature/Film Quarterly* that deal with Shakespeare are not adduced. Three useful essays by Michael Mullin in *Literature/Film* (fall 1973, on Welles's *Macbeth*; Spring 1976, on Richardson's *Hamlet*; and July 1983, on Brook's *King Lear*) are not cited in the articles that deal with those films. It may be that important essays by Peter Donaldson on Branagh's *Henry V* and by R. B. Parker on the films of *King Lear*, both in a 1991 issue of *Shakespeare Quarterly*, appeared too late to be incorporated.

Willems's very useful piece claims that the BBC series brought no equivalents to the Manvell and Jorgens books on films or any analysis of Shakespeare on television similar to the work on film of Bazin, Laffay, or Metz, and then provides an updated footnote that identifies work that incorporates precisely what she found lacking in 1986, including Sheldon Zitner's brilliant essay on Shakespeare and television that Willems does not use to update and expand her own thesis ("Wooden O's in Plastic Boxes: Shakespeare on Television," *University of Toronto Quarterly* 51 [1981]: 1–12, anthologized in a book Willems cites). Pilkington cites an essay by Michael Pursell in the October 1992 *Literature/Film Quarterly,* but important articles on Olivier's and Branagh's *Henry V*, the Brook *King Lear*, Zeffirelli's Shakespeare films, and Howell's First Tetralogy also in that issue are neither included in the materials that deal with those productions nor cited. Much of this objection could have been met by the inclusion of a bibliography with a cutoff point of 1992. Editing an anthology is never easy, but the editors should have insisted on essays that were "appropriately updated and revised," as the Preface promises was done. In some cases, it seems, any updating was deemed "inappropriate."

The book's major blind spot is television. We are given some excellent essays on the subject, particularly Willems's, and some acute analysis of specific productions: Manheim's of the Barton-Hall, Howell, and Bogdanov history plays, Crowl's of the Nunn *Antony and Cleopatra*, and Taylor's of the Bennett-Jacobi *Hamlet* (although he calls it a film [191] and is thus very confused about what it could and could not be as television production). But we get little guidance on what television is and how to talk about it when discussing "television's being neither a play script, nor a stage play, nor a film," as Rothwell says (228). To call productions made for television "films," even if they were recorded in 16-mm formats, as a number of these essays do, is to blur distinctions at precisely the point where precision is demanded.

Davies's brief "Retrospect" (1–15) is useful but this field keeps growing and requires the constant monitoring of *Shakespeare Bulletin, Literature/Film Quarterly, Shakespeare Quarterly,* and *Shakespeare and the Classroom.*

Peter Holland's "Two Dimensional Shakespeare: 'King Lear' on film" reformulates Jack Jorgens's categories of "theatrical, realist, and filmic" (50) to apply to versions of *King Lear.* The theatrical mode is

usually made up of very long takes, the camera's long breaths trying to match the sustained acting paragraphs of the theatre rather than the rapidity of shots and brevity of editing normally used in the cinema. Camera positions are usually medium and long shots rather than close-ups, mimicking as much as possible the position of the theatre audience with its independence and controlled selectivity of observation from its fixed point of view in the auditorium (its individual seat), rather than film's fascination with the detail of a face or a gesture; the style reflects and adopts the theatre's interests in groups of characters seen, now on screen at once. (51)

Olivier's deep-field, black-and-white *Hamlet,* for example, can include a lot within its frame, but as in a theater, we will look at what the director wants us to see, in spite of the amount of detail included in the shot. "Occasionally, and intriguingly, theatrical films work better when made for television," Holland says. "The sustained close attention of the stage-version, conceived for small spaces in which the audience is, in theatrical terms, as close to the action as to a television screen, translate[s] perfectly to television" (52). That is true, of course, particularly when the acting style required of small spaces like the Other Place, which produced Trevor Nunn's *Macbeth* and *Othello* and the television studio is scaled down to the proximity of audience and camera or microphone. Holland goes on to say that "film . . . cannot respond to its audience" (52). Television can, however. "All in the Family" was taped before a live audience, and Jane Howell brought people in to create a version of audience for her *Henry VI* sequence. Furthermore, it is not necessary for television to engage in "an imaginative recreation of the language of the play into the terms of the film" (57), as Nunn and Howell consistently demonstrated in their successful television versions of tragedy and history plays. It is worth noting that seldom has a comedy moved from a stage to a television format—the BBC's late 1970s *Comedy of Errors,* a musical, and Branagh's Renaissance Theatre *Twelfth Night* being the exceptions. Comedies have been televised in performance, of course; the Papp and the Epstein *A Midsummer Night's Dream*s, for example. There the third dimension, the audience, helps us suspend our disbelief of the stage fictions.

"Realist" films include Zeffirelli's *Romeo and Juliet* and Kozintsev's *Hamlet* and, says Holland "are bound up with a traditional liberal-humanist ideology" (55). The *"filmic* mode," says Holland, is exemplified by Olivier's *Henry V* and Branagh's version, which "is filmic in a different sense because the film defines itself in relation to Olivier's film" (56).

The three categories "chart different distances of the film from the theatre." Holland cites three more of Jorgens's categories that define "degrees of distance from the original: presentation, interpretation and adaptation." To those categories, Holland adds "deconstruction of the text" (57) and cites Godard's 1988 *King Lear*. Of the Brook film, Holland usefully describes the way the camera insists that "the spectator become . . . an enforced participant in the action, made to watch, as confused and distressed as the characters themselves" (66). Holland's essay is a useful reiteration of Jorgen's categories—useful because the discourse is extended in the direction of televised Shakespeare.

Willems's well-known essay, which I discussed in Chapter 3, describes the BBC approaches to televised Shakespeare as "naturalistic, pictorial, and stylized" (74). Willems argues that the BBC would "have benefitted from a preliminary reflection of the best ways of bridging [the gap between stage] and the electronic square" (70). What remains troubling is that Nunn's excellent *Antony and Cleopatra* was available to provide BBC at least one model of how it could be done. That had been a stage production, of course, so it had a "maturity" behind it. Television, Willems argues, does not demand the "duality" that theater requires. In the latter, the spectator experiences simultaneous participation and detachment. The " 'viewing' situation [however] does not necessarily include listening or imagining" (71).

In the "naturalistic" mode, "Shakespeare's language is transported wholesale on television. The message is dense, polyvocal; layers of significance qualify and enrich the basic narration. Now naturalism, instead of trying to find ways to transpose this complex language, retaliates by superimposing its own favourite representational idiom. The visuals [become) successions of purely referential shots" (75), and the language becomes "everyday informative prose" (78).

The notorious example on film is Eileen Herlie's voice-over of Jean Simmons's cruise down the river in Olivier's *Hamlet*. On television, with its paucity of depth and detail and its linguistic heritage, the conflict between language and image is less intense than on film. What suffers, though, in the translation to television is the metadramatic element of Shakespeare's stage plays: plays within plays, eavesdropping scenes, and comedy itself. In the "naturalistic" mode, Willems argues, "only the literal meaning is transcribed" (76). The "realistic logic . . . emphasis[es] social context [and] in comedy . . . reinforces the incompatibility between convention and representation at the expense of laughter" (77). Furthermore, television's scale does not easily accommodate huge characters like Anthony Quayle's Falstaff or his effort to treat us, the viewers, with quiet confidentiality (77). Drama's translation to the television medium means that tragedy is concerned, as Jonathan Miller says, not "with the fall of the great, but with the disintegration of the ordinary" (78). Television turns laughter to puritan sobriety (as in Miller's version of *The Taming of the Shrew*) and domesticates tragedy (as in his *Othello*).

The pictorial approach Miller and Moshinsky adopted creates "an abundance of visual signs . . . at the expense of the words which are often diluted in obtrusive visual detail and interfering sound" (79). Nor does this approach "negotiate [the] play-within-the-play . . . any better than the naturalistic" (79). Indeed, the pictorial approach tends to emphasize one of television's limitations: its lack of a depth field. Color flattens perspective and stops the eye at the first point at which it encounters color, thus shallowing out even a shallow medium. Television also lacks the larger frame of Shakespeare's stage within which smaller productions can be reframed for an inner audience.

Willems praises Jane Howell's *Henry VI* sequence. Its "metonymic mode of expression brings television much nearer to the theatre" (80) and incorporates metadramatic elements like doubling and televisual techniques like slow motion. The "settings . . . often proclaim that they are mere settings" (80). Willems also praises Rodney Bennett's direction of "The Murder of Gonzago" in the BBC *Hamlet*, again picking out a good example of how Shakespeare can work on television through what she calls the "metonymic mode."

This essay remains, along with Sheldon Zitner's essay, required reading for teachers who use televised versions of the plays in their classrooms.

The Taylor essay, "Two Types of Television Shakespeare," a contrast between the techniques of Howell and Moshinsky, makes some useful distinctions. Taylor quotes John Ellis to the effect that "TV offers relatively discrete segments, small sequential unities of images or sounds" (87). That accounts for the tendency of the plays as televised to come across as "spots of time" rather than productions unified by some deeper premises. The segmentation may result from the need for commercial breaks, another of television's inheritances from radio. The effect is not post-modern, but rather is a variation on modernism, in which television, unlike film, seems trapped. "Television," says Taylor, "produces an effect of immediacy even within dramas of historically remote periods by reproducing the audience's view of itself within its fictions" (87). Its fictions are designed to sell something, within and around what Taylor calls "television's rhythms of very short, ateleological segments" (87). Not only is television ateleological, but it exists in what Moshinsky calls "the constant present, which is a weakness if you are trying to build up a narrative structure" (Elsom, 1989, 124). Taylor argues that "Shakespeare will always be subject to the predominant conventions of the medium" (87), but does suggest variations within the conventions. Howell uses theatrical techniques, including doubling, which she expects an audience to notice (89). "Moshinsky's directorial style . . . involved keeping actors and camera comparatively still and providing movement through montage" (94). His "closer shots" put the "emphasis on individuals, psychological interpretations of behavior, and subjective experience" (94–95). "Moshinsky's *Cymbeline* was thoroughly subjective, exploring dream interiors in dream time" (95). For Howell, on the other hand,

Television's ability to simulate real time was combined with its frankness about the physicality of things, so that a pact was made with the viewer: these are the actors, this is the text, this is the set, this is the space in which we shall all be working. She operated within the known. [Moshinsky] discovered in television's sealed, iconic screen a denial of immediacy and intimacy. . . . He used television's preference for segmentation, and its ability to cut between shots, to create a cinematic montage that challenged the known. (96)

Moshinsky also uses a "pictorial" approach, as Willems suggests, that strikes me as very static when compared with the shuffle, sprint, and splinters of Howell's histories.

Russell Jackson's spritely essay, "Shakespeare's Comedies on Film," dismisses the specter of the "purist." Since Zeffirelli's *Romeo and Juliet*, it seems, the purist, who howled at the deletion of language from the playing script, has learned that film must subordinate language to image. Jackson notices that Shakespeare's films have a considerable "afterlife," as the recent reissue of the 1936 *Romeo and Juliet* attests. He condemns Christine Edzard's *As You Like It* as "a poor representative of the vigour and sense of relevance that 'modern dress' can bring" (101). Nevertheless, as I will suggest, Edzard's film does some fascinating things with androgyny, which is at the heart of the role of Rosalind. Emma Croft is brilliant as Rosalind, for all of the film's silly shifting of pastoral convention to the Thames dockside. The film's treatment of the Rosalind and Orlando story shows us much more than people who only get "to know each other in disguise" (118). I think the play does too. Shakespearean comedy on film suffers from the trait that Rilla notes: "at its most effective [film dialogue] is based on an essential inarticulacy" (1973, 89). "Shakespearian comedy," Jackson says, unfolds "in an unreal world in which speech has formidable power and value" (102). Jackson's knowledge of film as genre is particularly useful here, as when, for example, he discusses the ways in which Mickey Rooney, James Cagney, and Dick Powell bring roles and expectations from other films to Puck, Bottom, and Lysander in the 1935 Reinhardt and Dieterle *A Midsummer Night's Dream*. Jackson also deals deftly with Jarman's *The Tempest*, Greenaway's *Prospero's Books*, the Peter Hall film of *Dream*, and the Zeffirelli *Shrew*.

Manheim suggests in his "The English History Play on Screen," that Olivier, in his 1944 *Henry V*, created "the image of a victorious English leader for a country at war in a noble cause" and thus, "perhaps unwittingly, created what is probably the sole instance in drama of what Machiavelli really had in mind—and he did it by means of the medium most suited to the creation of illusion" (125). Olivier gives us

a sense of political leaders who are ahead of their time in depending more upon their talent for creating images of themselves upon the modes of morality and behaviour they were born into. . . . Branagh gives us a Henry who is at the beginning little more than a boy seeking his appropriate voice and direction. . . . Branagh's characterization radically divides our sympathies because along with his ingenuousness, sincerity, and apparent decency—he is also a ruthless murderer. (128, 129, 130)

Thus the film could be said to be postmodern in that it does not provide a single coherent point of view about its title character.

Manheim suggests that the Hall-Barton *Wars of the Roses* of the early 1960s displays "a sense of arrogant, self-centered swagger in a senseless political maelstrom," elements deriving from Kott and Beckett. Paralleling this "existentialism" is "the 1980s/90s Neo-Marxism of the Bogdanov/Pennington version" (133), which "appear[s] duty-bound to discredit aristocrats" (136). While Manheim questions the postmodernist eclecticism of the costuming in the Bogdanov-Pennington production of *Henry V*, where the "French wear Napoleonic costumes" and the English "twentieth-century military dress," he credits that approach with suggesting "quickly what it takes Olivier and Branagh many elaborate (and expensive) scenes to suggest: the inventiveness of Henry's tactics at Agincourt versus the glamourous but essentially tired militarism of the French" (142). That is a point worth making, particularly since Shakespeare does not "explain" the English victory at Agincourt, other than demonstrating French overconfidence and Henry's rousing oratory and postbattle piety. But the Bogdanov is a TV version of a live stage production. It probably can rely on metonymic modes that would be ludicrous in film. I find such postmodernism a distracting imposition by the director of his "concept" on the script and have found Bogdanov particularly culpable in this regard. Manheim's essay will serve as an excellent introduction to films and TV versions of the histories, though I wish he had looked at Giles's BBC Second Tetralogy rather than merely citing Ace Pilkington's books on the Second Henriad.

Crowl's "The Roman Plays on Film and Television" makes the fascinating point about "intention" and "historicity" that John Houseman hoped his 1953 production of *Julius Caesar*, directed by Joseph Mankiewicz, would "evoke memories of the Fuhrer at Nuremberg and of Mussolini ranting from his high balcony overlooking the wildly cheering crowds" (149). What happened, though, Crowl suggests, is that the film derived response from the contemporary "hysteria about supposed subversives" and the country's involvement in "the extension of America's international influence" (149).

Regardless of what Houseman intended, the film emerged into and was seen to reflect its immediate zeitgeist. Crowl nicely describes the performances in this film—Brando's use of eyes, for example (150–51), and the ways in which direction enhances characterization—and the images, for example, that suggest "the dry and tangled nature of Brutus's tortured reasoning" (150). He rightly condemns Jason Robards's performance in the Burge *Julius Caesar* (151), the "museum piece" BBC *Julius Caesar* (152), and Miller's BBC *Antony and Cleopatra*. The last is "an intellectually clever mis-

reading, transforming Shakespeare's most poetically and spatially flamboy-
ant play into something small and oddly barren" (157). Heston's film ver-
sion "not only fails, visually and verbally, to capture the dynamics of
Shakespeare's play but also fails to create an interesting epic inspired by a
Shakespearean source" (159). Crowl praises Nunn's televised version of the
RSC production of *Antony and Cleopatra*, with Janet Suzman and Richard
Johnson, and Elijah Moshinsky's BBC *Coriolanus*, with Alan Howard, Mike
Gwilym, and Irene Worth. These, "in their very individual ways, make pal-
pable the dynamic tragic tensions Shakespeare's imagination seized upon
when engaged in conceiving Rome and its legacy" (161). Crowl is kinder to
Miller's *Antony and Cleopatra* and harder on Herbert Wise's *Julius Caesar*
than I, but he is a keen-eyed and accurate guide to the Roman world as re-
depicted by Hollywood and White City.

Ace Pilkington, in "Zeffirelli's Shakespeare," suggests that resistances to
Shakespeare productions—à la Lamb, indeed, that "the old prejudice which
saw the theatre as superior to—because more Shakespearean than—film"—
are breaking down (163). The combatants, however, are still "the purists
and the popularizers," he says (164). I doubt that. Shakespeareans today are
sophisticated enough to understand that any film of a script is a translation
of the script, just as any stage version is an interpretation. The battle lines
are drawn by the materialists, who inveigh from the safety of their secure
careers against commercialization and by the variety of critics who simply
ignore the fact that these plays *are* plays. At any rate, Pilkington is correct to
call Zeffirelli "popularizer-in-chief," although Branagh may be vying for
that title. Pilkington details the indebtedness of Zeffirelli's *Hamlet* to
Olivier's. "Hamlet's 'To be or not to be' soliloquy follows his confrontation
with Ophelia," for example (166). On the other hand, Olivier's soliloquy is
spoken from the top of the parapets, as Hamlet looks out upon a literal sea
of troubles. Gibson's soliloquy is delivered in the crypt where his father is
buried. "Though they are mostly visual, there are some first-rate ideas in this
film" (174). Pilkington isolates "Hamlet lying on the graveyard grass, head
to head with Yorick's skull . . . the sheer vitality and happiness of Claudius
and Gertrude, paired and contrasted with the cautious shuffling of Polonius
and the sullen skulking of Ophelia" (174–75). One could add to the list
Claudius's holding his hand over his right ear as "Gonzago" breaks up and
Trevor Peacock's Gravedigger crossing himself on "But, rest her soul, she's
dead." Pilkington also deals effectively with Zeffirelli's *Shrew*—"While
Petruchio educates Kate, she domesticates him" (171)—and *Romeo and
Juliet*—"The town seems to crowd and compress the characters so that the
individual violence and the riots look like attempts to escape from a maze,
and the briefly deserted squares and streets provide a chance to breathe before the tension builds again to critical mass" (172).

Neil Taylor, in "The Films of *Hamlet*," argues that "films of the play inevitably provide audiences with less visual evidence of the actor playing

Hamlet than do theatrical productions. A stage Hamlet will be visible even when he is not speaking" (181). It depends on what the camera shows, of course, but that statement is probably true of Hamlet, in that he calls attention to himself even when he is not speaking: in the black garments that conflict with the splendor of the court, for example, in the second scene, and in that his soliloquies do not have "visual equivalents," as in Olivier's sea for "To be or not to be." Taylor points out that in the Olivier film, "Olivier was also scrutinizing and presenting himself as a director"—in the Players Scene, for example (182). The Kozintsev *Hamlet*, a conscious response and contrast to Olivier's, shows Hamlet's "isolation [as] political rather than merely psychological or emotional. . . . He is subject to larger and stronger currents than those of one Family Romance" (185). The film, says Taylor, "can be read both as a critique of a specific political situation in Russia and as a fatalistic statement about the individual's experience of history" (187). Williamson's Hamlet is "a neurotic outsider, spasmodically distressed and overwrought" (188). Director Richardson excludes "all reference to a material setting beyond the actions of the actors. . . . Hamlet is defined as being, not just the hero, but the total subject of the film" (188–89). And one must ask whether this film, with its many close-ups of Hamlet's bitter face, does not give us more of Hamlet than some stage productions. Taylor includes the Bennett BBC version under the category of film and thus somewhat misses the point about soliloquies shot "in a single long take" and the point about Porter, Bloom, and Stewart playing Polonius, Gertrude, and Claudius, respectively, as "warm, sensitive, reasonable people," and the point about "close-ups and reaction shots" (190). If television does not demand these techniques and approaches, the medium encourages them.

Taylor praises the Orlova cartoon version as "a distinctive folk-tale" (192). It does capture a remarkable amount of the script in a half-hour, but it also shows that Hamlet must be played by an actor, not a voice behind a painted face. Still, it is remarkable to see Hamlet "robbed of his divine verbosity" (192). The animated version should make for an introduction to the play for young people. The problem is that it is likely to become a substitute for any other experience of the script. Zeffirelli "cavalierly re-organizes the order of the text, advancing and delaying speeches in a bewildering manner" (192). Having seen productions that follow Q1's order of scenes, I did not find the reordering bewildering, but then Taylor seems to want to pose as the purist that Pilkington invents. "Zeffirelli's prime purpose is to simplify the narrative" (192). Of course, it is a film. Terrence Rafferty's objection to the brisk and too-cadenced pace of the film is more cogent (1991). Taylor suggests that, as in the 1968 *Romeo and Juliet*, "Zeffirelli wishes only to . . . create an a-tragic world of people going about their daily business in a glamorous, open, sunlit, cinematogenic environment, and then tell the unglamorous story of that society's ability to waste its young" (193). His, Taylor asserts, is "the slightest of the six [*Hamlet*] films" (193).

Davies's "Filming *Othello*" contrasts theater with film by quoting Bazin on film's "concession to solitude" and "betrayal of action by refusal of social responsibility" (197). (Film, as propaganda, can be a powerful inducement to social irresponsibility.) While Olivier's film is "both a record of Olivier's unique performance and a historical document revealing an interaction of theatre with society" (196), its "visual strategy sets up a relationship between specific character and the film viewer rather than one between character and a dramatic ambience created on stage" (197). But does that create a more "theatrical" effect in the film? And was not that effect responsible for the charge, by Bosley Crowther, that this was a filmed play and therefore should not be considered for an Academy Award? As performance, Olivier's *Othello* is still fascinating as he plays stereotype into stereotypic expectations, believing he is controlling his environment and its inhabitants. As film, with its close-ups and undefined settings, it is television, a medium in which Iago becomes far more prominent than he was in the stage version. Davies attributes the problems of the film to differing flows of energy, to "an aesthetic clash between the centripetal function of the actor on the theatre stage and the centrifugal dynamic of the cinema frame" (198). Furthermore, without a proscenium arch, "one is constantly aware that one's concentration is being restricted to only a part of a theatrical presentation designed for a different audience" (199–200). The Olivier film does show, however, partly because of its "intensely selective" camera, that "part of Othello's tragedy is . . . his readiness to make symbols more important than the abstractions for which they stand" (199). The Yutkevich version develops "an ironic relationship between exterior and interior (psychological) action" (202). Othello's "Are we turned Turks . . ." "is spoken like a soliloquy, as though even at this early stage, opposing forces of order and chaos have become internalized" (203). Although Welles "tends to juxtapose images and allow the composite effect to mature in the viewer's mind . . . the film lacks an intensity of theatricality which, at its core, the play demands" (209). Davies alludes to the Buchman essay on Welles's *Othello* that originally appeared in *Shakespeare Studies* and to the superb Trevor Nunn RSC version, which, emerging from a stage production, indeed incorporates an "intensity of theatricality." It deserves a fuller treatment than it gets, since it suggests that television can deliver this script in ways that film cannot. (See my chapters on the Nunn production in *Performance as Interpretation* [stage], 216–19 and *Watching Shakespeare on Television* [television], 93–104.)

Perhaps the most original essay in this collection is Hapgood's on Kurosawa. Kurosawa's films, Hapgood says, "have their own integrity and can be enjoyed on their own terms without reference to Shakespeare" (234). Although they take "liberties with the original, they are faithful . . . to some essence in it" (234). Hapgood isolates two Japanese film genres: *jidai-geki* (period pictures, a category that includes *Throne of Blood* and *Ran*) and *gendai-mono* (modern-story films like *The Bad Sleep Well*). The former two "are set in the *Sengoku Jidai* or 'Age of the Country at War' (1392–1568). . . . *Ran* seems the later of the two, both in weaponry . . . and decadence" (235). "Kurosawa has explained that [the] initial inspiration [for *Ran*] came not from *King Lear* but the Japanese warlord Montornari Mori (1497–1571) and his three sons" (236). Hapgood deftly outlines the sources for the films: scrolls, *The Tale of the Heike*, Noh drama, and the Buddhist hell to come, "presided over by the demon Ashura, where warriors continue their destructive ways" (237). "Where *Ran* sees the present moment as hell on earth, *Throne of Blood* emphasizes its persistence through the ages" (238). "*Throne of Blood* is more than anything else a mood piece . . . [and is] one of a kind" (238, 239). "The most distinctive hallmark of Kurosawa's general approach to Shakespeare is his constant pull toward the graphic, the immediate, the concrete, the simple, the extreme" (242). In *Throne of Blood,* we "come to see how the two of them [Washizu and Miki] have been doomed to doom themselves—the film's deepest thematic resemblance to *Macbeth*" (247). Those who use Kurosawa's films in their teaching will find Hapgood's essay indispensable, particularly on *Throne of Blood*. For a very useful contrast between Kurosawa's *Ran* and the *Lear* films of Brook and Kozintsev, see R. B. Parker's essay (*Shakespeare Quarterly* 42, no. 1 [spring 1991]).

Pearlman argues that modern film versions of *Macbeth* offer readings counter to the inherited script. He makes an assertion with which the cultural materialists disagree: that "*Macbeth* unabashedly celebrates a semi-divine monarch in terms specific to the first years of Stuart absolutism. . . . The play's satisfaction with the traditional order, though severely tested by the reign of the tyrant, is confirmed when a second exemplary monarch succeeds his father" (250). The play "assumes that misgovernment enters the community not because of defects in the system of monarchy, but at the behest of agents of darkness. . . . Monarchy remains the only conceivable form of government" (251). "Orson Welles," Pearlman argues, "unsuccessfully labours to strip *Macbeth* of its political content" (252). The "film inadvertently generates a rudimentary political vision of its own [becoming] an exploration of both dictatorship and the cult of personality" (252). At the end of the film, "the threat of dictatorship still looms" (252). Polanski's "vision is even more despairing. . . . Both Christianity and monarchy are deliberately and systematically replaced by satanism. . . . Unlike Welles's world, which is menacing and brooding, or Kurosawa's spare and joyless universe, Polanski's world is characterized by song, dance, and even a degree of joy. Yet there is a sinister underside to this apparently prospering community. It is permeated by . . . gratuitous violence" (253). "The massed ugliness of the naked witches in their cave is an imaginative expansion of the misogyny of the original play" (254). "Shakespeare's confidence in the triumph of justice has been transformed into our favourite contemporary cliché—that all events are merely accidents of an indifferent universe" (255). "In Welles's *Macbeth*, the alternative to monarchy is anarchy; in Polanski's version, the alternative is diabolism" (255). "Unlike *Macbeth*, where the witches invade a basically healthy universe, Kurosawa's universe is devoid of political virtue. . . . The society is characterized . . . by narrow self-interest, distrust, constant fear, and the easy recourse to violence" (257). But, while "Kurosawa offers no easy answers, neither does he permit his film to succumb to authoritarian or demonic presences . . . the rotten feudalism for which [Washizu] stands cannot be brought to its knees by one individual, but can be overcome by the people acting in concert" (259, 258).

The films now emerging will lead to more commentary. What is presented above becomes background for what is soon to come.

REFERENCES

Buchman, Lorne. 1991. *Still in Movement: Shakespeare on Screen*. Oxford: Oxford University Press.

Collick, John. 1989. *Shakespeare, Cinema, and Society*. Manchester: Manchester University Press.

Coursen, H. R. 1992. *Shakespearean Performance as Interpretation*. Newark: Delaware University Press.

———. 1993. *Watching Shakespeare on Television*. Madison, N.J.: Fairleigh Dickenson University Press.

Cox Report on Media and Education. 1990. London: Westminister.

Donaldson, Peter. 1990. *Shakespearean Films/ Shakespearean Directors*. Boston: Unwin Hyman.

Elsom, John. 1989. *Is Shakespeare Still Our Contemporary?* London: Routledge.

Erskine, Thomas, and James M. Welsh, eds. *Literature/Film Quarterly* 1, no. 4 (Fall 1973), 5, no. 2 (Spring 1976), 5, no. 4 (Fall 1977), 11, no. 3 (1983), 20, no. 4 (1992).

Jorgens, Jack. 1977. *Shakespeare on Film*. Bloomington: Indiana University Press.

Miller, Mark C. 1980. "The Shakespeare Plays." *Nation*, 12 July, 46–61.

Mowat, Barbara, ed. 1991. *Shakespeare Quarterly* 42, no. 1.

Pilkington, Ace. 1991. *Screening Shakespeare from "Richard II" to "Henry V."* Newark: University of Delaware Press.

Rilla, Wolf. 1973. *The Writer and the Screen*. London: Macmillan.

Skovmand, Michael, ed. 1994. *Screen Shakespeare*. Aarhus, Denmark: Aarhus University Press.

Zitner, Sheldon. 1981. "Wooden O's in Plastic Boxes: Shakespeare on Television." *University of Toronto Quarterly* 51, 1–12.

II

APPLICATIONS

The assignments that follow, with varying degrees of complexity, can involve students from senior high to graduate school. For each, I give an example, exploring one of the myriad possible topics. These chapters bring the individual works to the light as I have seen them. I do not disavow my own subjectivity or the factors—political, emotional, and intellectual—that have gone into my construction as observer and commentator. I have limited each response to a defined point of view, using a specific critical mode or selection process in looking at the visual material. My reasons are to focus the response and to point out to students that a limited point of view is probably inevitable in responding to film and television and perhaps helpful in pulling together the disparate elements of a critique. This part hopes to suggest that exploration and research in the field of Shakespeare on film offers many exciting possibilities for students on many levels. I also hope to bring some recent films to the attention of students, who should debate my own evaluations.

Assignment Take three scenes from three different productions of the same play and compare and contrast them through the use of a particular critical point of view. Here, I take *Twelfth Night*, specifically the scene in which Malvolio is visited by Feste in prison (4.2). I apply both generic and "Christian" points of view.

I also look briefly at Christine Edzard's *As You Like It* from a feminist perspective in my discussion of that film.

Fallacies: Unless the approach is itself historical, the results will be ahistorical. A generic approach takes the production out of history and assumes that events and expectations emerge from a prototype. If modern psycho-analytic insights are applied, for example, the results may be anachronistic, in that a recent theory may be applied to a work that did not have the theory available at the time of its creation. To see the comedies as emerging from a "Christian" rhythm—a movement from error to enlightenment—is debatable. Some critics would howl and cry, "That's thematic criticism!" That approach may also, like a feminist interrogation, involve the application of point of view that can smother what the film or TV production is trying to do. A work of art does not have to adhere to Christian or feminist or politically correct formulas.

Assignment Review a film, based on a Shakespeare script, using a particular mode of analysis. Here I look at the editing of the Parker *Othello* (1995) and the mise-en-scène—the world created for the script—of the Edzard *As You Like It* (1992) and the Loncraine *Richard III* (1996).

Fallacies: This may be ahistorical, and it may limit response to the thesis. Students will notice that I go beyond my own thesis to suggest other aspects of my response to each film.

Assignment Take a film that is based on or is an offshoot of a Shakespeare play and write about the film, particularly about how the film relates to the source. Examples are *A Double Life, Forbidden Planet*, Kurosawa's *The Bad Sleep Well*, Goddard's *King Lear*, and *Men of Respect*. Here, I look briefly at Kenneth Branagh's *A Midwinter's Tale* (1996).

Fallacies: The film itself may be devalued as a separate work of art if it is used only for the sake of paralleling it with the Shakespeare script. On the other hand, the film may be overvalued though its association with the Shakespeare script.

Assignment Take the openings or endings of films or television productions of a particular script and suggest how the director decides to tell the story or how to conclude the story that has been told. Here I look at the opening scenes of filmed *Hamlet*s.

Fallacy: In this case the critic may well have a strong sense of the "ur-story" that the script tells—that is, an interpretation that will tend to suggest what story should be told.

Assignment Take a version of the same scene from different productions that have appeared in different decades and historicize the segment, showing how zeitgeist and film or television production values help define the different versions. Here I look at depictions of Pistol, a minor character in *Henry V*.

Fallacies: "History" is a notoriously subjective construct. Experience of and research into a given moment in time will invariably represent the idiosyncrasies of the observer.

7

Genre and Production: The Madhouse Scene in *Twelfth Night* (4.2)

John Dexter, British Broadcasting Company (1970)
    Malvolio: Alec Guiness
    Feste: Tommy Steele
    Toby: Ralph Richardson
    Maria: Sheila Reid
    Sebastian: Joan Plowright

John Gorrie, British Broadcasting Company (1980)
    Malvolio: Alec McCowen
    Feste: Trevor Peacock
    Toby: Robert Hardy
    Maria: Annette Crosbie
    Sebastian: Michael Thomas

Kenneth Branagh, Renaissance Theatre Company (1988)
    Malvolio: Richard Briers
    Feste: Anton Lesser
    Toby: James Saxon
    Maria: Abigail McKern
    Sebastian: Christopher Hollis

Trevor Nunn (1996)
    Malvolio: Nigel Hawthorne
    Feste: Ben Kingsley
    Toby: Mel Smith
    Maria: Imelda Staunton
    Sebastian: Stephen Mackintosh

We look at a specific scene, 4.2 of *Twelfth Night*, particularly at what the scene tells us of Malvolio. I then go on to place Malvolio against the generic expectations of comedy. This kind of exercise can be conducted wherever two or three versions of a script exist. Students can observe the editing of the script, the editing of the shots (Who is in the frame? Who is not?), and the ways in which an approach to a specific scene contributes to an overall interpretation. The learning process builds from careful observation and analysis of the smaller component to a consideration of the larger. Each is a television production. The scene is limited in physical scope and number of characters and therefore should work on television.

Twelfth Night is the Feast of Epiphany, which celebrates the spreading of the light of the Gospels to the gentiles. Its symbol is the star that led the Wise Men—old believers, possibly pagan astrologers—to the new dispensation. Epiphany, then, celebrates the coming of knowledge, of a new way of knowing into what previously had been darkness. From the tiny point of the manger and its child emerge outward circles of divine energy. One does not have to believe that to accept that Epiphany is a fact of the Christian calendar.

For Christians, Epiphany is the answer to Plato's cave, where people huddle in darkness and accept shadows cast on a wall as reality. People might be blinded by reality and therefore must look at shadow shapes and mistake the shadows on the wall for what is real. For Christians, the light must shine from within—"let your light so shine." The experience can be blinding, as it was for Saul on the road to Damascus, but it is basically from the inside— from the insight—out, as in Christ's curing of the blind man, whose faith permits him to see.

Malvolio in his dark room refuses to see the light. That is obvious and probably the "meaning" of the scene. In a famous production that John Barton directed for the Royal Shakespeare Company, Donald Sinden played Malvolio as terrified of the darkness. Sinden stressed every reference to darkness, thus emphasizing his desperate need for light (1985, 63–65). But other questions also come up. I suggest that the available versions of the scene do not help us very much in understanding it.

In looking at the available Malvolios, we notice several things. Guiness does seem to be on the edge of madness; he has trouble controlling the need to become a woodcock. Joan Plowright is utterly unconvincing as Sebastian on TV, a medium that seldom tolerates gender destabilization. We get a good sense in the BBC production of the dimensions of Malvolio's cell and the limits it places on his mobility. BBC gets it all wrong by emphasizing the contrast between Malvolio and Sebastian. Part I ends. Part II begins with light and twittering birds in the garden and Sebastian waiting for his cue. We scarcely see Richard Briers in the Renaissance Theatre version. He has been virtually entombed. We notice Feste's anger at having to play roles for the likes of Sir Toby; apparently Feste is in love with Olivia but does require the occasional crust for sustenance. His angry, "Nay, I am for all waters," apparently intends to mean that he is for better waters than these. That interpretation—giving Feste a character or at least a subtext—confuses all issues that Feste helps to clarify for us in his designated role as Fool. But Renaissance gets it right by dissolving from the window that closes on Malvolio to the door opening for Sebastian as he gives himself a reality check.

We also notice the editing. The Plowright production cuts the line about the Egyptians in their fog, as does the BBC. Perhaps the reference to Exodus is deemed too difficult for a modern audience. But surely an allusion to an unenlightened people in the Old Testament is a significant cue to how we are to perceive Malvolio. The ninth plague, right after those grasshoppers, was, according to the Bible, "darkness which may be felt" (Exodus 10:21). That moment is one of the Old Testament precursors of Epiphany: "They saw not one another, neither rose any from his place for three days: but all the children of Israel had light in their dwellings" (Exodus 10:23). The line about Malvolio's fearing to kill a woodcock is also cut in all the productions, which is to chop the punch line of the joke. BBC excises the entire Pythagoras catechism—this in a series that promised fidelity to the texts. The Renaissance has Feste ask, "Are you not mad?" but eliminates the double-bind, "or do you but counterfeit?" The scene is confusing as written (to me at least), and the editing of these productions makes it incomprehensible.

What is going on in the Madhouse Scene? I am helped by critics like Barbara Lewalski and Chris Hassel, who point at the feast of Epiphany and Malvolio's failure to see the light, but I look in vain at the available productions, and at Bill Alexander's essay, "Directing the 'Dark Room' Scene" (1990), Billington's interviews with directors in *Approaches to Twelfth Night* (1990), and the Folger's celebrated *Shakespeare Set Free* ("Teaching *Twelfth Night* and *Othello*," 1995), which ignores the scene, just as the series tends to ignore most of the tricky dramatic issues of the plays it deals with, instead reducing them to a set of teenage stereotypes that presumably make them easy to teach. Folger would deny this and point at page 120 of its volume on *Twelfth Night*, which clearly says, "Show the Videotape," meaning the BBC production. But what does the teacher do with the student who says, "Hey! They left out that line about the Arabs, and all that stuff about the woodcock, a proverbially silly bird"?

What I think is going on is that Shakespeare pushes against the limits of comedy. I suggest that it is not just Malvolio's incapacity that is to be noticed here, but the incapacity of the genre itself. Feste need not have disguised himself as curate. He knows it figuratively, and Maria knows it literally. Malvolio can only hear Feste. In fact, Feste's roles conflate; he is fool and clergyman in the closing song of the scene, where he bids farewell to the person who will not be redeemed: "Adieu, goodman devil."

Malvolio is right to say that a fool works best with infirmity. In fact, infirmity of spirit is the reason for a fool, as incapacity of soul is the reason for a priest. Malvolio epitomizes the indictment of Sonnet 62:

> Sin of self-love possesseth all mine eye
> And all my soul with all my every part.
> And for this sin there is no remedy,
> It is so grounded inward in my heart.

Malvolio can only babble of his sanity, committing the sin of righteousness, reverting to the rigidity of a position he abandoned with alacrity when he believed that Olivia also knelt at his altar of self-worship. He can only demand an external light—something equivalent to ego or consciousness—which blinds him to the glimmerings of innerness, the epiphany that, as Paul says in Ephesians, helps "all men [to] see what the fellowship of the mystery is." Self-glorification leads only to darkness. The "obstruction" of "cross-gartering," of which Malvolio complained earlier, becomes the "obstruction" of darkness of which he complains later. Whatever we say of Malvolio, he does not represent that psychic prism through which shines the light of developing selfhood. Viola perceives rhythms beyond those of the individual will. She yields to those larger, shaping patterns: "Time, thou must untangle this, not I / 'Tis too hard a knot for me to untie." She presents to us a version of what we would call faith.

But while we experience Malvolio's refusal to grow—to laugh at himself—does not Shakespeare press Malvolio against an impossibility? Is not Feste's role itself clownish as curate and theological as clown, so that we do not know which is which? Malvolio may be able to distinguish the two voices in his darkness; he is certainly not mad. But Malvolio is proof against both fooling and preaching, a setter of the limits of comedy, occular and di vine, a character in a problem play, an Angelo who only dreams of the power that Angelo wields.

Feste suggests that Malvolio's heritage is fixed, allowing of no change; he is the grandson of a woodcock. The soul must change and be born again. It is immortal perhaps, as Hamlet says, but it is not static. Malvolio's rigidity in not accepting that souls must change, transmigrating to new birth, makes him another kind of fool. Malvolio will not play the game, in contrast to Orlando in *As You Like It*. Malvolio is snug in his certainty, smug in his self-valuation, and absolute in his unearned self-esteem. He cannot smile without looking strange and he cannot laugh at himself. Thus he cannot be redeemed into the comic analogue of Christian salvation. Again, contrast Orlando at the Duke's feast in the forest. Orlando surrenders his assumptions and is able to bring Adam to this community, this communion, re-creating for an instant a ceremony of innocence in a world contaminated by experience.

We know the two scenes I put together on tape are linked thematically because Sebastian says, "This may be some error, but no madness." In a production years ago at the Theater at Monmouth (Maine), Malvolio exited from 4.2 (the madhouse) to a few chords of "O, Mistress Mine, where are you roaming," which we had heard earlier. Sebastian entered to the same music. Sebastian steps into the light. Malvolio remains in darkness. Olivia is roaming with Sebastian. The presumed fluidity of Shakespeare's dramaturgy, with one scene flowing into another without interruption, makes the point automatically. In Shakespeare and Company's 1993 production, Tom Jaeger doubled as Malvolio in a severe, dark steward's robe and as Sebastian in a loose shirt, cream-colored trousers, and boots. Sebastian was what lies under Malvolio, as shadow lies under consciousness. Malvolio had read Olivia correctly, even if only in the direction of his own gratification. In a production choice that I would not have approved, John Barton permitted Sinden's Malvolio to babble unintelligibly and out of sight as Sebastian entered (1985, 65).

I do not think anyone has commented on Maria's line, "He sees thee not." The disguise seems to be for our benefit, so that we can believe that Malvolio is deceived. The emphasis is on hearing, and we could construct an allegory here easily enough. In an illiterate society, a culture held in a version of darkness, the word of the Lord was heard. "Hear what comfortable words our Saviour Christ saithe to all them that truly turn to him," says the priest in the Anglican communion service. Christ emphasizes having ears and hearing—not just listening, but taking the word in. The voice from the cloud in Mark—the voice of God—commands, "Heare him" (9:7). If the word is not heard then, as John says, "The light shineth in the darkness, & the darkness comprehended it not." We have an unprofitable servant cast into "the outer darkness," where "there shall be weeping and gnashing of teeth." In Malvolio's case, we have an analogue to the Pharisee who says, "O God, I thank thee that I am not as other men," as opposed to the blind man who receives his sight: Thy faith hath saved thee." "He that heareth and dooth not" is the man who has built his house on sand. The Madhouse Scene certainly shows comedy failing, since it works only when spirit, the inward person, can be moved. But I think that it is all too easy to hold scripture up to Shakespeare's text and make the play come out as exegesis.

Malvolio is isolated and humiliated at the end. We may dismiss him as we do at the end of the BBC version. Alec McCowen recognizes what has been done to him and hardens his heart. At the end of a production a few years ago at Regent's Park in London, Bernard Breeslaw was brought in having been stuffed down a well. We were horrified. Malvolio's revenge was in our recognition that the man had been deeply wronged. We notice that we scarcely see Richard Briers in the Renaissance Theatre version. He has been entombed, a poignant fact for a British audience accustomed to seeing him playing sympathetic characters in West End comedies.

Tragedy and history alternate between the public and the private, until finally, the private and personal, which has attracted us and involved us in its agenda, is canceled. The public—the political—wins out. *Richard II*, for example, alternates between public and private scenes in its first act, preparing us for the outbreak of private concerns of which Richard makes much in the Deposition Scene. His musings in prison about king and person are finally interrupted by Exton's executioners. Although Bolingbroke will be troubled by this regicide, as will his son, the final ceremony of *Richard II* is Richard's funeral. Bolingbroke can mourn—and there is a lot to mourn for since kingship has lost its essential qualities—but he is king. Hamlet can bring his private grief into a coronation scene and interrupt Claudius's kingship, but it is finally young Hamlet's funeral that Fortinbras orders, "with sorrow" perhaps, but with a sure sense of how the funeral carries with it Hamlet's "dying voice" in favor of King Fortinbras of Denmark.

Comedy tends to blend public and private concerns once a character decides, as Orlando does, that he "can live no longer by thinking" or as Kate does, that she need no longer defend herself by shrewing, or as Beatrice and Benedict do, once they are tricked into recognizing that their fascination with each other is actually love. Marriage is the ceremony that signals that individual insights have been achieved so that mutuality and social goals can be realized. It is like the world of Jane Austen. We probably do not care that Jaques declines, claiming that he "is for other than for dancing measures," and we may agree that Shylock has disqualified himself from participation in comic closure. But what of Malvolio, who, after all, wants only what any young man in comedy wants: to wive it wealthily, beautifully, and sensually?

Is Malvolio eligible to play the game? Suppose he learns to laugh? Suppose he accepts his humiliation, as Falstaff does at the end of *Merry Wives*: "Well, I am your theme. You have the start of me" (5.5.162). Falstaff is not a servant in that world of Windsor. In fact, Sir John Falstaff outranks those who have bested him. Malvolio remains "a steward still, the fellow of servants, not worthy to touch Fortune's fingers" (2.5.143–44). Shakespeare has created a world like that of *The Merchant of Venice* into which some people cannot intrude. Shylock is revenged upon, perhaps most viciously in his forced conversion to Christianity, but Malvolio promises revenge with his last line.

Shakespeare provides the opportunity for revenge inside the play.

The comedy at the end requires the sorting out of gender roles, a reestablishment of convention, as Orsino recognizes:

> Cesario, come;
> For so you shall be, while you are man;
> But when in other habits you are seen,
> Orsino's mistress, and his fancy's queen.

In a recent Stratford, Ontario, version of the play, Lucy Peacock, as Viola, came out for her curtain call in her wedding gown. It was a stunning fulfillment of Orsino's wish and a continuation of the drama into a postdramatic convention. It is reported that in another production, "Viola opened a trunk during Feste's song [at the end], exited briefly, then came on dressed in her 'woman's weeds' and danced with the Duke" (O'Brien 1995, 121). But the play ends with Feste's unoptimistic song in which change, but not necessarily evolution or individuation, occurs. Malvolio has the key to the trunk in which Viola's "maid's garments" (5.1.267) lie—or at least Malvolio has the key to the captain who has the trunk and is "in durance at Malvolio's suit." Malvolio has been denied the opportunity to leave Olivia's garments strewn near that daybed of which he daydreamed. But he controls the clothes on which the imperative of Viola's gender transformation depends. The comic ending, if it is to occur, must go through Malvolio, must enlist this obdurate ill-wisher, this killer of revelry, and must meet a point of absolute resistance to what is supposed to happen. It is to speculate into areas where no evidence exists to say that he will deny a command to free the captain, but Shakespeare builds in a moment that reinforces Feste's song, not the ending dictated by the aristocrats of this coast washed first by storm and then by laughter. Rebuffed, rejected, baffled, and "notoriously abused," Malvolio can revenge by delaying the festive ending, reminding us that although Orsino can command that "golden time convent" (5.1.369), "The rain it raineth every day."

Shakespeare comes up against an issue that is not soluble in the comic solution: Feste reaches the end of clowning, as he will in a deeper sense in *King Lear*. Malvolio becomes a character in a problem play. His revenge is generic. Further negotiation, undramatized and beyond the ending of the play, blocks the comic closure. It would seem that Shakespeare at the end of this last festive comedy had already built in to it a countervoice that would not be overruled, as Egeus is overruled in *Dream*, or coerced into conformity, as Shylock is in *Merchant*, or self-exiled, as Jaques is in *As You Like It*. The problem play would emerge from this complex vision, and the tragedy where Armin as fool can sing, "He that hath and a little tiny wit, must make content with his fortune fit." In the storm, in the bleak moors outside the walls of Lear's comfortable castles, the rain rains in the night as well.

By Malvolio's revenge, I do not mean Cromwell and the Puritans, an old idea that does crop up, as in the English Shakespeare Company production of 1991, in which at the end Malvolio directed the dismantling of the set as metaphor for the closing of the theaters in 1642. Malvolio is not a Puritan and not quite the hypocrite we tend to make of him. Bill Alexander, who directed the play for the Royal Shakespeare Company in 1987, says that Malvolio "will do *anything* he thinks will advance him. . . . His pose is the pose of a puritan because that's what, for him, gives him his own sense of authority, dignity, and purpose within the household" (Billington 1990, 76).

One might add that the pose gives him an identity in a household character-ized on the one hand by the stasis of mourning and on the other by constant revelry. Obviously Malvolio is seeking an identity—"to be Count Malvo-lio"; he is eager to advance to the status that others were born to. Shake-speare is exploring that space that still exists between birth and merit. He gives the story a spin. Usually we cheer for the Horatio Alger hero, the hero-ine of the Harlequin romance, and Cinderella, even if in the older versions of the story her father was a king who had lost his kingdom and had not told anybody. Malvolio, though, is hard to cheer for.

What has been celebrated in *Twelfth Night*? The comic spirit? A way of wasting time? Illyria hardly imitates the dynamic of Arden. Orsino's funded infatuation? Olivia's phony mourning? Toby's drinking? Sir Andrew? Feste points at the waste, and even Olivia acknowledges it. Like *The Great Gatsby*'s Daisy and Tom Buchanan, a few escape at the end into their aristocratic lifestyles. Any epiphany awaits us beyond the play, which is done. "When that I was and a little tiny boy": the reference to Corinthians is obvious, but wherein lies our maturing? Is that glass any clearer through which we see now? If so, we see what the people up there on stage have missed.

Peter Reynolds contrasts the successful lovers of *Twelfth Night* and *As You Like It*:

Unlike the lovers of *As You Like It*, who enter the Forest of Arden as adolescents and *use* the time to play out love-games in which they rehearse and test the behaviour required in adult married life, and consequently by the end of the play are recognized as mature, Orsino and Olivia seem locked into adolescent illusions. (1990, 98)

Malvolio has been locked into those illusions as well and has been ruthlessly jarred from them. He has lived "in such a dream," as Toby says, "that when the image of it leaves him he must run mad." Both Olivia and Orsino have been rejected, but they are rewarded at the end, so their rejections merely fade away as part of their adolescent state, which invariably incorporates mourning and being in love, as Peter Blos (1952) says in his study of ado-lescence. Each has found his or her "fancy's queen" or king, but have they learned anything? It may be that the Malvolio experience lies ahead for them, even as they now, like Malvolio earlier, believe they are stepping into their daydreams. "The uninterrupted continuance of the game . . . will al-ways be exposed to the resentment and resistance of those acquainted with anxiety," says Graham Holderness (1990, 107). The happy ending "has been attained only at the cost of ejecting an unassimilable fragment," he continues (105). Feste's final song reminds us of everything else that has not been assimilated: drunkards, thieves, marriages that are not goals but gaols, the passage of time, our own irrelevance within the "long time" of the world's history, everything out there to which we, temporarily assimilated into the golden time of the play, return, unassimilable fragments, more like

Malvolio, regardless of our love of plays, than any of the happy young people who marry at the end of the play. Malvolio holds the key to our own ability to doff our disguises, the pleasant reveries of Illyria—illusion and lyricism—disguises that are a wickedness and a danger in the world to which we return, stripped now, as Olivia and Orsino are not, of such a dream and the image of it.

Suppose Malvolio saw what was really being said—that he must laugh at his frailty and accept himself as fallen man in a fallen world? Would he then see into the fellowship of the mystery? Perhaps. But is there any fellowship for him there in *Twelfth Night*? Olivia calls Malvolio "fellow," but not as Malvolio translates the word. There is no comic world in this play into which a reformed and illuminated Malvolio can move.

At the end, Guiness's Malvolio resigns, dropping his chain in the dust as he had previously discarded Olivia's ring. Be it his who finds it. He limps off with what dignity he can muster, still obstructed by that cross-gartering. Mc-Cowen begins to calculate. He has been had. How can he get back at them? Briers retrieves the letter—as evidence for his hearing? He departs, broken and brokenly. Sinden says that Malvolio's vow of vengeance is "a totally empty threat. . . . There is but one thing for Malvolio—suicide" (1985, 66).

Of the recent film version, directed by Trevor Nunn, Anthony Lane says, "Nunn is rightly intrigued by the vengeful vows with which Malvolio gashes the happy ending" (1996, 74). Nigel Hawthorne is a most cruelly treated Malvolio. He is imprisoned in what looks like a recently vacated chicken coop. When he comes in at the end, bedraggled and besmeared and waving Maria's letter, having clawed his way out of his imprisonment like Lady Madeline Usher, he stops the party cold. The others, of course, have forgotten about him in the comic analogue to "Great thing of us forgot!" in *King Lear*. We, too, have forgotten about him. Feste has not, however, and in a moment more stinging than any Malvolio has known so far, Feste comes down the staircase wearing Malvolio's toupee. This symbol of Malvolio's desire to join and rule over the play's youth culture completes his humiliation. That the culture is hardly worth joining—if Orsino is the criterion—merely means that Nunn has undercut a conventional comic ending on both sides of the equation. Malvolio may have deserved what he got, but those who gave it to him and forgot about him are not particularly deserving either. Like a James or Fitzgerald novel, the film shows one thing that the play *can* show—that the upper class, that which is desired and aspired to by every one else, is empty among its golden objects and hollow within the seeming solidity of its many mansions.

Perhaps the best scene in the film is that in which Malvolio is tricked into believing that Olivia is in love with him. The fountain in front of the garden and the walls of its inner yard are made up of shells from the sea. Elements of a wild and unseen kingdom have been domesticated into designs without being understood as themselves. The statue of an armless Venus in the middle of a pagan garden becomes a substitute for Olivia. It is an emblem of Malvolio's desires, a fusion of ideal and sensual, like Keats's urn, and it cannot speak back. It cannot fend off. It can only absorb and, in its voluptuousness, encourage fantasy, a perfect object for his projections upon it, a stand-in for the still-unravished Olivia.

This is a very "stagey" scene, and it is here. It reminded me of the scene in which Roger Allam's Benedict was tricked into believing that Susan Fleetwood's Beatrice loves him in the Royal Shakespeare Company *Much Ado About Nothing* of several seasons ago. Nunn's camera, however, convinces us of something that can strain credulity on stage—that is that Toby, Andrew, and Fabian can keep out of sight around the hedges as Malvolio gives himself a spurious "reality" check.

An effective allocation of what on stage must be separate scenes is Nunn's intercutting between Malvolio's imprisonment in the fowl coop, as he attempts to prove to Feste and Sir Tophas that he is not mad, and Sebastian's effort to give himself a reality check and to prove that Olivia is not mad. In the script, Sebastian steps into the sunlight immediately after the dark room scene of Malvolio's incarceration. Sebastian steps into Malvolio's fantasy. Nunn clearly understands the relationship between Sebastian and Malvolio. Malvolio knows that Olivia is a potentially pagan goddess. For all of her mourning, she would like to escape the role, but she has committed to it. Her narcissism cannot release, but Olivia's (Helena Bonham Carter) snapping black eyes are on the prowl. She is happy to relinquish her role as a young Victoria and accept Feste back from his wanderings. From this declension, the attractive, articulate, and nonthreatening Cesario is an easy step. Sebastian is the beneficiary of this rhythm. Carter splendidly captures the two extremes of adolescent game-playing: mourning and being in love. Nunn cuts back and forth between the madhouse—the slimy place where Malvolio is trapped—and Sebastian's questioning of his own and Olivia's sanity. Sebastian applies the reality checks that Malvolio had used earlier, but the verification is not spurious and Olivia arrives immediately afterward with the parson.

The two scenes are neatly brought together as Feste, having wandered away from Malvolio in the turkey pen, says "Adieu, Goodman Devil" as he sees the newlyweds, Olivia and Sebastian, hug each other outside the chapel and looks in on the wedding of Toby and Maria. Feste says goodbye to Malvolio, his enemy, and goodbye to the repressed sexuality that has troubled the neighborhood.

Malvolio would have seized the day. Youth is a stuff—a fabric, a material—that will not endure. Are we being told that only those freed of pretension and hypocrisy can seize the day? If so, who would that be in *Twelfth Night*? The fun and games are over on stage, and for us there is no extra time borrowed from the inexorable calendar, or if there has been, we have just borrowed it. Feste's song points back at Illyria, recapitulating its excesses, but also defining for us the inevitable movement of time and our implication in a process that is not necessarily progress. The sun is setting by this time—and that helps make the point. The globe has revolved while we have gazed at Illryia, and even the long English afternoon must end as the zodiac begins to wheel into view against the spires of the city across the river. Our play is done. Our play is just begun. We leave the lovers there in golden time. We exit to confront Malvolio.

REFERENCES

Alexander, Bill. 1990. "Directing the 'Dark Room' Scene." In *Twelfth Night*, edited by Linda Cookson and Bryan Loughrey. London: Longman. 83–89.

Bible. 1560. Geneva: Rovland Hall.

Billington, Michael. 1990. *Approaches to Twelfth Night*. London: Nick Hern.

Blos, Peter. 1952. *On Adolescence*. New York: Free Press.

Folger's Library. 1995. *Shakespeare Set Free III: Teaching* Twelfth Night *and* Othello. New York: Washington Square Press.

Hassel, R. Chris. 1969. *Renaissance Drama and the English Church Year*. Lincoln: University of Nebraska Press.

———. 1980. *Faith and Folly in Shakespeare's Romances*. Athens: University of Georgia Press.

Holderness, Graham. 1990. "Happy Endgames." In *Twelfth Night*, edited by Linda Cookson and Bryan Loughrey. London: Longman. 100–107.

Lane, Anthony. 1996. "Tights, Camera, Action!" *New Yorker* 25 November, 65–77.

Lewalski, Barbara. 1965. "Thematic Patterns in *Twelfth Night*." *Shakespeare Studies* 1, 168–81.

O'Brien, Peggy, ed. 1993. *Shakespeare Set Free: Teaching* Romeo and Juliet, Macbeth, *and* A Midsummer Night's Dream. New York: Washington Square Press.

Reynolds, Peter. 1990. "Illusion in Illyria." In *Twelfth Night*, edited by Linda Cookson and Bryan Loughrey. London: Longman. 91–99.

Sinden, Donald. 1985. "Playing Malvolio." In *Players of Shakespeare*, edited by Philip Brockbank. Cambridge: Cambridge University Press.

8

Editing for Film:
The 1995 *Othello*

Othello. Castle Rock Entertainment, 1995. Directed and adapted by Oliver Parker. Director of photography, David Johnson. Music, Charles Mole. Designer, Tim Harvey. With Kenneth Branagh (Iago), Laurence Fishburne (Othello), Irene Jacob (Desdemona), Michael Maloney (Roderigo), Nathaniel Parker (Cassio), Anna Patrick (Emilia), Michael Sheen (Lodovico), Andre Oumansky (Gratiano), Nicholas Farrell (Montano), Pierre Vaneck (Brabantio), Indro Ove (Bianca), Gabriele Ferzetti (Duke). Running time: 125 minutes.

Implicit in my discussion of Shakespearean films is my assumption that the Shakespeare film is itself a genre. What makes it so is its emerging from a written script, an originating and at times inhibiting set of words often in conflict with themselves in their original form. That conflict occurs when a particular play has several versions—Quarto and Folio, for example—that actually create different plays, as in the cases of *Hamlet* and *King Lear*. Different scripts have grown up around even scripts that have only one original source. *Macbeth*'s "Banke and Schoole of Time" in the 1623 Folio is almost invariably translated into "bank and shoal," as if Macbeth is standing on a promontory surrounded by a vast and murky ocean of eternity. The genre of Shakespearean films depends on plot—the action imitated—and on language. Films at the greatest remove from the Shakespeare, like those of Kurosawa, pursue an archetype inherent in the script: ambition or despotism and their consequences, for example. Films in foreign languages (Kozintsev and Lyth, for example) rely on subtitles, often annoyingly when the imagery of the film is making very clear what a well-known script is doing at any given moment. Silent films rely on subtitles, which can interfere with the action.

The genre incorporates a world that is not ours—usually an aristocratic zone that includes castles and combat with sword or horse. In the film, those horses can become real, as opposed to elements mentioned by characters reporting on battles being fought just offstage. In dealing with Loncraine's *Richard III*, Peter Holland talks of the film's "avoiding the fake medievalism of conventional representation" (1996, 19). But *Richard III* is perhaps the most "medieval" of Shakespeare's plays (as I have argued, 1986, 1–8), so that the idea, to my mind, is not to modernize it, "eliminating archaisms in order to prevent a surface obstacle being placed between viewer and film" (Holland 1996, 19), but to eliminate "fakeness" and language that gets in the way of film as film. The genre, like that of futuristic films, asks us to anticipate a world we do not necessarily recognize until we get to know it, as opposed to a world close to our own in its assumptions, structures, and language. The most radical translations become almost "non-Shakespeare" films (*Joe Macbeth, Men of Respect*, and *China Girl*, for example), more removed from their originating source than even ballet, which often mimes the action of, for example, *A Midsummer Night's Dream, Romeo and Juliet*, or *The Tempest,* more precisely than filmic offshoots reflect and reinforce whatever the original may be. "I like 'dis place. The air smells good here," as in *Joe Macbeth*, comes closer to parody than to a modern equivalent of Duncan's lines as he approaches Dunsinane.

The Shakespeare film does not ask us to suspend our disbelief. It educates us to believe in the mise-en-scène the camera creates for us and in the conventions of the genre. Those conventions include a speaker's addressing us directly, something we would not anticipate in most films, which, like television, assume a fourth wall between characters and audience. I have been told that such direct address insists that I suspend my disbelief. My response is, no, I merely accept that as a convention within this unique genre, that is, a film that emerges from a play text, no matter how dimly that *praxis*—the action the characters perform (Goldman 1985, 3–16)—may manifest itself in a film. Anthony Davies attributes the direct address aspect of the genre to Olivier's *Richard III*: "Olivier's use of the direct address to the camera, which defies the naturally assumed aesthetic laws of the medium, is another of those brilliant strokes whereby he brings a distinctly theatrical action to film and then gives it an impact which only cinema can [achieve]" (1988, 69). In other words, since 1955 we have had to accustom ourselves to this convention in the Shakespeare film genre.

In a film as realistic as the recent *Richard III*, Loncraine even dug up a De Havilland 89 Dragon Rapide for the Duchess of York's escape. This was a lovely twin-engine biplane that came into service with British European Airways in 1934. It provides an "authenticity" intended to make us believe that the events depicted occur in a literal world to be taken literally. That is to play against genre and, in that film at least, does not work.

A further definition of Shakespeare film as genre argues that such a film, like other genre films, must "concentrate not on the reality of a society or the reality of the past, but on the individual's perception of those super-human orders and what they mean" (Braudy 1976, 122). It follows that overspecificity of mise-en-scène, as opposed to suggestiveness—Olivier's dream castle for *Hamlet*, Branagh's sun-soaked hillsides for *Much Ado*—is likely to get in the way of the perceiving and perceptive camera. The film, Braudy argues, depicts a character's "psychic relationship to a society, a community, a world of others" (1976, 123).

Bert O. States agrees. The Shakespeare film as genre places "the character against the rhetorical sky of the play's world" (1992, 85). What we see is a "scenic pointer to ambiguous regions in human character that cannot be explained in terms of motive" (85). Braudy suggests two versions of the genre: the open and the closed. The latter is "a burrowing inward, an exploration of inner space, an effort to get as far as possible into the invisible heart of things, where all connections are clear" (1976, 66). The character in the open film learns that the "possibilities of the self [are] a freedom rather than a prison" (225), "and the private self is, paradoxically, discovered within the teeming activity of the world," as Kathy Howlett says (1997, 16). Howlett argues that the Olivier *Hamlet* is an example of the closed film, and the Zeffirelli version an example of the open. These categories and descriptions would seem to refer to the most frequently made Shakespeare films, the tragedies, but the open film would seem to fit comedy, where, as Braudy says, the characters experience an "interplay between artifice and the reality that refuses control" (1976, 66), as, for example, in the defaming and rebirth of Hero in *Much Ado*.

Certain scripts are more susceptible to open or closed forms, of course. It is hard to believe that Othello, for example, can be the subject of an open film, that is, until his anaganorasis (recognition of error) at the very end of the script. Macbeth, however, who knows from the beginning that what he is doing is wrong, can become much more the focus of an open film, as he tends to be in the Polanski version. "The impulse towards freedom of self-definition is the central desire in the open film," says Howlett, "although the protagonist may have to combat the structures that attempt to enclose him" (1997, 16). Macbeth must finally be enclosed by those structures, which assume the garb of the cosmic facts themselves. It may be that Kate, in *Shrew*, surrenders to the structures that attempt to enclose her in order to achieve a harmony, reconciliation, even a pleasure otherwise denied her. The effort toward "freedom of self-definition" invariably meets resistance, but in different ways in comedy and tragedy. The conflict can be dealt with in different ways in closed and open films, the one winding inward until the frame becomes the imagery of psychic depth, the other circling outward and incorporating the concentricity of the expanding image or, as in *Macbeth*, the widening vista of the forces opposing the expansive will.

Other aspects of the Shakespeare film as genre might include assumptions about the spoken language. It would be more elegant, stranger to the modern ear, better spoken, and perhaps more poetic than most film dialogue, assuming that the film has dialogue spoken in English. As Dennis Kennedy has pointed out, foreign directors have an easier time changing Shakespeare's language to a contemporary rendition because they are not obliged to repeat what the script provides (1996, 133–48). For a Hamlet to say, "Ay—that's the point!" instead of "that is the question" would be for an audience to be disturbed, although the former reading has the authority of the First Quarto behind it. A stage convention like doubling (fairies and artisans in *A Midsummer Night's Dream*) might work on film, as it did in *The Wizard of Oz*, another film based on dream and fantasy. The space itself might be stylized, with the same sets, altered in interior content, doubling as brothel and convent, tavern and room of state, while avoiding fake medievalism.

Our perception of Shakespeare on film has changed and is changing. In 1936 it was necessary for MGM to assert that all the words of their *Romeo and Juliet* were Shakespeare's. Olivier was criticized for modernizing the language of *Hamlet* ("lowered lids" for "vailed," for an example among many) and for incorporating other than Shakespearean language into his *Richard III*. We now accept the necessity of editing the language that does everything on a stage that enjoyed few special effects but that a camera can make redundant.

It may be that if more comedies are filmed, we will come to accept certain conventions that are difficult, perhaps impossible, in realistic media like film and television. Two that are difficult to translate from the stage are the use of identical twins, as in *The Comedy of Errors* and *Twelfth Night*, and the use of a woman disguised as a man, as in *The Two Gentlemen of Verona, As You Like It*, and *Twelfth Night*. We suspend our disbelief for the stage productions of these scripts. Can film permit us to believe what the other characters accept—the one twin for the other or the girl for a boy? These are questions that remain to be explored within the area Goldman calls *theoria*, that is, the action of the spectator in possessing the dramatic experience (1985, 3–16).

Any work of literature translated to film moves from word to image. We do not have to be told about a house as in Dickens, Henry James, Daphne DuMaurier, or Shirley Jackson. The camera can show it to us, with dark clouds and ominous music in the background. In *Macbeth*, Banquo and King Duncan talk about how "pleasant" the place is where Duncan will be murdered. A film does not need language to show us the castle. In the Polanski film of *Macbeth*, we see a pig being captured to be part of the banquet for the visiting king. We will see that pig with an apple in his mouth a little later. And a little later than that, the king will be slaughtered. Words must be cut from the Shakespeare script and replaced by the imagery of film. I also argue, though, that the editing of the Parker *Othello* is a major problem of the film, particularly for those who do not know the play.

Quickly and wordlessly, the film of *Othello* establishes the imagery of subterfuge, secrecy, and voyeurism. The heavy chords of cellos ride under the darkness of a Venetian canal. A gondola plies toward us. We get a fleeting glimpse of someone inside it—a woman. Next to her, an apparently black man puts a white mask over his face. They are observed by people in another gondola. The woman runs along a damp alleyway, the fish market of Venice. Desdemona is slipping out to marry Othello. But if that was Othello with her, why does she run alone though the alleyways? Perhaps it was an allegorical "Tragedy" in the boat with her? Her pursuers, Iago and Roderigo, observe the ceremony through a window.

We see Brabantio awakening, sweaty from a bad dream of which Roderigo and Iago will immediately remind him. Iago hides behind the prow of a gondola, forcing Roderigo to negotiate face to face with Brabantio. Roderigo is appalled by Iago's obscene allusions to Othello and Desdemona. The Doge's palace becomes the film's first illuminated space. Director Parker does not try for an "Old Masters" effect, as Zeffirelli did in *Romeo and Juliet*. Instead, we get a contrast between Othello and Iago. The Moor stands over the huge map of the Mediterranean, a dark god with a thick black scar on his bald scalp and the brand of slavery on his left palm. If he dominates this grand geography, it is by dint of a statue-like magnificence.

Fishburne gets most of Othello's speeches to the senate. About twenty lines of his "Most potent, grave, and reverend signoirs" are edited out, including the reference to "a friend that loved her" and the line about heaven making "her such a man," a line Welles touched with a dangerous trace of smugness. Fishburne cools these speeches, making them sound unrehearsed. He looks at Brabantio as he says "drugs," "charms," and "conjurations." This is Brabantio's language, Othello implies, a language foreign to him. Some of the big words and strange images—"Anthropophagi and men whose heads / Do grow beneath their shoulders," for example—are spoken over a flashback to the scenes of Othello's wooing, so that the imagery takes over. In the flashback, we see Othello wipe Desdemona's tears with the handkerchief that will appear and disappear and reappear so fatally later on. The flashback technique will be absorbed into Othello's psyche, as he imagines the scenes at which Iago hints. Crowl says that "Parker's camera deserts the actor" (1996, 41), but any long speech can be difficult on film, and even Welles and Olivier do not escape the difficulties by keeping the words in the senate chamber. Olivier's "My life upon her faith" is the grand gesture of the narcissist with a possession that he has absorbed into his self-image. Fishburne says what he means. It may make his downfall a bit less motivated in an Aristotelian sense, but it makes it more powerful in a human sense.

At the end of the scene, Iago toys with chess people. His is the tactical skill, the knowledge of what move to make in response to the board immediately presented to him, and his is the ability to reduce great things to their miniatures.

The movement to Cyprus is rapid and accomplished without a storm. Oars pull in to an uncontested beach along a placid bay. The Venetians land to the delight of the Cypriots in scenes reminiscent of the newsreel shots from Sicily in 1943. Othello rides up the hill and into the square on a magnificent black charger. His superb and hubristic speech on landing at Cyprus ("I fear, / My soul hath her content so absolute / That not another comfort like to this / succeeds in unknown fate") is almost completely erased in favor of a long kiss delivered to Desdemona as the crowd looks on. The crowd is uneasy; the war is not officially over after all. If they "resent and envy his triumphs," as Janet Maslin suggests (1995, C-11), the envy is muted. Racism, if there, is certainly subtly conveyed. In the Olivier film, Frank Finlay's Iago keeps glancing at Othello's very black hand clasping Maggie Smith's very white one. We get the point. Here, Othello simply announces that the Turks are drowned. Perhaps their boats were leaky. Perhaps they all followed each other in formation onto the rocks. We get no sense of Cyprus having had a close brush with a brutal occupation. And if that external agent is removed, we get no sense of the Turk rising from the stormy sea ("the Pontic") within Othello to beat a Venetian and traduce the state. Nor, if his fatal absoluteness as he sees Desdemona before him is cut, do we get any sense that what happens is a tragedy.

When the film was shown at a school in Louisiana in February 1996, a white woman covered her eyes as Othello and Desdemona kissed. A young African American man told me, "That's all he has to do. He doesn't have to *say* anything." Although I agree that the script contains an explosive racial subtext, I believe that tragedy is motivated by Othello's hubris. We cannot overlook the racial-racist element of the play in performance, however, particularly when Othello is played by a black actor, as is almost invariably the case in today's productions.

Our belief in what happens in the Parker film—and film does not ask us to suspend our disbelief—rests on Iago's four slow syllables, "I hate the Moor." We get a hint of sexual jealousy in Iago's reference to Othello's having done Iago's office betwixt Iago's sheets, but we are meant, I think, to take this hatred as motiveless malignity. That is particularly so since Branagh follows Henry Irving's advice and plays Iago as extremely affable, a chap you would be likely to invite to dinner after a brief conversation, a fine fellow. That makes him extremely plausible within the fiction. What makes him believable to us is that he addresses us directly in close-up. It takes a very confident actor to bring this metafilmic technique off. At one point, after Roderigo learns, to his ecstasy, that Cassio has been cashiered, Iago turns to us. Roderigo returns to clap Iago on the back. Iago gives us an exasperated look. In other words, the reason we believe in Iago is that he believes in us. Iago's only problem is Roderigo, who keeps leaping at him unexpectedly, like Coyote in a Roadrunner cartoon. One of the best scenes in the film is Roderigo's confrontation with Iago (4.2). Here Maloney holds a dagger close to Iago's left eye, as Iago translates the threat into, "Why, now I see there's mettle in thee." We sense that Iago is beginning to get in over his head, and it is Roderigo who makes the point.

For those who know the play, the editing will seem a bit strange—not just the scaling of the language down to a subordination to image but the shifting of bits and pieces of the inherited script. The editing, however, has one major payoff. The first part of act 3, scene 3, the long and central scene of the play, begins as a workout in the tiltyard; it moves inside as Othello and Iago towel down and then into the armory. Othello has heard about unfaithful wives, it seems, and jealousy. He does not think it can happen to him but is calmly prepared for it if it does occur. This early phase of Iago's manipulation works well as he quickly translates Othello's mode from conceptual to experiential. We see Othello through a sword rack, in a kind of prison as he begins to hallucinate images of Desdemona and Cassio. A close-in shot of Othello's ear and Iago's whispering mouth captures the sensuous power of Iago's insinuations. Othello wears a pearl in his left ear, suggesting the "pearl" he will throw "away." Roderigo's painful glimpse through the church window at the outset becomes Othello's "inner life." It is as if that psychic nightmare is implanted there already. Any innocent image of the past—a smile, a glance—is transformed to a primal image, a primal scene, that becomes increasingly controlling within Othello once Iago deploys the handkerchief. That object shifts the scene back into the prior generation and places Othello in an oedipal conflict relative to Desdemona (see Coursen 1993). Othello will have these glimpses—Desdemona smiles at him to say that these stolen moments are hers—will flash back to his "My life upon her faith" and to Brabantio's "She has deceived me," as Iago reshapes the past for Othello and makes it strange for him. He becomes an alien not just to Venice but to himself and what he knew.

Iago hardly has to mention Cassio before Othello takes the bait. While Iago is given some of the Venetian material ("In Venice they do let God see the pranks / They dare not show their husbands," for example), he does not need it. Cassio (Nathaniel Parker) is a conventionally good-looking man, and even Roderigo (Michael Maloney) is darkly handsome and not the abject reject that some companies make of him. Nor does the film make anything of an Othello perhaps slightly older than his comrades. This Othello is not "declin'd / Into the vale of years," nor does he say he is.

What would have helped Iago and our belief would have been his ability to interrupt Othello just as the latter is consummating his marriage. The contrast between revelry, as Desdemona dances and Othello picks her up and swings her around in a dizzying turn, and the strapping on of swords in the barracks is nicely drawn by cross-cutting, dance against drill, marriage against martial law. If the sounds of the brawl had reached Othello's ear just as the last whispers of clothing had melted to the floor of the bridal suite, we would have needed no explanation for Othello's subsequent rage. Iago's "Friends all but now, even now, / In quarter and in terms like bride and groom / Divesting them for bed," which was cut here, would have been at once a blandly innocent simile for Iago and a devastating thrust at Othello. As it is, when the script might have been well served, Oliver Parker decides for "one of the most erotically charged productions ever committed to film," as Michael Medford's blurb on the film's advertisement has it. The isolated erotic kinesis, however, is achieved at the expense of the larger motions of character and action.

We had seen Othello, in a flashback to his telling her of his adventures, wipe Desdemona's tears with that handkerchief. Emilia gives it to Iago in a wonderful scene in which she dangles it in front of him and pulls his head up and around with it. He is a fish following a lure, and Emilia enjoys her moment of control. Iago tosses the handkerchief in the air. The scene shifts to a beach, with Othello standing on a promontory staring across the waters and Iago narrating: "The Moor already changes with my poison." In the scene after the drunken brawl, Othello had slapped Cassio, a prelude to his later striking of Desdemona. In the seaside scene, he almost drowns Iago in his rage in a foreshadowing of his strangling of Desdemona.

After Othello's "If it be that," the still-aloft handkerchief flutters into Cassio's chamber. He leaves it with a sleeping Bianca, and we hear Desdemona wondering, "Where should I lose that handkerchief, Emilia?" Then Othello terrifies Desdemona with its origins as he tumbles into that pagan past from which he thought he had escaped, even if by a "hair breadth." That moment occurs after act 3, scene 3 in the script. The scene shifts to Cyprus's dungeon for what is act 4, scene 1 in the script. Here, as Iago works Othello into a fit, the Moor collapses into a mime of incarceration, holding the chains of the dungeon walls as if held by them. Iago puts Othello in a cell to eavesdrop on Cassio. The transitions here are not as logical as those from tiltyard to armory. What is Cassio doing down here? How does Bianca get here? It is as if this dungeon were the Rialto. Again, the scene shifts to a parapet, and the end of act 3, scene 3 occurs. Othello consummates the relationship with Iago in an embrace. Iago's "I am your own forever" seems to be the culmination of his own goals—not a homoerotic triumph but the gaining of an absolute control for which he had been striving from the first, the marriage of a concept and its realization. The moment seems painful to Iago, particularly after his amused and cynical embraces of Roderigo and Cassio, when Iago looked over their shoulders at us. After he embraces Othello, the rest seems almost irrelevant to him. He has captured a man greater than Iago will ever be and the rest will be anticlimax. Ian McKellen, in Trevor Nunn's splendid Thames TV version, plays the moment as overwhelmingly emotional—his feelings for "wrong'd Othello" just too much for his sensitive nature. He can barely find language to express his anguish. Finlay, cocky in the face of Olivier's frantic pagan gestures, ties the handkerchief in a knot after Othello exits and says, mockingly, "I am your own forever." Ron Moody, in the Bard version with William Marshall, is a cerebral, detached Iago, not at all involved in Othello's pain; he is a chilling presence of evil, perhaps already in hell, like Marlowe's Mephisto.

The payoff for Parker's rearrangements is that Othello can peak in increments, fueled by cannily placed hallucinations of Cassio and Desdemona naked in bed. The results of this imposed rhythm are potent, as Othello's buildup of rage begins to flow toward a "reasonable" conclusion: revenge on behalf of all humanity. The rhythm is particularly powerful since Laurence Fishburne splendidly underplays the words, which are the more potent for their coming from Othello's effort at control. "Fishburne, with his masculine beauty and fine, dark voice," says Lloyd Rose, "is a troubled and moving Othello" (1996). Holland, with whom I strongly disagree on this issue, has only "awful memories of Laurence Fishburne's *Othello*" (1996, 19).

The film has a lot of background music, presumably so that its images will translate to television, which cannot abide silence. The music supports meaning, as opposed to mood, only behind Desdemona's "I cannot say 'whore': / It does abhor me now I speak the word." On the wall near Desdemona is a crucifix, one of the film's few references to the play's strong Christian content. The music shades toward a minor key and sounds like "Greensleeves." That song, whose refrain can relate to a woman often on her back and elbows or to the Virgin Mary ("What Child Is This?"), nicely captures the terrible rent in points of view that the play exploits: our knowledge that Desdemona is "chaste" and Othello's belief that she is "that cunning whore of Venice." The film effectively reiterates the dichotomy. As Othello holds Desdemona, he thinks the lines about "a cistern for foul toads / To knot and gender in," a moment when his action and his mind are terribly disjoined. On their wedding night, Desdemona and Othello had mutually blown the lamps out. As he enters her chamber to kill her, he blows out the candles. As he kills Desdemona, her hand brushes his face, even caresses his skull, then drops away, a synecdoche of affection and death in a powerful visualization of the "unnatural" death "that kills for loving." Othello hears Emilia calling from outside the chamber but thinks it is Desdemona. "Not dead? Not yet quite dead?" The instant shows him incorporating a sound into the waking nightmare he is having.

Later Cassio helps Othello up from a kneeling position and slips him a dagger. Cassio remembers what it is to lose one's reputation and gives Othello a way out. Cassio's "thought he had no weapon" becomes a lie here. This overwhelming closure is compromised for me when Iago, still alive, slumps on to the bed and lies there as Cassio opens the curtains. What are we supposed to get from that? At the end of the BBC-TV version, Bob Hoskins is led away to the accompaniment of his own maniacal laughter. Since Anthony Hopkins had been so fair and elegant an Othello, the only place that Hoskins's Iago could go was into extreme psychopathology. At the end of the Nunn production, McKellen stares at the laden bed, contemplating his own lack of any response.

Another element that works in this film is the tendency for characters to complete lines for other characters. "Put money in thy purse," Roderigo says, after Iago has said it several times, showing that Iago is a kind of ventriloquist. "Bianca," she completes, as Cassio says "fair" with a question mark. That adjective, as in the Nunn production, is ironic, perhaps even racist, since a black Bianca belies her name.

Anna Patrick is a strong Emilia, definitely shaped by having been Iago's wife for so long. She would have been helped had she been given the lines about "some squire . . . That turned [Iago's] wit the seamy side without / And made [Iago] suspect [Emilia] with the Moor," lines that argue the falseness of the rumors that Iago has heard. As her surrender of the handkerchief demonstrates, this Emilia is pathetically in love with an Iago who despises her. Patrick does bring the necessary countervoice to the final scenes. She is cynical but much more sympathetic to Desdemona than, for example, Zoe Wanamaker opposite Imogen Stubbs in the Nunn version. While Patrick dominates Desdemona, the latter, Irene Jacob, uses her difficulty with the language to advantage. She "struggles . . . noticeably with the English her role requires," Maslin says (1995), but that struggle gives her a tentativeness and a vulnerability that make her effort to understand what is happening to her absolutely piercing. Rather than trying to mitigate this linguistic issue, director Parker makes it central to Jacob's characterization of Desdemona. Her plea to Iago, invariably moving, is particularly poignant here and completely believable because of her innocence and his credibility.

Fishburne is perhaps "an unusually hot-blooded Othello" (Maslin 1995), but does not, for me, display "an improbable loftiness, sounding very much like the rarefied thesbian beside Mr. Branagh's regular Joe" (1995). That remoteness is in the speeches, particularly in the exotic adjectives with which Othello loads up his nouns. Fishburne plays Othello as if the role of great man does depend on an acquired language and a constant reiteration of his narrative. It won Desdemona, after all, as the film shows us. Fishburne's approach to Othello's language is much cooler than that of the other film Othellos, Welles and Olivier. Iago does offer a contrast to such "bombast . . . horribly stuff'd with epithets of war" and manages to shift the circumstances from which Othello's story emerges.

In the Burge film, Olivier plays at stereotype, savoring the fascinated response of the Venetian senate. This sets his Othello up neatly for Iago's insistence on the female stereotype of Venice. Olivier's film, which never quite cools down from its Old Vic manifestation, is likely to be misunderstood in these politically correct times. He is likely to be accused of embracing the stereotype as a white actor searching for a mode of characterization. As Paul Robeson demonstrated long ago for Margaret Webster, the role does demand a black actor. Fishburne is "dangerous" and "smouldering" (Maslin 1995), qualities that work on film. He is not as powerful as Robeson, who had been an all-American when only eleven men made the Walter Camp team, but Fishburne does suggest the athlete in an effete world. Willard White, in the Nunn production, also depicts the strongest physical presence in the play, a fact that becomes poignant as we view him behind the bars of the bed on which he rapes/strangles Desdemona. At the moment of that production, he became Willie Horton, whether the production intended that allusion or not. William Marshall's sonorous Othello is less dangerous than Fishburne's or White's, indeed very much in control, as when he uses Cassio as an example of Desdemona's "a friend that lov'd her" in his speech to the senate, signaling the role Iago will soon invent for Cassio and Othello's credulous acceptance of that story.

John Kani's African Othello, learning the language as he goes as opposed to having mastered the "Othello music," in the Janet Suzman production, evokes a remarkable anguish as he continues to love Desdemona even as he comes to believe Iago's story. Fishburne's agony as he goes through with his execution of Desdemona is visually magnificent. Many of his lines are gone ("But if I quench thee, thou flaming minister" and "When we shall meet at compt," for example), and thus some of the larger dimensions of life, death, and afterlife are not suggested in this version. The film, however, can be placed with confidence against the other Othellos we have on film and tape.

This is a film designed ultimately for television. It has its establishing shots—a torch-invaded Venetian street, a fortress on a hillside, glimpses of the sea surrounding Cyprus, a scene in the courtyard as Desdemona prepares for bed on the final night—but the film exists primarily in two-shots and close-ups. It does not try for the spectacle of the Welles film: the opening funerals, with the mournful chorus, as if the earth itself were responding, even as Iago is hurried to a cage that will be raised so that crows can pick out his eyes, or the tracking shot along the parapets, as Iago and Othello walk, and Othello sees Desdemona far off in the deep field, already becoming "ancient" history. Sitting halfway back in the Paris Theater in New York City, I found this new version uncomfortably close. It demands to be scaled down, and it will be once it becomes a cassette.

The final images show an open boat pulling out to sea. Sailors tip a board, and Othello and Desdemona plunge full fathom ten down the dark altitudes of the Mediterranean. This shot picks up Iago's earlier dropping of chess people into a pool. He has turned something approaching perfection into manipulatable pieces and, finally, into corpses. That translation would have been much more potent here had Othello been permitted to phrase the perfection as he lands on Cyprus.

Still, the film is powerful, if not profound. It is a splendid addition to the growing body of performance materials of this great and still disturbing play.

REFERENCES

Braudy, Leo. 1976. *The World in a Frame*. Chicago: University of Chicago Press.

Coursen, H. R. 1986. *The Compensatory Psyche*. Washington, D.C.: University Press of America.

———. 1993. *Watching Shakespeare on Television*. Madison, N.J.: Fairleigh Dickinson University Press. (Chapter 6 on the Nunn production; Chapter 8 on the "psychology" of Othello and on other television versions of the play.)

Crowl, Samuel. 1996. *"Othello." Shakespeare Bulletin* 14, no. 1, 41.

Davies, Anthony. 1988. *Filming Shakespeare's Plays*. Cambridge: Cambridge University Press.

Goldman, Michael. 1985. *Acting and Action in Shakespearean Tragedy*. Princeton: Princeton University Press.

Holland, Peter. 1996. "Hand in Hand to Hell." *TLS*, 10 May, 19.

Howlett, Kathy M. 1997. *Shakespeare Framed and Reframed: Spatial Interpretation and Film Adaptation of Shakespeare's Plays*.

Kennedy, Dennis. 1996. "Shakespeare Without His Language." In *Shakespeare, Theory, and Performance*, edited by James Bulman. London: Routledge.

Maslin, Janet. 1995. "Fishburne and Branagh Meet Their Fate in Venice." *New York Times*, 4 December, C-11, C-20.

Rose, Lloyd. 1996. "When All the World's a Screen." *Washington Post*, 28 January, G1, G8.

States, Bert O. 1992. *Hamlet and the Concept of Character*. Baltimore: Johns Hopkins University Press.

9

Playing against the Allusion:
A Midwinter's Tale and *Hamlet*

A Midwinter's Tale. B/W. Writer/Director: Kenneth Branagh. Producer:
David Barron. Associate Producers: Iona Price and Tamar Thomas. As-
sistant Director: Simon Moseley. Photography: Roger Lanser. Design:
Tim Harvey. Costumes: Caroline Harris. Editor: Neil Farrell. Music:
Jimmy Yuill. Principal Players: Robert Briers (Henry), Hetta Charnley
(Molly), Joan Collins (Margaretta), Ann Davies (Mrs. Branch), Nicholas
Farrell (Tom), Mark Hadfield (Vernon), Gerald Horan (Camforth),
Celia Imre (Fadge), Michael Maloney (Joe), Julia Sawalha (Nina), Jen-
nifer Saunders (Nancy), John Sessions (Terry), and James D. White (Tim).
Running time: 1 hour 38 minutes.

Branagh's film does trade on clichés: the director who threatens suicide in
front of his company (and almost has to go through with it, since the coun-
terthesis is a long time in announcing itself), the actor who cannot remember his lines, the cynical older actor who has never played Shakespeare, the
ingenue who says that this ragtag group is her "family," the designer whose
concept is "space" and then "smoke," the agent who would pull her client
out of the opening night for a three-film Hollywood contract, the Ophelia
who actually slaps Hamlet during a performance. Add to the stereotypes
that the actor who cannot recall his lines also drinks to forget the rest of his
life, that the ingenue is virtually blind but will not wear glasses and thus features limb-threatening crashes as entrances, and that the director will spend
precious moments patiently trying to get Francisco to recall a time when he
was terrified, so that "Who's there?" will carry conviction, and you have un-
promising material indeed. Then consider that the production, which finally

does occur, brings a son to his father, a mother to her son, and a father to his daughter, two lovers (Hamlet and Ophelia, of course) together, Hollywood contracts to a very minor actor and a helpless designer, and Christmas bells to a village named Hope—and you cry "Oh no!"

But out of this comes a very funny and moving film that transforms the bleak midwinter into a Christmas card from Branagh to his public, that is, to those who like Shakespeare. The film is caviar to the general, almost all subtext—some of it having to do with the recent history of British theater, some to do with the play itself. The film is superbly edited and timed, insisting in a Capotesque way that we overhear the lines as one brief sequence dissolves to the next. The director is a "sweat prince," but ends up as "sweet prince." He takes his company to the wrong church at the outset but, in an allusion to the increasing emptiness of English churches, finds the right one for his performance. The church also serves as "digs." Two actors sleep in the crypt—"cryptic actors," as one of them says. But what begins as murder in the cathedral ends as a community of the spirit, so that the setting gradually exchanges its ironies for its sacramental qualities.

Gerald Horan makes much of the tiny part of Francisco. He lays down his pike to mime changing a tire—his most frightening moment and his best job of acting until the obliterating smoke of the "design" forces him to get "Who's there?" right. He also sops up the company's wine supply—"so much," as one of his colleagues says, "that you'll affect the next harvest." He also has a line to cover his forgetting his lines. Some actors say, "Angels are bright still, though the brightest fell." Jon Finch used the instructions he found on the back of his furnace when he was a lad: "Roll back the burner to its full extent." Francisco, who doubles as Horatio, says, "Crouch we here awhile and lurk." He tends to exit in the wrong direction and at one point is told, "Go practice your rotation exercises."

It is unfair to a wonderful ensemble to single out Horan or, for that matter, Nicholas Farrell, whose "Go, Captain" from Fortinbras is delivered in an excruciatingly slow Norwegian accent and whose subtext as that significant figure Reynaldo is that he is "foxy." John Sessions, who plays Gertrude in the inner play, is also very funny, particularly as he elicits objections from Richard Briers, who "doesn't mind the occasional diesel" as Gertrude, but draws the line on drag. Celia Imre—"Fadge" or "Fur" to her good friends—is wonderful in her shy scene with Julia Sawalha ("Please call me 'Fur' ") and even better as she gazes at her "design concept," which is a model of the church the troupe is already in. Her major contribution is to construct cardboard audience members. Shakespeare observes his audience filing in, and a stoic Native American refuses to rise for the final ovation, validating the theory of multiple response. Jennifer Saunders is a Hollywood producer who compares the production to an Andy Hardy backyard extravaganza: "It was like one of those Judy Garland movies . . . Judy and Mickey, keep it up!" Mark Hadfield's Polonius gives the line,

"And let him ply his music" the power and conviction of a Coriolanus dealing with the Roman senators.

Other very funny moments include Gertrude and Claudius suddenly appearing as a curtain is drawn open dressed as bag ladies or Dickensian tarts (I did not pick up the allusion, but that did not matter) and the director wishing to have a word with them about costuming, and the hilarious reversal in which busty Salwalha doubles in a beard as "a Gentleman" and listens to an artificially endowed Gertrude. It also seems that Polonius is about to go on at one point as a nineteenth-century conception of Shylock—Henry Irving's version at that. Earlier, Briers had imitated Irving's Othello for a bewildered Maloney.

Hamlet is the text against which all this subtext is played. The play elicits disabling emotion: Ophelia cannot sing, "And will he not come again," because her Royal Air Force husband has pranged. Gertrude is overwhelmed in his scene with Hamlet because of his estrangement from his own son. That scene, in which Hamlet pinions Gertrude and shouts at him from close range, is a wry glance at Branagh's scene with Scroop in the 1989 *Henry V*. But *Hamlet* turns out to be an enabling context for these actors, one that elicits the romance ending, in which the marble of the church comes alive as it echoes the words of the play, and cardboard rises from the seats—sons and mothers and fathers come backstage to the sanctuary for reunions and reconciliations. It is very much a formula, but because we have come to love these hapless actors, it is also very moving. Why not—it's Christmas! The G. T. Holst setting for Christina Rossetti's poem strums in the background, reminding us that though "Earth stood hard as iron, Water like a stone," the world around the tragedy of *Hamlet* can still observe "that season wherein our Saviour's birth is celebrated."

Joe Morgenstern complains that Branagh's actors "are pitiful children with perfect vacuums in place of brains . . . there's no baseline of sanity or competence against which to compare the group's lunacy" (1996, A8). Perhaps not, but does such a baseline exist in *Hamlet*? In the film, *Hamlet* as script is, ironically, the context against which the company's incompetence is projected. In this instance, art reflects art. "I wanted the making of the film to have the speed and financial makeup of the play in the film," says Branagh. "We shot it in 21 days. Everyone got a flat rate—Joan Collins, the electrician, the truck driver. It became a profit-share thing" (Carr 1996, 61). James Wolcott says, "All that this antic movie asks of us is our fond indulgence (It's a luv-in)" (1996, 85). I did give the film fond indulgence and recommend it for students who have just read *Hamlet*. Richard Briers, for example, may play a cliché as "a bitter has-been" (Wolcott 1996, 85) but he does so with wry and understated brilliance. Furthermore, Briers is the king who was never a prince. The film picks up *Hamlet* in other ways as well. Fortinbras, a minor prince in the play, goes off to become a Hollywood star. The woman playing Ophelia is already working through the loss of a

lover as she takes on the role. The actor playing Gertrude resolves his problem with his son: the issue of the actor's sexuality. The director, of course,
has an identity crisis, which he resolves with emotional (but not financial)
satisfaction. In other words, the film is in many ways a *Hamlet* story with a
happy ending.

REFERENCES

Carr, Jay. 1996. "Branagh's *Midwinter's Tale*." *Boston Globe*, 18 February, 61.
Morgenstern, Joe. 1996. "Review." *Wall Street Journal*, 16 February, A8.
Wolcott, James. 1996. "Review." *New Yorker*, 12 February, 85.

10

Mise-en-scène:
Christine Edzard's *As You Like It*
and Richard Loncraine's
Richard III

As You Like It. Directed by Christine Edzard. Sands Films. With Charles Armatrading (Charles), Celia Bannerman (Celia), Ewen Bremmer (Silvius), Emma Croft (Rosalind), Cyril Cusack (Adam), James Fox (Jaques), Valerie Gogan (Phebe), Roger Hammond (LeBeau, Corin), Don Henderson (both Dukes), Miriam Margolyes (Audrey), Murray Melvin (Martext), Andrew Tiernan (Oliver, Orlando). Running time: one hour and fifty seven minutes.

Richard III. Directed by Richard Loncraine. Based on the stage production directed by Richard Eyre. United Artists. With Ian McKellen (Richard), Annette Bening (Queen Elizabeth), Jim Broadbent (Buckingham), Robert Downey Jr. (Rivers), Nigel Hawthorne (Clarence), Kristin Scott Thomas (Lady Anne), Maggie Smith (Duchess of York), John Wood (King Edward), Adrian Dunbar (Tyrrel). Running time: one hour and forty four minutes.

Edzard's *As You Like It*, produced in Great Britain by Sands Films, and released in October 1992, deserves to be distributed in the United States. It will serve as a useful contrast to the available versions: the Czinner film of 1936, with Olivier and Elizabeth Bergner; the BBC-TV version of 1978, with Helen Mirren; and the Stratford, Canada, version of 1982 on the festival stage, a performance of which was televised.

The film is reviewed by Sam Crowl in the summer 1993 *Shakespeare Bulletin* (41). I recommend that review for its sensitive discussion of aspects not treated here.

My problem with the film is in its placement of Arden on the concrete of a construction site with Thames bridges in the background. True, such places, in London, Los Angeles, and New York, are the homes of the homeless. We grasp the director's metaphor. In Mark Rylance's recent *As You Like It* in New York, Arden was a junkyard.

Television, as we know, demands realism, but film and stage do not. When we go to a play, we agree to suspend our disbelief. Film's special effects, even something as simple as a dissolve between scenes or a wipe in which winter becomes spring, suspend our disbelief for us. "Pastoral," however, is difficult for any medium, partly because it is not a genre but a convention, which ends with Milton (some would argue Tennyson or Lewis Carroll). Vestiges may survive in the austere New England of Robert Frost or the sentimentalized forest outside Nottingham, where Robin Hood makes merry and woos Marian, but pastoral is a mode, not a location. This fact was brought home by the BBC-TV version of *As You Like It*, which was taped near Glamis Castle, Scotland, but which was "far too earthbound, too specific for the elusive joys of the Forest of Arden" (Bulman 1988, 174), where "the relentlessly realistic setting . . . the sunny hills of Scotland . . . threw a curious shadow over the play's magical aspects" (O'Connor 1988, 251), where "seldom have natural settings been used to less effect" (Jorgens 1988, 251). Television may be a realistic medium, but it seldom goes on location. Alan Kimbrough suggests that "the location shooting . . . forces some disquieting contradictions between what the characters say and what we see" (1988, 252).

If that is true when the play is produced in a natural environment, it is certainly more true when Arden becomes a concrete expanse bordered by a fence built of railway ties. A literal location summons an inevitable literalness in the viewer. References to trees and a forest are indeed disquieting, as are, in a modern dress production, allusions to curtle axes and doublet and hose, and a statement that a sword has been dropped when what clanks to the pavement is palpably a .45-caliber pistol. The site offers no sense of magic or of the possibilities of transformation. It is a dead end.

When a play as conventional as this is shifted to a contemporary locale, the language has to be edited or altered, or it makes no sense. It may be that a culture in which song lyrics are merely part of an overall cacophony has lost its grasp on signification. Charles's evocation of Robin Hood and the Golden Age is cut in the Edzard production. But to bring a solitary lost sheep on with Corin is simply to invite unkind laughter. That pastoral is an un-Christian mode (cf. Theocritus) is a factor that Shakespeare exploits in having Duke Senior respond in parallel phrases to Orlando's lines about "better days . . . where bells have knoll'd to church." Those lines are cut in the Edzard script, but Touchstone's "Then thou art damn'd" to Corin is left in. The colloquy is effective here, perhaps the only aspect of Touchstone that works, but it works largely because Roger Hammond's Corin observes

Empson's dictum that "the proper tone [of pastoral] is one of humility" (1960, 13). Touchstone is not drawn clearly enough here to "forestall . . . the cynicism with which an audience might greet a play in which his sort of realism has been ignored" (Barber 1959, 232). That is to make a larger point: that the contrasting levels of love in the script are not effectively delineated in the film.

Any production of *As You Like It* faces the difficulty that Barber isolates when he says that the play "makes fun of [the] assumptions [of Lodge's *Rosalynde*]" (1959, 227). What are those assumptions? In *Dream* we probably have little trouble "assuming" the assumptions of "Pyramus and Thisbe," because we witness an inversion of "the willing suspension of disbelief" in the Mechanical's fear that their play will be taken literally. What we are likely to miss as we laugh at the play within is its insistence on a grim, red-clawed determinism that makes it bootless to ask nature why she framed lions. The assumptions of pastoral romance are difficult to retrieve unless a production somehow educates us to them. The wealth of notes in a typical RSC program cannot substitute for what the play must do. Nor is it possible for pastoral and its undercutting to be realized on a puddled slab of concrete. Even if a modern version of the script cannot reconstruct "Arcadia, a pastoral landscape embodied in an ancient and sophisticated literary tradition" (Bevington 1980, 358), this one gives us no sense of a return from a "green world" (cf. Frye 1957, 181–84) to the world of the court. Crowl says that "surely Northrop Frye and C. L. Barber have taught us that Arden is a metaphor" (1993, 41).

Shakespeare's stage makes its metaphors with a word: Arden, Ilyria, Elsinore. It is infinitely capable of absorbing implied comparisons between unlike things, partly because our own imaginations participate in constructing the bridges. In a different medium, however, we must for an instant consider the speaker mad who mistakes a bare construction site for a forest. Is this Kate on the road to Padua? And in this script we probably want a contrast between court and woods, particularly from a literal medium like film. In *As You Like It*, one of the primary contrasts is between what Frye calls "the *vegetable* world . . . garden, grove, or park" and "the *mineral* world . . . a city" (1963, 20). Suffice it to say that the issue of the pastoral mode helps explain why this script, so popular as a stage play, is seldom translated to film or television.

Edzard's film realizes a splendid moment when Rosalind puts down Jaques, as Crowl notes (1993, 41). Here, Jaques is not just "the refuser of festivity" (Frye 1957, 218) but one whom festivity rejects. Jaques is not given his final summation of the future of each couple, perhaps because Andrew Tiernan doubles Oliver and Orlando, though that should have been no problem for an inventive camera. Again, however, distinctions are blurred by a huddled, hurriedly edited finale. Rosalind does not get her epilogue, very effective in the Czinner film, where the camera cuts between Bergner in doublet and hose and in wedding dress. The strength of the film is in Celia Bannerman's splendid Celia, wonderfully able to adopt to life in a construction shack, and Emma Croft's fetchingly boyish Ganymede, speaking truths about love that she discovers as she utters them. In an interesting comment on disguise and twins, she "arrives in Arden wearing an outfit—jeans, hooded sweatshirt, and black stocking cap—that mirrors Orlando's scruffy attire" (Crowl 1993, 41). She "comes to discover her fuller, richer witty self through the liberation provided by her androgynous escape to Arden" (41). Indeed, here the post–World War II tendency toward unisex clothing really works, as abetted by Croft's winsome performance.

The "film ends up as damp as the dockside wasteland on which most of it takes place," according to Betsy Sherman. Doubling Andrew Tiernam as Orlando and Oliver "means that in their big confrontation in the first scene, the characters cannot share the screen. Cutting from one to the other dissipates the scene's power." The film's "gender-bending kinkiness" involves not only Rosalind's disguise as a boy but that "she tests Orlando's love for her by encouraging him to fall in love with her male alter ego." As Sherman says, however, Emma Croft's "spritely Rosalind [is] an androgynous dreamboat" (1994, 63).

Regardless of the film's heavy-handed translation of pastoral, Croft alone makes this one worthwhile.

Another element that comes through in the production is the cold. It helps to watch the tape in Maine in February, of course, but the wind whistled up the Thames during the filming, and thus one aspect of the metaphoric Arden was fully realized.

Richard Loncraine's *Richard III* offers students a vivid contrast with the more traditional Olivier version. The latter does plenty of editing of the script and borrows lines from the third part of *Henry VI*, but it places the events in Elizabethan times. The Loncraine film is based on Richard Eyre's stage version, which opened at the National Theatre (London) in 1990 and subsequently toured the United States. The play and film depict a 1930s fascist takeover of Britain's crown and develop many analogies between a fifteenth-century king and national leaders between the two world wars. The film offers students an opportunity to look back at European history, not excluding Great Britain, during the 1930s. The following response to the film is based on its effort to place the script in that specific moment of history.

Having seen the Richard Eyre stage production of *Richard III* in London in August 1990, I went to see the film version when it finally arrived in my neighborhood with considerable anticipation. The film, after all, arrived with positive advance notices:

" 'Richard III' offers action-adventure in 'Masterpiece Theater' trappings. Its welcoming title character and sinister host, Mr. McKellen, plays a black-hearted Alastair

Cooke daring us to join him in a party game of murder for power. Who could resist?" (Holden 1995).

"This movie is the fetid, enthralling goods, the *Nixon* that Oliver Stone didn't quite dare to make" (Corliss 1996).

"This smart 'Richard III' looks terrific, moves like the wind and rides the nerve of McKellen daring us not to enjoy its central monster's evil panache" (Carr 1996).

"The film is screen fantasy at its finest, combining elements of Hollywood spectacle with British acting tradition, and big-budget production design of 1930s sets with eternal themes of male power lust" (Meltz 1996).

"This lush yet ravaged backdrop, with its suggestions of Visconti and Bertolucci films set in the same period, established a familiar sense of an anxious, desperately hedonistic wartime society in which the usual rules of society are suspended. It is the perfect clay for Richard's purposeful military hands" (Brantley 1996).

"Loncraine and McKellen are as jazzed as we are by the film's evil energy, and they implicate themselves along with the audience. . . . This production seduces the audience. In that sense, in spite of all the liberties and all the cuts, it's a masterly realization of the play" (Rose 1996).

Shakespeare's stage works suggestively. *We* must imagine. Shakespeare's stage does not offer literal sets, à la Chekhov or O'Neill. The 1990 stage version of *Richard III* suggested a fascist takeover. We filled in the details, making up for the lack of any real links between a Richard and a Hitler, a Mussolini, or a Franco. The film fills in all the details, creating a mise-en-scène, or physical environment, that renders the events it depicts utterly unconvincing. What we get in the film, Samuel Crowl says, "is visual overload . . . a ripe, garish cartoon . . . visual jokes, which, unfortunately, only work to fragment and dissipate the propelling energy of McKellen's performance" (1996, 38).

What I experienced was a parody of Hollywood films, at times mildly amusing, most of the time simply grotesque—a shallow, meretricious shadow of the stage production. Any review is subjective, emerging as it does from the reviewer's experience of an immediate event and his or her experience as it circles inward and outward, perceived and unperceived, from the event. In this instance, the stage production becomes a negative background for the film. Those who did not see the stage production would not be similarly conditioned. Nor, I assume, would those who were not alive in the 1930s respond in quite the same way as those of us who were to the recreation of that era in this film. But that is merely to introduce another aspect of the subjective nature of responding to a film. What we do with our subjectivity, and that includes our recognizing it, is what counts in any critical inquiry.

The film does more than strain credulity. At the beginning, Prince Edward and King Henry, together at Tewkesbury, forget to post any guards. A tank rumbles up and crashes through their headquarters. Richard leaps out and kills them. King Henry does not even have time to ask where his Switzers are.

At the end, the abandoned Bankside Power Station, which had been the Tower for this film, becomes, it seems, Richard's redoubt for the final battle. Shrewsbury resembles the small unit struggles in the factories of Stalingrad during that pivotal battle. The analogy is that history itself can turn on the hinge of a tiny moment within a larger war. If Richard had had a horse to pull his staff car out of the mud . . . But Richard, the Nazi here, has no air force. Until Dunkerque and the Battle of Britain, Hitler's Stukas and Me-109s had dominated the skies. But here, Air Marshall Stanley (who had never won the British Distinguished Flying Cross, one noticed) has the only airplane! If one imitates history, particularly on film, that history must be depicted with fidelity and not be "transparently fake" (Holden 1995), particularly when the rest of the late 1930s details, from that DeHavilland 89 down to the smallest Tiffany pin, have been so meticulously re-created. But then it does not matter by the end of this travesty. We have to see horses, since they are mentioned in this botched-up filmscript, but they are as heavily anachronistic in an otherwise mechanized world as is an army that has Tiger tanks but neither an air force nor some early warning system to show the blips of enemy planes.

Richard delivers the first part of the opening speech into a microphone at the Tewkesbury victory party and then to himself in the palace men's room. He includes a slighter borrowing from *III Henry VI* than had Olivier. He notices us halfway through the speech, accusing us implicitly of being Toms peeping on his peeing. Unlike Kenneth Branagh's engaging Iago in Oliver Parker's *Othello,* McKellen's Richard never does ask "us to join him," as Holden says he does (1995). He sneers at us as he sneers at the feeble characters he manipulates in the film. The result is an alienation from him, as opposed to the fascinated emotional participation in his schemes and our sharing in his response to their success that Branagh's evil schemer invites.

Clarence's big speech is delivered irrelevantly to his guard as the former moves onto a grim circle of concrete surrounded by a foul moat. Clarence is willing to stay outside during a London soaker because it is his exercise period. The speech demands quiet and a reengendered fear. Here it is not only pointless but largely lost to the downpour. Clarence is not drowned in that droll butt of malmsey but has his throat cut in a bathtub, a borrowing from the enforced suicide of the old capo in *The Godfather.*

Robert Downey, Jr. (Rivers), apparently an American seeking a title, is imported into this production to provide a dash of sexuality and to be dispatched suddenly. He reads his few lines as if reciting today's specials. While simultaneously smoking, drinking brandy, and being massaged by his friendly air stewardess, he is startled to see, with his final sunny beams, a knife emerge from his stomach. Trick or treat! This also borrows from *The*

Godfather, where a hood and his moll are tommy-gunned in bed while the christening is going on and Pacino is denouncing Satan with heavy irony.

Richard III's final chase scene up the steps and along the floor of a ruined building is on loan from a thousand old films. How many detectives and courageous cops have pursued their culprits upward into the scaffolding? How many criminals have fired blankly into the dark, run out of ammunition, and tossed their guns away in disgust? How many crooks or crookbacks have tumbled from their perches? Richard falls away into the flames, a Faustian end, as Al Jolson warbles the 1925 song, "Sitting on Top of the World." Yes, it is meant to remind us of James Cagney walking the last mile in *White Heat*, but the sudden intrusion of Jolson is inconsistent with the tunes that have been a leitmotif here. Marlowe's "Come Live with Me, and Be My Love" is sung by a chanteuse at the outset, as a band leader made up to look like Glenn Miller waves his stick. It might have been fun had we heard versions of "It Was a Lover and His Lass" or "O, Mistress Mine" with Bert Ambrose or Ray Noble settings in the background from time to time, but the promising beginning is not pursued.

Richard does put on a record as he delectates over photos of Hastings's execution by hanging. Hitler had watched the films of the slow strangulation of the Stauffenberg plotters in July 1944. Later, Richard eavesdrops on the garroting of Buckingham, who is cut off, it seems, with piano wire, as the Stauffenberg conspirators had been. In the 1990 stage version, however, Hastings's head had been brought to Richard in a bucket. He reached delicately into the bucket, apparently to close Hastings's eyes. It was macabre but funny.

The film erases the play's rhythms. Richard's brilliant step-by-step progress to the throne and the nemesis that begins at the moment he "is seated" are gone here. Even the sequence of frantic reports in act 4, scene 4 is edited out, although we do get Richard's striking of the messenger who brings word of Buckingham's capture and Richard's subsequent "I cry thee mercy." In the inherited script, however, the striking is motivated by Richard's belief that here is more bad news. What we get, as Holden says, "is little more than a collection of famous speeches connected by the Cliff [*sic*] notes" (1995). The film does not establish a rhythm of its own—Richard's "bustle," for example, as opposed to upper-class ennui. It is as if some of the original words are obligatory amid the dreary drift of a 1930s world ignoring the Great Depression around it and colluding in a slide toward war. Holden calls the film "a glib equation between the rise of Fascism and upper-class ennui. But it makes that equation with such a campy exaggeration that it finally seems tongue-in-cheek" (1995). If so, why? It is Richard who shows us how effete or naive his rivals are. All that reinforcement from the film diminishes Richard's brilliant skill in exploiting weaknesses that would probably be survivable if not for his malevolence. And,

of course, the reality of Hitler's prewar Germany needs no fictional embell-
ishment. Many upper middle-class German men were happy to accept hon-
orary colonelcies in the SS and thus join the fashionable uniformed set of the
late 1930s. We see Buckingham do precisely that here.

This production has almost no humor. Richard does turn to us to say, "I
am not made of stone," but otherwise the film's literalization of what even
Richard recognizes as improbable fiction flattens the story into sheer and
unrelenting grimness. We do not want a comic Richard—this is an evil character!—but we do need some variation in tone and not just "visual overload" (Crowl 1996, 38).

Richard does not appear "aloft, betweene two Bishops" (First Folio) but
is secreted in a room with two manicurists. That is a modern analogue to
that old-time religion, one assumes, but it is not as funny as the scene can
be as scripted.

Buckingham does not get his amusing line, "This general applause and
cheerful shout / Argues your wisdom." Buckingham and Richard do not create for the Lord Mayor the farcical pretense that Lovel and Radcliff are enemies approaching (3.5.18–19). And Richard does not say to Buckingham,
after all the talk of bastardy, "Yet touch this sparingly, as't were far off; / Because, my lord, you know my mother lives."

The effort here goes into a simulation of Nazism. Like Hitler, Richard
operates from a railway car. Buckingham, in uniform, looks just a bit like
Herman Goering, Ratcliff like Martin Borman, Catesby like Rudolph Hess,
and Tyrrel like the model of a perfect Aryan. The hall—the University of
London Senate House—in which cheering brown shirts greet Richard is a
colorized replica of the one filmed by Leni Reifenstahl on the night of the
1934 Nuremberg Party Conference.

We get a brief touch of Zeffirelli at the end. Richmond and Elizabeth have
been married. Their wedding night is also the eve of battle. Dawn comes to
their rumpled sheets. Kate Steavenson-Payne, who had been pulled empty-
faced from place to place throughout the film, finally gets a line. I expected
her to say, "Wilt thou be gone? It is not yet near day." Richmond blows her
a kiss and strides cheerily off to war. He rides around in a gun truck turning
the battle, firing his machine gun at anything that moves.

The film does have a few good moments—for example, a cut from King
Edward pulling oxygen into his wasted lungs to one of Richard dragging on
an Abdulla and about to burn Clarence's pardon. We observe Edward's survivors from his deathbed, as if his shade has hung around for an instant before
its journey down through the royal wine cellar. As young York says, "That
you should bear me on your shoulders," he jumps on Richard's back and
throws him to the platform of the railroad station where Richard writhes in
agony. This is a violent homage to Olivier, who had shown his naked hatred
for a terrifying instant when York had taunted him about his lumpy back. We
watch Richard's coronation and then, after a glimpse of Lady Anne's vacant

face, see the same thing in black and white. It is as if Lady Anne were hallucinating until we realize that we are in the royal screening room as the royal party watches a newsreel. Later we learn that Lady Anne is a heroin addict. We know that she is dead when a spider crawls over an unblinking eye. The young princes play at war, one wielding a biplane above a toy locomotive. But the film provides no sense of Richard's "playing," as either actor or no intellectual athlete. McKellen's "Richard," Terrence Rafferty says, "is a dull, sufficient, affectless sort of monster" (1996). He was not much more than that in the stage version, but a more complete script permitted McKellen to suggest the concentric circles of institutionalized evil radiating outward from the still, spidery center that his presence created. The effect was achieved because he stood alone on a vast stage, not surrounded by the busy 1930s mise-en-scène that Loncraine constructs.

As with other anachronistic productions of a script—I think of the Papp-Antoon *Much Ado* of the 1970s—we have two plays competing against each other, with the Shakespeare script a distant runner-up. On stage, McKellen did not need Olivier's "startling, animal vitality" (Rafferty 1996). On film, however, he needed Hitler's mesmerizing presence. Another actor might bring that to Richard III, but I do not think it is inherent in the role. Hitler was hypnotic in public, dull in private conversation. Richard is the reverse. The script and the analogy are probably incompatible, as some critics argued of the stage production (Berkowitz 1991; Nightingale 1990), but it worked on stage because it was suggested in the ways stage can suggest, rather than enforced in the ways film must convince.[1]

Richard Eyre's stage version was the imitation of an action. We watched the virtuoso performance of McKellen and Richard. On stage, McKellen, with one hand, extracted a cigarette from a silver case and lit it, a performance in itself. The closest he comes to this facility on film is to pull a ring from his hand with his teeth, then place it on Anne's finger. On stage, McKellen accosted Lady Anne as he pursued the gurney on which Henry VI lay. His wooing was self-amused and convincing. On stage, McKellen established ironic distance which the many close-ups in the film erase. In the film, the scene occurs in a white-tiled mortuary, as Anne mourns not Henry VI but bonny Prince Edward, plugged through the head. As Rafferty says, the sequence lacks an "appalling magnetism . . . potent enough to win the grieving widow over. As the charmless McKellen and the wan Thomas play it, Anne's capitulation is wholly incomprehensible, not a breath of sexual passion is visible" (1996). Furthermore, McKellen seems to a playing the scene straight in the film. Afterward, says Ben Brantley, "he waltzes though the casualty-cluttered corridors of a hospital to a jazzland beat, like the boy who has just won the girl in a 30's musical" (1996). That is all wrong. The cynical manipulator withdraws after his success into a savoring of his cynicism. On stage, McKellen had a mourning band already in place as he entered the scene in which the others learn that Clarence is dead. That band predicted the fascist armbands to come. Buckingham threw his own armband on to the empty throne as he said, "Made I him king for this?" In the film, Buckingham says the line just before his windpipe is shut. In Richard's stage dream, Lady Anne (Eve Matheson) danced briefly with Richmond (Colin Hurley), and Richard, suddenly desiring what he had cast away, felt a stab of sexual jealousy. In the film, a sweating Richard hears angry voices from the past. The formal, stylized dream is discarded, one assumes, for something more psychologically plausible. But a surreal moment had come earlier when a boarfaced Richard embodied Stanley's dream. That is an isolated effect that might better have tasted the cutting room floor, like the rest of the film. McKellen virtually throws the postdream soliloquy way, sweating and mumbling. The style of this film can make nothing of an Augustinian anagnorisis.

We suspended our disbelief for the stage version and were pulled into a nightmare world of black uniforms, klieg lights, and summary executions. The metaphoric approach, which Dennis Kennedy suggests is a major element of recent Shakespearean productions, (1993) worked. The stage forced us to fill in its suggestions with our imaginations. The grim rooms around the single light bulbs under which prisoners were interrogated became visible to us and multiplied into other countries and other times. We could sense, just out of sight, the thousand outstretched arms of the Reifenstahl film and the clump of the goosestep down the Champs Elysée (or Oxford Street) in 1940. The spider convinced us of the web. By trying to make it real, the film, stuck with its metaphor in a nonsuggestive way, does not permit us to believe any of it.

Peter Holland found the translation from stage to film effective. The film offers "a precise cinematic analogy to the Shakespearean history play" (1996, 19). I take it that, Holland means that Shakespeare did not try to place his history back in time. His characters and their sentiments, their meat, drink, and clothing are stalwartly Tudor. The stage version provided, Holland says, "an alternative history extrapolating from the perception that the English aristocracy's close potential alignment with fascism could make Richard into an English Hitler." On film, "*Richard III* becomes a superb political thriller in an England that is a subtly distorting mirror of reality—or a reality adjacent to our own" (19). The film, however, does not so much distort reality but represent it, and the reality cannot be adjacent to our own unless we ourselves are situated in 1936. The style of the film is so relentlessly realistic that it cannot be called a distorting mirror, even though a mirror is used as Richard tells us how *he* will employ distortion as one of the tactics in his grand strategy. The film is too faithful a mirror of a time and a place to pick up the tinge of surreality Holland imputes to it. I agree with Crowl, who says that when stage directors "mount modern dress productions of Shakespeare . . . they do so by inviting our own imaginations to fill in the details of their period suggests." Loncraine's "locations distract by rivaling, and often swallowing, the performances they contain" (1996, 38).

Holland goes on to argue that the mixture of accents, British and American, in the *Richard III* has a point that Branagh's *Much Ado* misses. *Richard III* "finds reasons within the conventions of filmic naturalism for its choices, so that Queen Elizabeth (Annette Bening) [is an] American arriviste ... with hints of Mrs. Simpson clustering around. . . . The meaningless conjunctions of styles and voices that Branagh has been prepared to accept are here turned into a carefully controlled polyphony" (1996, 19). This is an aspect to which a British ear is apparently much more attuned than is my own. My own criterion is for clarity of diction, regardless of the national coating in which the words are wrapped. But, again, the response to the inflection of the words is a highly subjective aspect of overall response to a film.

Olivier's film is Oliviercentric, as are all the other films in which he directs himself, contains more language than film can easily accommodate, and is indebted to other than canonical sources (Cibber's "Off with his head. So much for Buckingham," for example). But Olivier brings a malign sexuality to the role, plays "a renaissance wolf among medieval sheep" (Jorgens 1977, 136), and gives a splendid Shrewsbury, his map in the dust suddenly materializing into soldier, halberd, and horse. It also has Claire Bloom, John Gielgud, and Ralph Richardson. It is hardly Olivier's best Shakespeare film, ranking well behind his *Henry V* and *Hamlet*. The Olivier version, however, looks very good beside this new *Richard III*. This film "is as unnaturally proportioned as its hunchbacked central character," says Rafferty (1996). The inherited material has been pulled, twisted, and hollowed out into a *Friday the Thirteenth* or *Pulp Fiction*, with more than just a hint of Richard Dreyfuss's ludicrous Richard III in *The Goodbye Girl*. To witness Shakespeare subjected to the most blatant of Hollywood clichés is to be reminded of Doctor Johnson's statement on another topic: "It is not done well, but then, one is surprised to see it done at all."[2]

NOTES

1. On the Richard Eyre stage production, see my "*Richard III*: Large and Small," in *Reading Shakespeare on Stage* (Newark: University of Delaware Press, 1995), pp. 232–40.

2. I am grateful to Marion O'Connor of the University of Kent for an incisive critique of my response to the Loncraine *Richard III* and the Parker *Othello*.

REFERENCES

Barber, C. L. 1959. *Shakespeare's Festive Comedy*. Princeton: Princeton University Press.

Berkowitz, Gerard M. 1991. "The London and Stratford Seasons: 1991." *Shakespeare Bulletin 9*, no. 4, 8–10.

Bevington, David. 1980. *The Complete Works of Shakespeare*. 3d ed. Glenview, Ill.: Scott, Foresman.

Brantley, Ben. 1966. "Richard III and Iago, Mesmerizing Men of Ill Will." *New York Times*, 21 January.

Bulman, James. 1988. *"As You Like It* and the Perils of Pastoral." In *Shakespeare on Television*, edited by James Bulman and H. R. Coursen. Hanover, N.H.: University Press of New England.

Carr, Jay. 1996. " 'Richard' Served Up '30s Style." *Boston Globe*, 19 January.

Corliss, Richard. 1996. "Pulp Elizabethan Fiction." *Time*, 15 January.

Crowl, Samuel. 1993. *"As You Like It." Shakespeare Bulletin* 11, no. 3, 41.

————. 1996. *"Richard III." Shakespeare Bulletin* 14, no. 2, 38.

Empson, William. 1960. *Some Versions of Pastoral.* New York: New Directions.

Frye, Northrop. 1957. *Anatomy of Criticism.* Princeton: Princeton University Press.

————. 1963. *Fables of Identity.* New York: Harcourt, Brace, and World.

Holden, Stephen. 1995. "An Arch-Evil Monarch, Updated to the 1930's." *New York Times*, 29 December.

Holland, Peter. 1996. "Hand in Hand to Hell." *TLS*, 10 May, 19.

Jorgens, Jack. 1977. *Shakespeare on Film.* Bloomington: Indiana University Press.

————. 1988. "Review." In *Shakespeare on Television.* Hanover, N.H.: University Press of New England.

Kennedy, Dennis. 1993. *Looking at Shakespeare: A Visual History of Twentieth Century Performance.* Cambridge: Cambridge University Press.

Kimbrough, R. Alan. 1988. "Review." In *Shakespeare on Television.* Hanover, N.H.: University Press of New England.

Meltz, Marty. 1996. " 'Richard III' Sumptuous Feast for Discriminating Filmgoers." *Portland (Maine) Press-Herald*, 17 March.

Nightingale, Benedict. 1990. "A Very Modern Nightmare." *Times*, 26 June.

O'Connor, Joseph. 1988. "Review." In *Shakespeare on Television.* Hanover, N.H.: University Press of New England.

Rafferty, Terrence. 1996. "Time Out of Joint." *New Yorker*, 22 January.

Rose, Lloyd. 1996. "When All the World's a Screen." *Washington Post*, 28 January.

Sherman, Betsy. 1994. "A Soggy, Not Snappy 'As You Like It.' " *Boston Globe*, 31 March, 63.

11

Hamlet on Film

As I write, a new *Hamlet* film is being edited by Kenneth Branagh. This film will permit us to see previous films of this script in different ways, as T. S. Eliot argues that the "individual talent" alters "tradition," even if only imperceptibly (1960). We will try to look at the Branagh film with fresh eyes, as if we were looking at any other new film that did not derive from a book we had read, another film, a television series, or a historical event. But it will be impossible to look at Branagh's film without some knowledge of its source. It will certainly be impossible to look at other *Hamlet* films, once we have seen the Branagh, without using the latter as an imaginative filter through which to see another version. Film is a storyteller, and *Hamlet* is an ongoing cultural narrative. The issue is not, What is the Hamlet story?, but How is it told? It becomes a different story on film and in time, as a different film picks up the narrative as it interthreads a particular moment in history.

A student can look at a tiny segment of several different versions of a script and emerge with useful conclusions about each production and the continuing possibilities that that script presents for production. I look here at a few moments of many *Hamlet*s as its film manifestations begin. Television must be more conventional—more like the stage—and more predictable as it opens into this play, though I leave that conclusion to be explored and possibly refuted.

Robert Weimann makes an extraordinarily useful distinction that allows us to separate a script, an edited version of a play that exists as words on a page, from a production of that script, which occurs in a specific place at a precise moment in time: "What the Shakespearean text seems to project are two different (and potentially divisive) locations of authority: the represented *locus* of authority *and* the process of authorization on the platform stage" (1988, 402). "The Elizabethan theatre was not, by any stretch of the imagination, a subversive institution, hostile to the Tudor balance of socio-economic forces old and new" (409–10), but "the mirror of representation, the rules of decorum, the language of privilege could be challenged or confronted by a different 'impertinent' or 'antic disposition' of dramaturgy" (410). This process "negotiate[d] two differing locations of authority in the theatre [and] could involve a subversion of the dominant uses of authority" (410).

Weimann calls these two competing authorities *locus* and *platea*. *Locus* incorporates the original text in all of its conservative, hierarchical, class-structured sense, in its role as ostensible champion of the values of the dominant ideology, and as a product of a historical moment. *Platea* involves the production of the script, which can incorporate an undercutting of the conservative locus and does inhale a different zeitgeist than did the original production. In Shakespeare's plays, as "traditional modes of correlating theatrical space, language, and social status begin to collapse or at least show signs of strain, the supple art of crossing from *locus* to *platea*, and vice versa" also begins, and manifests the energy of a "bi-fold authority" (416).

With a seventy-year history on film, *Hamlet* provides a wonderful opportunity to chart and describe the ways in which *locus* has been challenged by *platea* in the twentieth century. Clearly this enigmatic script picks up and amplifies the enigmas that history has formulated, and invariably the film versions are aware that the script is an exploration of depth psychology. This is more true in a black-and-white film like Olivier's, in which the camera can delve into physical depth and where it itself does some wild whirling—bouncing in and out of focus as a giant beat shakes the parapets and swish-panning up and around staircases—than in Zeffirelli's opulent color film, which seldom pauses to contemplate its *locus;* but the film versions of the script, when unearthed a thousand years from now, will confirm that ours was, among other things, a century of the psyche.

Roger Manvell calls *Hamlet* "the least immediately filmable of the great poetic tragedies" (quoted in Davison 1983, 52). Robert Duffy talks of "the resistance of the source play to cinematic adaptation" (1976, 142). "Much discussed 'epic' qualities," Duffy says, "particularly the emphatic and rapid shifting of locale and time frame—so often cited as one of the most 'cinematic' of Shakespeare's techniques—simply do not operate to any great extent in the play" (141). Films of Shakespearean scripts, says Anthony Davies, "can be articulated to varying degrees through the relationship of men to things, of ideas to the concrete world and of motives to actions, without conscious distortion. But of all the plays of Shakespeare," Davies suggests, "*Hamlet* is least of all a play which readily enlists spatial detail and the world of objects for its major thematic developments" (1988, 40).

Some of the soliloquies in *Hamlet* are, as Peter Davison says, "bravura set-piece[s] for an actor, and . . . require . . . amplitude and a theatre audience to make the most" of them, like the "rogue and peasant slave speech," for which "there was no place," Davison says, "in Olivier's film" (1983, 51). We may recall him racing through a midnight palace shouting so loudly of "the conscience of the king" that even a wine-sodden Claudius might have started from his slumber. And if films erase Fortinbras, as Olivier and Zeffirelli do, they also eliminate the splendid, "How all occasions do inform against me!" soliloquy, to say nothing of political closure.

The words themselves fight against the medium. Peter Hall indicts Shakespeare for "bad screen writing. A good film-script relies on contrasting visual images. What is spoken is of secondary importance. And so potent is the camera in convincing us that we are peering at reality, that dialogue is best under-written or elliptical" (1969). Kozintsev goes so far as to call the text "a diffused remark that the author wrote to acquaint actors as thoroughly as possible with the heart of the action to be played" (1966, 215). The sheer amount of language in *Hamlet* must stretch a director's imagination as he or she seeks visual equivalents for it. A film of *Hamlet* demands transitions that, in this play, often occur in the mind of Prince Hamlet and not in some exterior and potentially cinematic space. Yet for all of the problems, *Hamlet* is one of the most filmed of all the plays, and successfully filmed at that.

Of all the plays, *Hamlet* has summoned the greatest artists in response to it, and that includes filmmakers. I deal here only with films, not with television productions, like the Franz Peter Wirth–Maximilian Schell (1960), the Christopher Plummer (1964), Ian McKellen (1971), Rodney Bennett–Derek Jacobi (1980), and Kevin Kline (1990), but including films that seem to have been designed for television and destined for cassette, like the Tony Richardson–Nicol Williamson (1969) and the Ragnar Lyth (1984). The "straight" films I will consider are the Sven Gade–Asta Nielsen (1920), Laurence Olivier (1948), Grigori Kozintsev (1964), and Franco Zeffirelli (1990). My question is, How does the director get us into the *Hamlet* story? That is another way of asking, What does the director believe the *Hamlet* story to be, or not to be? Since the films considered cover a seventy-year period, their examination constitutes a history of *Hamlet* on film and must treat the assumptions about Shakespeare and film that conditioned the production of each film.

The Gade version succeeds perhaps because it tells a story other than what most believed the *Hamlet* story to be as of 1920. It is also much more than "extended pictorial allusion . . . to the source play," as Duffy calls most silent films up until the Gade (1976, 141). The "Gade version," he says, "makes evident the central reality of *Hamlet* adaptation: cinematic effectiveness demands the sacrifice of some traditional, even, sacrosanct, Shakespearean values" (142). Robert Hamilton Ball says of the Gade-Nielsen film that "by adaptation and acting appropriate to pictures in motion, the least Shake-spearean *Hamlet* becomes the best *Hamlet* film in the silent era" (1968, 278). It "succeeded," Ball claims, "because it started with, developed from and ad-hered to a conception of the *Hamlet* story, which, however unShake-spearean, made cinematic sense" (279). The star, Asta Nielsen, was an actress of power and grace, with a remarkable ability to suggest nuances of emotion without the exaggeration we often associate with the silent screen. A con-temporary review remarked her "mature art [in which] appearance, gesture, even the movement of an eyelid—show forth the soul of . . . Hamlet" (quoted in Ball 1968, 277).[1]

The film opens with an ominous piano score, obviously added at some point, and, after her name appears, a picture of Nielsen. Edward P. Vining is given a credit for suggesting that the problem of *Hamlet* is that Hamlet is re-ally "eine Frau"! (Sarah Bernhardt should also be credited with playing Hamlet, though she did not embrace the Vining thesis in her portrayal.) The opening of the film is a series of crosscuts, with title cards, depicting events on a battlefield and back in Elsinore. (The technique is pure D. W. Griffith.) The king of Denmark defeats Norway on a muddy hillside as battle ebbs and sways against a gray wash of sky. Denmark himself is wounded and hurried off on a stretcher. At Elsinore, a crowd of *danische Volk* awaits a royal birth. "Ein Prinz fur Danemark?" asks the queen. "Nein, meine Koni-gin," says the nurse. "Es ist eine Prinzessin." A messenger reports the severe wounding of the king. The queen and nurse devise a scheme. They will claim that the child is a boy and so maintain the line of succession. The conspiracy is sealed with an iris close. From the steps of the palace the good news is de-livered: "Ein Prinz ist geboren!" The king rises from his stretcher, however, returns, and is let in on the secret by the queen. Another iris close links the scene with the one between the queen and the nurse.

Hamlet grows; he is a winsome youth with luminous eyes framed in dark lashes. This Hamlet loves his father, dislikes his mother, and is suspicious of a really nasty looking "onkle." We get a strong depiction of the Electra complex in a film uncannily aware of the gender issues it raises by making Hamlet really a woman, as opposed to a Bernhardt or a Judith Anderson de-picting a male Hamlet.

Jeff Hush (1991) suggests that

the precise way in which Hamlet's womanish heart (his delays and excuses), which Hamlet himself sees as being like a strumpet's heart . . . gained great prominence in the major strands of the late nineteenth-century acting tradition. Hamlet's becoming a woman is a pointed reversal of and commentary upon the slanders heaped on women in Shakespeare's *Hamlet*.

I have argued elsewhere that Hamlet is characterized as out of touch with his anima (or "femaleness": 1986). The film makes that point poignantly by creating a Hamlet forced into a role that defies her "nature," at least as consciously constructed (persona). We have Viola's story without a Sebastian to permit her to reassume her desired gender role. Nielsen's Hamlet is in love with Horatio but has no genre to save her. It is a moving and deeply realized film, both in its grasp of the ramifications of the femininity of Hamlet—the taking literally of the insight that Vining offers literally—and in Nielsen's remarkable performance.

Laurence Olivier was a director looking for a starring role for himself, and he may have perceived that the post–World War II world would accept a hero other than the dashing Henry V he had provided in 1944. After victory in World War II, Great Britain was absorbing the costs of victory within an austere, socialist landscape. One could argue that the external environment dictated a black-and-white film, but the use of deep-field photography permitted Olivier to explore the Freud-Jones thesis. Perhaps the reason for his taking on Hamlet, however, lies in the role. Olivier's films all feature characters who are also consummate actors: Henry V, Hamlet, and Richard III. Even his filmed version of his *Othello* shows him playing the stereotype rather than being it, as some critics charge in the light of recent racial sensitivity.

Olivier called his film an "essay on Hamlet" (1948, 11–15), and Robert Tanitch says that "it looks like a great silent masterpiece with a beautifully-spoken, dubbed soundtrack" (1985, 81), suggesting that film and the spoken word are basically incompatible. Jack Jorgens describes the opening this way: "Titles over waves pounding rocky shore at the foot of the castle in swirling mist. Boom slowly in toward castle from dizzying height" (1977, 297). Jorgens neglects to mention the muscular giant, naked to the waist, swinging twice and never missing at that J. Arthur Rank gong. For me, as a teenager in those days, that usually meant a thrilling and often mysterious film to follow, and Olivier's *Hamlet* is no exception. Bernice Kliman notices "the orchestra warming up," at the beginning, "suggesting a play more than a film" (1988, 24). Olivier cues us to his artifice by suggesting that his soundtrack has begun a few seconds too soon. The brief jangle of instruments may also be a wry glance by Olivier (not William Walton) at Strindberg's suggestion that "life is like an orchestra tuning up and never beginning to play." Davies observes "a screen which brightens slowly to show a visual composition of theatrical properties: a mask, a crown, standards, foils, and spears, a goblet, a dagger, a horn and a drum [props that send] a clear signal that *Hamlet* is essentially a theatrical construct to be played before an audience" (1988, 42). This grouping is assembled a moment before "Laurence Olivier Presents" appears above it. Raymond Ingram notes that "the credits . . . reverse contemporary practice by naming 'The Players' before their roles; this indicates that the film will focus on the art of acting" (1992, 15). Kliman suggests that Olivier "opens up space and moves the audience without losing the theatrical essence of nonrealistic space"

(1988, 25). Ingram puts it another way: "Olivier has selected types and lengths of shot that match his perception of what a theatre audience would look at, had it the mobility of the camera" (15).

The film carries forward the overt theatricality of *Henry V* and in its way predicts the theater-like qualities of *Richard III* and *Othello*, the latter indicted by some critics as merely a filmed play. The effect of theater is not just a function of the period 1944–1964, in which distinctions between filmed and staged Shakespeare were still being formulated and debated, but is clearly Olivier's choice. What distinguishes the film from films of the 1930s and Olivier's *Henry V*, and, I would argue, his subsequent Shakespeare films, is the relationship of the set to the action. The "film is in motion," says Roger Furse. "The designer's business is to do everything he can to assist the mobility and flow; *not* to freeze it into a series of orderly compositions" (1948, unpaged; my emphasis). The setting takes on a kind of personality, beginning with its introduction as a dream castle floating in clouds, and it is in this respect like Hill House in *The Haunting* (1962), though not actively malevolent. Olivier may also be indebted to Xanadu in *Citizen Kane*.

In the *Hamlet* opening, spectator and director share the same subjective experience in space, and perhaps the spectator, at moments, resists the point of view being imposed on him or her. Although it is not true that the spectator of a stage play can look where he or she wishes to look (although we are told that all the time), it is certainly true that Olivier's camera makes us very aware of its selective presence and movement. Peter Donaldson suggests, furthermore, that "visually, we cannot always locate ourselves quickly or unambiguously [in the film]" (1990, 65). That effect is intentional, of course, even if André Bazin overstates the case in claiming that Olivier uses film "to produce *theatre* precisely as [he] feel[s] and see[s] it" (1970, 124, my emphasis).

The opening gives us Olivier's reading of the "So oft it chances in particular men" speech, voiced over the words themselves. The camera booms in on Hamlet's funeral procession on a circular platform at the top of the castle. Horatio stands nearby, a condensation of the *Citizen Kane* approach.[2] The rest of Olivier's film will be a flashback leading to this final procession and ending just before the silhouetted soldiers reach this high stage. Donaldson demonstrates, using evidence from Olivier himself, that the final shot "is the generating image for the film as a whole" (1990, 39).

The "image changes," says Davies, "from the close freeze-frame of the six figures on the highest tower . . . to an identical replication of the composition photographed from a distance in long shot" (1988, 43). These figures, according to Sandra Singer, "appear to be crude little dolls. The 'real' people on the 'real' tower have been replaced by small wooden figures which, in the next moment fade from the scene, leaving only the empty toy tower." Singer's conclusion is "that the scenes that unfold before us do so under the control of an all-powerful storyteller, who manipulates his figures to suit his narrative" (1978, 121). This manipulation is accompanied by another voice-over, one that haunts the film and its critics: "This is the tragedy of a man who could not make up his mind." Certainly Olivier's "subtitle" for his "essay" has been a filter through which the film has been viewed, so that response has emphasized the camera's entrance into Hamlet's mind in the "To be or not to be" soliloquy, for example, which occurs after the confrontation with Ophelia and again at the topmost part of Elsinore. (Zeffirelli puts the soliloquy in the same place in his script but moves it down to the crypt.) The voice-over seems to make the film "a study of a tortured intellectual in which a great actor plays the part of a prince trapped in the labyrinth of his own mind" (Collick 1989, 63), twisting us securely into his metaphor of torture and entrapment. Some, however, reject Olivier's description of Hamlet and claim, as Anthony Dawson does, that "Olivier's portrayal itself gave us a caged and vigorous melancholic rather than a contemplative one (several of the soliloquies were cut)" (1988, 154). Parker Tyler suggests that Olivier wanted "to pretend to honor the traditional 'mystery' of Hamlet's hesitation while he patently accepted the quasi-scientific Oedipal interpretation" (1949, 529).

We see the battlements from a medium low-angle shot. The castle is shrouded in mist, floating in a zone of its own, a dream castle, vaguely ominous and detached. If it were color, we would think we were entering a medieval fantasy. A soldier moves up a stone staircase. Bernardo and his pike cast a huge shadow against the stone. He pauses as if reluctant to continue. A soldier (Francisco) marches by above. Bernardo's pike appears above the stones before he does, and he shouts his challenge, to be rechallenged immediately by Francisco. The latter's "I am sick at heart" receives unusual emphasis. It comes after a pause and elicits a glance from Bernardo. Horatio is skeptical ("Tush, tush"). "Yon same star" gives way to the melodramatic, in-and-out-of-focus beating that accompanies this mist-shrouded Ghost, framed between two pikes. The Ghost approaches and fades as a cock crows, leaving the guards on a suddenly demisted tower. The guards seem to make a prisoner of Horatio between their pikes, until he assents to the story he had scorned. The guards ponder the possible truth of local folklore about ghosts. Anthony Quayle gives us more of the "season wherein our Saviour's birth is celebrated" than film productions usually grant. Horatio, who has been thinking as he listens, smiles and "in part" believes it, suggesting that he wants to cling to his skepticism, regardless of what they have all just witnessed. He remarks the approach of a personified Dawn. Now, on the left of the frame, Horatio commands the pikes as he suggests that they tell young Hamlet of what they have seen. Something is rotten, and the sun suddenly climbs above the wall to touch the faces of the watchers.

The staircase looks very solid. The camera tracks down with seeming randomness, picking up thrones, a tapestry, a door to the outside world—

Ophelia's entrance and exit, we will learn—and a big bed below a yawning backdrop. This "symbol," Donaldson says, "in proximity to [a] phallic cannonade, is a kind of declaration of the film's Freudian intentions" (1990, 52). The camera is "rewinding," as we will learn, traveling past symbols—throne, bed, cannons—that it will reemphasize at the ending that these objects have helped to generate, as the procession returns to that high platform against a pitiless twilight. We may begin to notice that Olivier's black-and-white camera can achieve considerable depth, in addition to the flexibility of the up-and-down movements it has already demonstrated. Black and white is a deep-field medium, as opposed to color, which tends to flatten perspective. We hear voices. Claudius drinks. He tosses the cup to a startled courtier. Trumpets and drums sound. An ample Gertrude leans beside him, showing no sign of recent grief. On "time be thine" we see Hamlet at last, slumped in a chair downcourt from the throne. We begin to notice Olivier's editing: *persist* for *persever* and *lower'd* for *vailed* (see Dent 1948 for the film script). Claudius pulls the power of the court with him as he moves down the long table toward Hamlet. Claudius makes his accusation of Hamlet very public and makes sure that his counselors signal agreement by bowing as he passes them. Gertrude lingers a bit too long in her kiss of Hamlet, and a furious Claudius says, "Madam, come!" He is still angry as he says "smiling to my heart" and as he pulls Gertrude from the court, giving her an if-looks-could-kill look. Basil Sydney's subtext as Claudius seems to be, "Dammit all—I have knocked off her husband. Now I have to worry about the kid! Curse Sigmund Freud!" (see Mills 1985, 241–49, for further description of Olivier's performance in the film).

All of this has already happened as we watch the film. Olivier's use of the oedipal configuration may mean to suggest as well that all of this has happened many times before (see Donaldson 1990, 31–67) and that Hamlet's story is merely a specific manifestation of an inevitable pattern. If so, all men, princes and the rest of us, are characters in an oedipal sideshow; that is the inevitable history dictated from the psyche independent of any eternal events or circumstances. Neil Taylor nicely captures the relationship between the opening and the closing sequences of the film: "An aerial view of Hamlet's pall-bearers reaching the top of the tower . . . provides the opening. . . . A companion low-angle shot of the same ascent provides the closing. . . . Between them they establish a cyclical structure which may be read as either regeneration or futility" (1994, 182). I think the evidence comes down solidly on the side of futility.

Max J. Herzberg argues that

on the screen Olivier's version in some ways moves closer to the Elizabethan manner of production than any other post-Elizabethan versions have done. For Shakespeare's theater largely disregarded the conventional acts and scenes in which printed editions of Shakespeare's plays appear; the Elizabethans had a constant flow of action and dialogue that resembles motion-picture technique. The great difference of course is that Elizabethan audiences had to imagine for themselves the backgrounds of scenes; photoplays today can reproduce these with living fidelity. (1949, 4)

Olivier's film does not try for "living fidelity" of scene (cf. Furse 1948 and Donaldson 1990, 65–66), even if language describing place is cut (except in the notorious example of Gertrude's voice-over of Ophelia's melodious cruise down the River Colne). Olivier's Elsinore is, Robert Duffy says, "midway between heaven and earth" (1976, 149), and the film incorporates what Sheryl W. Gross calls "chapters in a fairy tale . . . a kind of Never-Never Land" (1980, 64, 65). Our suspension of disbelief and extension of imagination—the contract we enter into as we encounter a live performance—do not pertain to film, which can make us believe but which tends to do our imagining for us. Herzberg's comment, however, must be read against zeitgeist. He writes at a time (1949) when Shakespeare on film was very rare, when Shakespeare was read as text, and where live Shakespeare was not only a random event but was framed by a proscenium. Olivier's film invites comparisons to theater because its deep-field technique makes "it possible to film long sequences with moving actors and/or camera without losing the focus, [thus] preserv[ing] unity of time and space" (Gross 1980, 65). Deep focus also "requires more active participation [on the part of the spectator] than is normally expected of a movie audience" (66).

   Mary McCarthy calls the role of Hamlet "mannerist" (1956, 65) and certainly the play contrasts its techniques with classical proportion, as represented by the Player's speech, for example, and in "Gonzago." The film itself incorporates some distortion of conventional expectations, in its in-and-out-of-focus responses to the Ghost and in its eerie independent camera, which can rove, ghostlike, up and down stone steps and along corridors. The constant movement of Olivier's camera and the time it took for the camera to cover distances caused John Mason Brown to label the film a "travelogue" (1948, 26).

Grigori Kozintsev's film shows us how far film can be from the linguistic premises of Shakespeare's theater, as Ingram says: "The film is rooted not in the play's words but in its references: 'something is rotten,' 'sulf'rous and tormenting flames,' 'sweet bells jangled, out of tune and harsh,' and 'o'erhear their conference.' The result is what Shakespeare himself might have conceived had he been a screenwriter" (1992, 17). The film is, as Jack Jorgens observes, quoting Kozintsev, "a cinepoem of stone, iron, sea, and earth" (1977, 223). It begins, as Jorgens says, with "waves wash[ing] though the shadow of Elsinore as a bell tolls. Titles over rock with a blazing torch to the right. Billowing banners of mourning" (300–301). The film is "After the Tragedy by William Shakespeare." The camera pans the wall of the castle, and the three opening chords of Shostakovich's somber theme sound. Bernice Kliman picks up the description: "Two horsemen give a signal from below for the flag signifying the death of the king to be flown, and in a reverse shot, we see flag after flag unfurled from the wooden veranda overlooking the courtyard of the castle" (1988, 88).

Hamlet pounds along on a white horse under an ominous sky. He and his three companions thump across the drawbridge. He dismounts and runs up some steps. A huge black flag unfurls as he rushes to embrace his mother, who is weeping. She is "all in black," Kliman notes, "noticeably well turned-out, with jewels adorning her fingers" (1988, 89). An officer orders cannons to be fired. Workers strain against the seven huge spokes of the wheel that pulls the drawbridge up. Jorgens notes "Gertrude's black-gloved hand embracing Hamlet while the drawbridge and huge portcullis close him in" (1977, 220). The teeth of the portcullis rise as the bridge slowly closes out the light. "The last, slow shots of the drawbridge and moat enclosing Hamlet effectively convey Denmark as a prison," says Kliman (89).

A final streak of sunlight plays against the stone and is erased. We hear a crowd. A soldier beats kettle drums, one on each side of his horse. Claudius's opening speech is read by a soldier from a parchment to the crowd in the courtyard. The black flag behind the soldier is withdrawn. The period of mourning is over. The proclamation ends with "taken to wife." The camera cuts to the inside of the castle, where the king and queen descend from a platform. He says, "In equal scale." Ambassadors stroll past, two speaking in German, two in French, as if to emphasize the cosmopolitan nature of this court. Claudius adjourns to his council room, the queen with him. The king mentions Fortinbras and has his council look out of a window, where, to martial music, Claudius's army marches out of the castle. It is an allusion to a May Day parade past the Kremlin, a display of power that needs no rhetorical amplification. Claudius deals with Laertes, but when the king looks for Hamlet, the chair is empty. Gertrude and then Claudius pursue Hamlet. He agrees to obey her, and Claudius orders a public celebration. Hamlet walks through the court as his first soliloquy drums through him in voice-over.

"The shots," Kliman says, "are always connected by straight cuts [that provide] no clue about the passage of time" (1988, 91). This camera technique is, as Jorgens notes, in contrast to "Olivier's dreamlike film [where] dissolves frequently link shots" (1977, 218). We begin to realize as we watch the black flags retract in the Kozintsev film that we are experiencing a skillfully orchestrated and total state control of events and their interpretation. Kozintsev emphasis what he calls the "theme of government," which he finds "very interesting" and which he feels "Olivier cut" (1966, 226). "Kozintsev's *Hamlet*," Collick says, "was intended partly as an anithesis to [Olivier's] psychological reading. [Kozintsev's is] a tragedy of man caught in a climate of political corruption, as opposed to one confronting his inner flaw" (1989, 135), that is, one assumes, his inability to make up his mind.

Kozintsev shows us immediately some of the monumental natural, forces that lie under and beyond politics. Olivier shows us "nature" almost exclusively through Ophelia, who can run in and out of landscapes but is crushed within the stones of Elsinore and must finally float down the river to muddy death.

Kozintsev gives a sense of something great and a priori around the closed-in construct of the castle. It is an Aesopian way of indicting Stalinism. Olivier shows us a single nature—Ophelia's—being drawn into a centripetal vortex that turns innocence to self-destructive nightmare. The dynamics dictated by Kozintsev's Claudius affect many, as in Kozintsev's *King Lear*, where a multitude of peasants gather near the great wall of the fortress to hear Lear's proclamation, and here, in the group gathered in the courtyard to listen to Claudius's announcement, which inaugurates and terminates mourning with a sweeping disdain for human issues but an accurate assessment of how political transition must function.

Hamlet has been out of the loop and returns to Elsinore as merely a prop in Claudius's coup. Olivier's camera closes in on Hamlet's mind. Kozintsev's Hamlet is a participant in a politics dictated by a smooth and plausible king and a Gertrude out of Thackeray, who glances approvingly at a mirror as she utters clichés about "all that lives must die." Narcissism is perhaps an inevitable reflex of tyranny, an effort to benefit from power by imitating it. "The politics of the court," says Kenneth Rothwell, "begin to rival the inner perturbations of the prince" (Melzer and Rothwell 1990, 69). Olivier obviously does not try for this balance. Kozintsev's Claudius is skillful enough to incorporate nature into the workings of his court, as Ingram suggests in describing this superbly self-referential film: "The billowing movement of banners is repeated not only by the Ghost's cloak, the curtains in Gertrude's closet and the enveloping mourning veil into which Ophelia is forced after her father's death, but in flames, breaking waves and streaming clouds" (1992, 17).

Of all the *Hamlet* films, Kozintsev's suffers the greatest loss when put on cassette. It is hugely scaled in Sovscope, a 70-millimeter medium that makes an epic of the play whether it wants to be or not. Some would argue that the size of screen and conception work better in Kozintsev's *Lear*, which, for example, contrasts the moves and countermoves of a great battle with the intimate reunion of Lear and Cordelia, iron and the clank of arms against the flowing garments and smiles of the captives. Edmund does not understand those smiles, goes into combat still troubled by them, and is defeated. Each film is in black and white, which gives the *Lear* a powerful documentary effect and lends to the *Hamlet* what Kozintsev calls "the cool greys of the North" (1962, 80). *Hamlet*, Kozintsev believes, must, like the screen itself, "convey the enormity of history, and the fate of a man determined to talk with his epoch on equal terms, and not be an extra, with no speaking part in one of the spectacular crowd scenes" (1972, 192). Kozintsev, the maker of films, is hardly an attendant lord himself.

Jorgens remarks a quality that Kozintsev's *Hamlet* shares with his *Lear*: the camera's attention to "a world beyond Hamlet's tragic action which is oblivious to it" (1977, 224). Kozintsev's camera captures the randomness that Auden describes, where in corners and untidy spots, as the torturer's horse rubs against a tree and dogs lead their doggy lives, "the dreadful martyrdom must run its course." It is the world we experience as we step over and around the homeless huddled near the steam vents of our great cities as we move briskly toward the snug theater. Kozintsev's art shows us what we tend to ignore in our pursuit of Shakespeare, but which Shakespeare does not ignore. The film, and the *King Lear* even more, shows us the history that formal history does not record, except in a table of statistics.

The Tony Richardson film provides the most close-up *Hamlet* of all. It is a filmed version of a production in London's Roundhouse and was designed to be filmed from the first. Richardson wished to "free the theatre from the tyranny of the proscenium arch and the social habits that go with it" (quoted in Manvell 1971, 232). And the film succeeds in this goal, as Arthur Knight affirms: "It eliminates all sense of proscenium, and the tatty stage scenery that proved so distracting in, for example, Olivier's . . . filming of *Othello*" (1970, 37). It begins with the credits against a rough, brick wall in the Roundhouse, once a switching station for the vast rail network that converges on London—"a metaphor for the world of the play," says Michael Mullin:

The brick, the dust, and the darkness form part of this world in the film as they did for audiences in the stage performances. . . . The film makes these images predominate, disregarding others—the seas foaming at the foot of the battlements, the russet sky overhead, the images of the Ghost itself, the vision of Hamlet at sea, Ophelia afloat in the stream and many smaller, but no less powerful images conjured up in reading and, in their time, enacted in stage and film performance. (1976, 124)

A jovial Horatio (Gordon Jackson, later "Mr. 'oodsin" of "Upstairs, Downstairs") joins the guards. He takes his glasses off and blinks before his "Tush, tush," perhaps to suggest that "the characters," as Duffy says, "seem confined by a vaguely visible edge of confusion and myopia" (1976, 151). He is shocked, however, by the Ghost, who is here a blinding light and a series of deep and ominous chords. "The text," says Manvell, "is cut back to the barest essentials . . . to emphasize the impact made by the Ghost" (1971, 128; see Mullin 1976, 130, for "Cuts in the Text"). Horatio yanks his hat off as he vows to "cross it, though it blast me" and puts his specs back on as the dawn appears as a blank light at an archway. We do get a crow, incidentally, and do not, I assume, have time to wonder how it got here, as the scene blasts on by. This Horatio acts as a Jamesian "reflector," preparing us for Hamlet, as Manvell suggests: "A bespectacled and middle-aged don . . . the friend and 'fellow-student' of Hamlet at Wittenburg University, he prepares us for a mature interpretation of the Prince . . . an academic summoned back home for his mother's marriage" (128) and, based on his colloquy with Horatio, for his father's funeral as well.

The camera cuts to a close-up of Claudius drinking wine, then feeding some to Gertrude. Claudius gets a big laugh on "impotent and bedrid." He is hardly impotent but will be seen shortly conducting state business from his bed, as Gertrude munches grapes beside him. Claudius seems only slightly upset that Hamlet will not join the party. We watch the candelabras and the king depart from Hamlet's point of view, frame left. Hamlet turns his forlorn face to us as trumpets triumph and a torch flares to the right. His thin voice begins its complaint, "his rough Midlands twang," Mullin says, "making each word new-coined and fresh" (1976, 128). I find the coins dull, however freshly minted. As Mullin also says, "Inevitably, as the naturalistic acting, closely observed by the camera, brings the verse to us afresh, the sweep and cadence of the verse may be lost" (129), as I have found it consistently to be lost in Williamson's performances of Shakespeare. Williamson is "more a peasant than a poet," Clive Barnes remarks of his Hamlet (1969). To be fair, however, one must acknowledge the difficulties of applying naturalistic acting techniques to verse drama (see Hornby 1988).

The "neurotic *Hamlet*," as Duffy calls the film,

deliberately frustrates the spectator's unconscious attempts to impose a spatial coherence on the mise-en-scène and establish a perspective drawing the disjointed visual impressions of film into a cognitive unity. . . . Richardson, in short, establishes a strategy of visual frustration, and the lack of perceptible depth of field in most scenes communicates what Richardson seems to view as the tragedy's subtext, a contagious inability to penetrate the context and mystery of human affairs. (1976, 150)

Richardson's "frequent cuts and soft-focus close-ups completely disorient the audience," says Sheryl Gross (1980, 67). Our own adjusting of eyeglasses does not help us see what cannot be sensed in normal and normative ways. Only Hamlet, Mullin suggests, "looks beyond the milling throng to see his fate" (1976, 129; on Williamson's interpretation of Hamlet, see Mills 1985, 268–82, and Trewin 1978, 146–48). Williamson's is an enraged, snarling prince of Denmark, a Hamlet of the 1960s, along with David Warner.

In the 1960s, the sense of displacement in society and alienation from the political process was strong among the college generation and need not be stressed here. The script provided plenty of opportunity for working from what was more than subtext in the culture and is more than subtext in the script. Authority was to be questioned in the 1960s and responded with force at home and a stepping up of its agenda abroad. The film launches the interrogation by refusing to provide an architectural buttress for politics—neither the spiraling staircases of Olivier nor the prison-like solidity of Kozintsev's castle. Instead "the production operates [in a] black void. . . . Elsinore is like the true Elizabethan court, a collection of courtiers following the king, a network of relations and values" (Taylor 1994, 188), but it is a network as fragile as a spider's web.

The Ragnar Lyth film begins with, "The time is out of joint, oh cursed spite that ever I was born to set it right," written in Swedish and translated into English in a subtitle. We hear laughter (and later learn that it is Claudius's ingratiating laughter, in which he will engage even after he has been given several superfluous stabs by Hamlet). An eye looks from a doorway. Is it Hamlet's? No. It is the eye of the head chef, timing the need for the next course. "Even as the film opens," Kliman says, "we see the spying that is a way of life at Elsinore" (1988, 209). The kitchen help place cherries in the pastry heads that adorn the game hens beneath. A strange wind invades the kitchen, blowing out candles and blasting the pastry heads to the kitchen floor. Silence. The candles are relit. A guard—Marcellus—appears and lights his torch from one of the candles. The screen tells us that this is the "Tragic Story of Hamlet, Prince of Denmark." A cold Horatio, hugging his robe about him, follows the guard's torch through corridors, past a door that creaks open as attendants tug at chains. Another guard joins them. "What, is Horatio there?" "A piece of him." He is skeptical. The procession continues as a clock begins to strike. It grows louder as the group goes up into an attic. Horatio looks down to the catacombs, many stories below and one story ago. There lies the corpse of the former king, arms folded and very corporeal. The film gives us a nice contrast between what is going on in the upper floors and Claudius's party below. It is a moment in the play from which Keats borrowed:

> The boisterous, midnight, festive clarion,
> The kettle-drum, and far-heard clarinet
> Affray his ears, though but in dying tone—
> The hall door shuts again, and all the noise is gone.
> "The Eve of Saint Agnes"

"Tush, tush, 'twill not appear," says Horatio. The torch flares. The camera follows it upward, as do the eyes of the two soldiers and Horatio. Pigeons flap excitedly and are replaced by a weeping, sighing sound. Horatio sees—what? As Kliman says, "The ghost appears only in the briefest of glimpses while he is speaking to Hamlet in the last scene of act 1, and is sensed rather than seen by the others" (1988, 210). For once, then, something (although I found this opening very confusing when I first watched it and was prepared to denigrate the film until I saw the rest, which is uneven but often powerful, particularly in its emphasis on Ophelia). Horatio asks whatever he sees to speak and even goes up a couple of steps to drive his demand home, but the thing evaporates. A soldier grabs Horatio by the shoulders: "Is it not like the King?" Horatio agrees reluctantly. The scholar has been confronted by something beyond his "philosophy." The camera cuts to the throne room, a large and relatively empty space (actually, a room in the abandoned Nobel dynamite factory). Claudius chuckles. Two young men fence. Each gives the other a hit. One of them is Laertes, as we will discover. A man hits a cue ball. A jovial Claudius hefts a bowling ball. A dark figure stands apart, staring out the window, suggesting the "Denmark's a prison" pattern that will be repeated, particularly for Ophelia, as Laertes inhales the light between him and Paris, and the door shuts darkness again into Elsinore. A bell jingles, and Claudius gets down to business.

Kliman suggests that Lyth's montage technique conveys "a more powerful sense of knowing the truth than more realistic methods might evoke. [Thus] to analyze the shots is to belie their summative power" (1988, 205–6). That is accurate. The film provides consistent disjunctivity: The time is out of joint, yet a clock chisels its precision upon midnight. Horatio demands speech of something *we* would not ask to speak. Hamlet broods and Claudius chuckles, but Hamlet is not just a self-exiled existentialist and is perhaps less than an exemplification of "the Swedish character [which can retreat] into the role of the aloof, misunderstood exile" (Milton 1993, 436). He is a spoiled brat, rock or tennis star, who wants nothing to do with responsibility and even engages in the adolescent display of trashing his room.

We have here a Hamlet of the 1980s: the man who continues his adolescence into chronological maturity. We also have a postmodernist production, in that what we experience as film audience is not always consistent with what the characters seem to be experiencing within the contexts of production, so that disjunctivity exists as our zone of interpretation. The film handles the political theme powerfully by suggesting the absolute cynicism and opportunism of the citizenry and benefits from feminist criticism in its portrayal of Gertrude as the power behind a figurehead Claudius and in its brilliant depiction of Ophelia, who is here an agent of discord and dismay that reaches beyond her personal destruction (see my discussion, 1992). This is a film that Olivier, had he wanted to, could not have made in 1948. Lyth makes *Hamlet* very much the story of 1984, reflecting an Orwellian perspective on a rotten society.

Zeffirelli permits us to look down from the parapets onto Claudius's celebration as Hamlet waits for the Ghost to appear (see Jorgens 1977, 220, on Kozintsev's depiction of this contrast). The view down for Ragnar Lyth is to the corpse of the former king. And Lyth, it would seem, permits the presence of a night visitor to pervade the kitchen, at least, of the building below. Whatever is on the parapets never comes to the attention of the king, in Lyth or in the script. Lyth's king attempts to chuckle his way past the problems he has created for his kingdom. Lyth's opening is not as spare or as nonspectral as Richardson's but it does, as, television tends to and perhaps must, put the emphasis on the viewers, as opposed to the thing seen. It may be that the supernatural, when framed for television, must become merely the psychological (see Dessen 1986). The Lyth film is among the many productions that exist but that have not become commercially available.

After that intimidating warning from the FBI, along whose parapets walks the ghost of J. Edgar Hoover, Zeffirelli gives us the name of the play in black against a sunlit Elsinore sitting solidly above the beginning and cease of ocean waves. The credits come up in white, and we cut to a closer shot of the battlements as Zeffirelli's name appears. The camera cuts to horsemen waiting in the courtyard of the castle and tracks aimlessly. They are waiting for something. We are told that this is the "Royal Castle of Denmark. Elsinore." We hear weeping. The queen approaches a bier. Claudius looks on. We see the corpse of the former king, as in Lyth, before we see the incorporeal version, although Scofield's Ghost is much more human than most others and needs no dry ice come from the fridge to tell his story. A hooded Hamlet drops dirt on the corpse. Claudius softly requests that Hamlet "think of us as of a father." Hamlet turns away. The queen weeps. A heavy cover is placed over the tomb. The tristful queen looks up and sees Claudius looking at her down the long length of the tomb. Hamlet sees this exchange of glances. Edward Quinn says that Gertrude's weeping is "one of several instances where a line in the play ['like Niobe, all tears'] is rendered visually rather than, verbally, and this one makes it clear who the visual star of this film is" (1991, 2). That is a somewhat perverse viewing of the film, although it permits Quinn to make the point that some actresses playing Gertrude can make, and that is that she be "impressive enough . . . to put to rest T. S. Eliot's . . . charge that the play lacks an 'objective correlative' " (see my discussion of Gertrude in *Watching Shakespeare on Television*, 1993). But certainly Zeffirelli makes the point that "Hamlet is 'a man who has a terrible problem with his mother' " (Jacobs 1991, 21). Hamlet exits up the stairs, "into the bright dissolving light of out-of-doors, as though [we] witness . . . his birth into the primal visual environment of the film" (Impastato 1991, 2).

We hear Claudius saying, "Though yet of Hamlet, our dear brother's death," as we look at the stone walls of the castle. It is not the public announcement of Kozintsev, but it is an inclusive political statement that incorporates those we see as the camera pans across the throne room. As Claudius says "taken to wife," he reaches across and takes Gertrude's hand. Polonius signals and the court applauds. (Olivier's Polonius, Felix Alymer, signaled the court by hitting the fingers of his right hand against the back of his left hand, though he gave an imperative signal to the trumpets to underscore Claudius's naming of Hamlet as heir.) Zeffirelli's room echoes with trumpets and cheers, and Polonius signals that the ceremony is over.

The camera cuts to Laertes entering a library and being asked, "What's the news with [him]?" Claudius and Laertes share a silent joke about Polonius's long-windedness. Claudius gives a jubilant Laertes a kiss on each cheek. A frolicsome Gertrude trips down the castle steps to a waiting Claudius. They kiss at length. Gertrude nods toward a closed door. We had better do something, she seems to say. They enter a room, Gertrude calling, "Hamlet! Hamlet!" Claudius follows with a goblet of wine in his hand: "Now, my cousin Hamlet, and my son." Hamlet, seated, says, "A little more than kin, and less than kind." Gertrude laughs at Hamlet's "too much in the sun." As Claudius sits, Hamlet stands, as if unwilling to accept any equal status with his uncle. Gertrude's right arm surrounds a model of a soldier in chain mail, an emblem of King Hamlet that she embraces unconsciously, but a visualization of Hamlet's archetype of parental grouping. Claudius gives his "courtier, cousin, and our son" speech, holds his arms out as if to say, "There!—I've done what I can!" and leaves. The dogs outside, waiting to hunt, yammer excitedly. The problem with this way of doing it is, Kathleen Campbell argues, "that private rather than public occasions diminish our sense of the king's power. [This] appears to be a conciliatory gesture undertaken at Gertrude's request rather than a delicate public negotiation with a potential claimant of the throne" (1991, 7). The dynastic theme here is far less emphatic than in Olivier's nonpolitical treatment. Here Claudius is as little concerned with Hamlet's inability to join the fun as Richardson's Anthony Hopkins. In Richardson, however, Gertrude (Judy Parfitt) also ignores Hamlet, which Zeffirelli's Glenn Close clearly does not.

Close's Gertrude continues Claudius's plea personally, almost romantically, looking past Hamlet's shoulder with her own veiled eyes at an irretrievable past. Hamlet's "Seems, madam!" is to her alone, and flattens out without its bite at Claudius ("actions that a man might *play*"). Hamlet agrees to obey Gertrude, and hers is the commendation of a "gentle and unforced accord"—merely, then, a mother's contentment at her son's acquiescence. She runs down the steps of the inner palace, is helped into a blue robe by a giggling attendant, and races out the door again. Hamlet begins to brood about "solid flesh." He looks out the window. Solid Gertrude is running down the outer steps again. "Things rank and gross in nature possess it merely. . . . That it should come to this!" Claudius leans from his horse to kiss Gertrude. "Satyr!" Gertrude rides off gaily on a white horse, courtiers oohing and aahing, Hamlet still complaining. He shuts the leaded windows, as if on a playmate abandoning him as he stays after school. Gertrude, Claudius, and party ride into the deceptive sunlight just outside the castle grounds. The effect of this opening is of a "return to normalcy" for Denmark and of a reawakening to life for Gertrude, with only a self-isolated prince shading the bright panorama.

The film has not met with as enthusiastic a response as that which greeted Branagh's *Henry V*, partly because, Max McQueen tells us, " 'Hamlet' has always been a tough nut to crack" (1991). Frank Ardolino finds that "so much of the text is cut that we do not experience the full personalities of the characters and their relationships" (1991, 5). In this "telegraphic version," Ardolino says, "the scenes remain isolated and detached because we have not been given sufficient motivation to understand their connections"

(1991, 6). Edward Quinn criticizes the film for "its neglect of important dimensions of the play. The loss of the opening scene eliminates the threat of war, the rottenness in Denmark and the hint of a sacrificial agent. Fortinbras is cut" (1991, 2; on the problems involved in cutting the opening scene, see Cohen 1989, 9–11). Television versions usually include Fortinbras, partly perhaps because television has been, at least in the United States, the medium of political transition, on which we watch funerals and inaugurations, conventions and computer projections of who is in and who is out. Once the reporter of such events, television now shapes and controls them. Thus, television anticipates the arrival of a Fortinbras and a speech by the new ruler that honors the past before announcing new agendas. Zeffirelli's film incorporates television's thematics in becoming what Ingram calls "a beautifully photographed account of familial lust and hate. This focus is established by replacing Act I Scene 1 with the burial of King Hamlet at which his bloat brother and tearful widow exchange a significant look across the tomb. Her son is disgusted. Zeffirelli has domesticated *Hamlet*" (1992, 18). Richardson had done the same thing, as Knight suggests: "Between Williamson's modern, uninflected readings, Richardson's unrelenting use of extreme close-ups, and the concentration of the plot upon King Claudius's domestic difficulties, this *Hamlet* often seems like a costumed version of television's 'One Man's Family' " (1970, 37). The effect of "angry young men" collides with the taming tendencies of the techniques whereby the rage is recorded and transmitted. Ace Pilkington says, "It is unfortunate that Zeffirelli, following Olivier in this as in so much else, chose to explain Hamlet with Freud, foregrounding the incest theme" (1994, 175).

Terrence Rafferty says of the Zeffirelli film that the "play's alternating rhythms of action and reflection have been flattened to a single tempo, brisk but monotonous" (1991, 22). That may be, but if so, it is because that is the "Claudius Rhythm," dictated throughout the film and, with only a few exceptions, capable of incorporating Hamlet within its beat. The tempo is Zeffirelli's acknowledgment of the political theme, which he otherwise ignores.

David Impastato defends Zeffirelli's technique by calling it "baroque . . . fluid, emotionally expansive, sensuously free. . . . The camera, like the Baroque frame, seems reactive, improvised—as if unable to predict where the human energy it witnesses might take it" (1992, 1). The film, then, cannot be unified on the basis of an auditor's sense of *Hamlet*, as play or as script, but represents an experience like that of any filmgoer who does not know the story. As Zeffirelli says, "The audience sits there in a big dark room, and I have to tell them the story from the beginning, making clear every single word of William Shakespeare" (HBO, 1990). In other words, "Zeffirelli has a distressingly low estimate of his audience's intelligence" (Pilkington 1994, 168). He anticipates a spectator innocent of even trace memories of his or her cultural heritage, and his mission is "to make this thing accessible to the distracted multitudes. . . . Everything that we do is [designed] to make people forget what has been achieved before us. We impoverish our culture in the end" (Jacobs 1991, 21).

That does not mean that the result cannot be judged by people who do know the play and the many shapes, guises, and disguises it has assumed as it has confronted the great, modern light-sensitive medium. Zeffirelli does, however, want his film to be judged against other contemporary films, not against other versions of *Hamlet*. It may be that Zeffirelli proves Ralph Berry's thesis that "Hamlet is not . . . a part that demands great acting. But it does demand the essential star quality of magnetism" (1993, 24). Zeffirelli was attracted, he says, to Gibson's "vitality, his mystery, his sudden changes of color, his humor. We've never had this humor in Hamlet, but it's there" (Jacobs 1991, 21). If Zeffirelli hoped to bring this classic effectively to mass audiences, he would seem to have failed, if Marty Meltz's ear is any criterion: "With only 70 percent of the dialogue comprehensible, it's still a film for the elitist" (1991). If *Hamlet* is taught in the schools, however—and it is—Meltz seems to suggest that there is no link in a student's mind between what happens in class and what happens at the local movie theater. That means that one *locus* is divorced from another *locus* and that the *plateas*—the teacher's interaction with text and with class and Zeffirelli's intervention in the history of the script—cannot usefully contrast with *locus* or with each other.

The script of *Hamlet* moves through time, picking up the shadings of history, its black and white, its deep fields and close-ups, its colorations, even, as Pilkington says of the Zeffirelli film, "the blue dimness of distance, the colour equivalent of black and white but with a suggestion that the characters are receding from the audience into a kind of mythic mistiness" (1994, 175). Any production is a reflection of zeitgeist. It cannot help but be and is meant to be, as Barbara Hodgdon argues: "Performance acknowledges, in its every aspect, its ephemeral nature. . . . Disturbance—one might call it transformation—is just what Shakespeare's texts are about" (1985, 65).

Gade's silent film explores and develops the very camera techniques that were making film the powerful medium it was becoming in the twentieth century. Olivier's dark and inward exploration of the deep fields of Hamlet's mind in 1948 contrasts with the technicolor need for a national hero only four years earlier. Kozintsev's anti-Stalinist fable of 1964 looks at recent and ongoing Soviet history from a stance Kozintsev could not have avoided had he wanted to. An effort to free the script from its moment would probably have resulted in an odd and schizophrenic film. Williamson's uncultured snarl is a look back in anger typical of the 1960s, which experienced the bankrupt rule of a Richard Nixon. Lyth's film offers no hero but does examine Ophelia from the perspective of a feminist critique available in 1984. Zeffirelli's despairs amid a culture at once illiterate and ignorant of its past and brings stars who have helped to create the Lethal Terminator XIII expectation to a classic text, along with some superb Shakespearean actors as well. It may be that his film will gain its place by its precise depiction of the marginal characters who surround the great ones: Helena Bonham Carter's Ophelia, Scofield's Ghost, Bates's Claudius, McEnery's Osric, and Peacock's Gravedigger, the only one I have seen who crosses himself as he says, "Rest her soul, she's dead."

Whatever we think of it, Zeffirelli's film implanted its images into the retinas and memories of students of the early 1990s as surely as the Olivier film did for my generation. It became their Hamlet, and it goes forward with them as part of their history. We wait for the impact of Branagh's version. Time's march invariably transforms the films, fixing them in their times but finding in them meanings undreamed of in their conscious composition. The point, of course, is to move from production back to the script and *re*-view the script as an energy that takes *Hamlet* into the future and shows that future what it is. We probably see that reflection only in retrospect.

NOTES

1. For more on Nielsen and the 1920 adaptation of *Hamlet*, see Lawrence Danson (1993).

2. Like the Olivier film, *Citizen Kane* features a back-lit castle, Xanadu, at the beginning and end. Welles used a similar setting for the end of his *Macbeth*.

REFERENCES

Ardolino, Frank. 1991. "Three Reviews," *Marlowe Society Newsletter* 11, no. 1, 5–6.

Ball, Robert Hamilton. 1968. *Shakespeare on Silent Film*. London: George Allen and Unwin.

Barnes, Clive. 1969. "Williamson's Hamlet." *New York Times*, 2 May.

Bazin, André. 1970. *What Is Cinema?*. Berkeley: University of California Press.

Berry, Ralph. 1993. *Shakespeare in Performance*. London: Macmillan.

Brown, John Mason. 1948. "Olivier's *Hamlet*." *Saturday Review of Literature*, 2 October, 26–27.

Campbell, Kathleen. 1991. "Zeffirelli's *Hamlet*—Q1 in Performance." *Shakespeare on Film Newsletter* 16, no. 1, 7.

Cohen, Michael. 1989. *Hamlet: In My Mind's Eye*. Athens: University of Georgia Press.

Collick, John. 1989. *Shakespeare, Cinema and Society*. Manchester: Manchester University Press.

Coursen, H. R. 1992. *Shakespearean Performance as Interpretation*. Newark: University of Delaware Press.

Cross, Brenda. 1948. *The Film "Hamlet": A Record of Its Production*. London: Saturn Press.

Crowther, Bosley. 1967. *The Great Films: Fifty Years of Motion Pictures*. New York: G. P. Putnam's Sons.

Danson, Lawrence. 1993. "Gazing at Hamlet, or the Danish Cabaret." *Shakespeare Survey* 45, 37–51.

Davies, Anthony. 1988. *Filming Shakespeare's Plays*. Cambridge: Cambridge University Press.

Davison, Peter. 1983. *Hamlet: Text and Performance*. London: Macmillan.

Dawson, Anthony. 1988. *Watching Shakespeare*. London: Macmillan.

Dent, Alan, ed. 1948. *"Hamlet": The Film and the Play*. London: Saturn.

Dessen, Alan. 1986. "The Supernatural on Television." *Shakespeare on Film Newsletter* 11, no. 1, 1, 8.

Donaldson, Peter. 1990. *Shakespearean Films/Shakespearean Directors*. Boston: Unwin Hyman.

Duffy, Robert A. 1976. "Gade, Olivier, Richardson: Visual Strategy in *Hamlet* Adaptation." *Literature/Film Quarterly* 4, no. 2, 141–52.

Eckert, Charles W. 1972. *Focus on Shakespearean Films*. Englewood Cliffs, N.J.: Prentice-Hall.

Eliot, T. S. 1960. "Hamlet and His Problems." In *Hamlet: Enter Critic*, edited by Claire Sachs and Edgar Whan. New York: Appleton-Century-Crofts.

Furse, Roger. 1948. "Designing the Film *Hamlet*." In *"Hamlet": The Film and the Play*, edited by Alan Dent. London: Saturn.

———. 1949. *"Hamlet": An Introduction to the Photoplay*. New York: Theater Guild.

Gross, Sheryl W. 1980. "Poetic Dualism in Olivier's *Hamlet*." *Hamlet Studies* 2, no. 2, 62–68.

Hall, Peter. 1969. "Shakespeare's *Dream*." *Times*, 26 January.

Herzberg, Max J. 1949. *"Hamlet": The Photoplay*. New York: Theater Guild.

Hodgdon, Barbara. 1985. "Parallel Practices, or the *Un*-Necessary Difference." *Kenyon Review* 7, no. 1, 57–65.

Home Box Office. 1990. "The Making of *Hamlet*." Documentary on the Franco Zeffirelli film of *Hamlet*.

Hornby, Richard. 1988. "Shakespeare in New York." *Hudson Review* 40, no. 2, 339–44.

Hush, Jeff. 1991. Letter to the author. 30 October.

Impastato, David. 1991. "Zeffirelli's *Hamlet*: Sunlight Makes Meaning." *Shakespeare on Film Newsletter* 16, no. 1, 1–2.

———. 1992. "Zeffirelli's *Hamlet* and the Baroque." *Shakespeare on Film Newsletter* 16, no. 2, 1–2.

Ingram, Raymond. 1992. "Angles of Perception." In *Audio Visual Shakespeare*, ed. Cathy Grant. London: British Universities Film and Video Council.

Jacobs, Tom. 1991. "Hamlet Is No Wimp." *Brunswich-Bath* (Maine) *Times-Record*, 7 January.

Jorgens, Jack. 1977. *Shakespeare on Film*. Bloomington: Indiana University Press.

Kliman, Bernice W. 1988. *"Hamlet": Film, Television, and Audio Performance*. Cranbury, N.J.: Associated University Presses.

Knight, Arthur. 1970. "Still There, Old Mole?" *Saturday Review of Literature*, 17 February, 37.

Kozintsev, Grigori. 1962. *"Hamlet." Films and Filming* (September).

———. 1966. *Shakespeare: Time and Conscience*. London: Dennis Dobson.

———. 1972. "*Hamlet* and *King Lear*." In *Shakespeare: 1971*, edited by Clifford Leech and J.M.R. Margeson. Toronto: University of Toronto Press.

Kustow, Michael. 1964. Review of Kozintsev *Hamlet. Sight and Sound* 33, 144–45.

Manvell, Roger. 1971. *Shakespeare and the Film*. New York: Praeger.

"Masterpiece." 1946. *Time*. Review of the Olivier *Hamlet*, 8 April.

McCarten, John. 1946. Review of Olivier *Henry V. New Yorker*, 22 June.

McCarthy, Mary. 1956. "A Prince of Shreds and Patches." In *Sights and Spectacles: 1937–1956*. New York: Farrar, Straus & Giroux.

Meltz, Marty. 1991. "Now Playing." *Portland* (Maine) *Press-Herald*, 31 January.

Melzer, Annabell H., and Kenneth S. Rothwell. 1990. *Shakespeare on Screen*. New York: Neal-Schumann.

McQueen, Max. 1991. "Mel Gibson as Hamlet: Not the Definitive Dane." *Kennebec (Maine) Journal*, 2–3 February, D-10.

Mills, John. 1985. *Hamlet on Stage*. Westport, Conn.: Greenwood Press.

Milton, Joyce. 1993. *Loss of Eden*. New York: HarperCollins.

Mullin, Michael. 1976. "Tony Richardson's *Hamlet*: Script and Screen." *Literature/Film Quarterly* 4, no. 2, 123–33.

Olivier, Laurence. 1948. "An Essay in *Hamlet*." In *The Film "Hamlet," a Record of Its Productions*, edited by Brenda Cross. London: Saturn.

Pilkington, Ace. 1994. "Zeffirelli's Shakespeare." In *Shakespeare and the Moving Image: The Plays on Film and Television*, edited by Anthony Davies and Stanley Wells. Cambridge: Cambridge University Press.

Quinn. Edward. 1991. "Zeffirelli's *Hamlet*." *Shakespeare on Film Newsletter* 15, no. 2, 1–2.

Rafferty, Terrence. 1991. "Zeffirelli's *Hamlet*." *New Yorker*, 11 February.

Singer, Sandra S. 1978. "Laurence Olivier Directs Shakespeare: A Study in Film Authorship." Ph.D. dissertation, Northwestern University.

Skovmand, Michael, ed. 1994. *Screen Shakespeare*. Aarhus, Denmark: Aarhus University Press.

Tanitch, Robert. 1985. *Olivier*. New York: Abbeville.

Taylor, Neil. 1994. "The Films of *Hamlet*." In *Shakespeare and the Moving Image*, edited by Anthony Davies and Stanley Wells. Cambridge: Cambridge University Press.

Trewin, J. C. 1978. *Going to Shakespeare*. London: George Allen.

Tyler, Parker. 1949. "Hamlet and Documentary." *Kenyon Review* 11, 517–32.

Weimann, Robert. 1988. "Bi-Fold Authority in Shakespeare." *Shakespeare Quarterly* 39, no. 4, 401–17.

12

Pistol in History

Students who have become interested in Branagh's films will probably have looked at Olivier's *Henry V* of 1944, suddenly visible as it had never been before by dint of Branagh's version thirty-five years later. A lot of history had passed, wars perhaps less horrible than World War II but certainly not as popular, so that Branagh's film not only portrayed war differently than had Olivier's, but our eyes were conditioned to look at war through different filters, those treated by TV's invasion of our living space with images of death in the jungle—this in spite of the fact that Branagh's French campaign is a replay of the Somme, its mud and superfluous death, of 1917. In a strange way, the Somme was available to a post–World War II audience as it had not been when an invasion of France was being generated in 1944. History becomes available when film versions of a particular script have been made at different moments in history. I am not a new-historicist, but the methodology can be valuable as we place productions in time and thus avoid the atemporal attitude that makes the texts mere museum pieces gathering dust as the days pass by outside, or which makes films merely artifacts, as opposed to dynamic spokespersons for their moment in time.

With different versions of the same scripts becoming increasingly available at reasonable prices, the opportunity to use contrasting interpretations in teaching continues to grow. The payoff for teachers is several-fold. When asked to discuss in detail two or more versions of a scene or character that interests them, students suddenly find themselves writing good prose instead of wallowing around in vague and shapeless generalizations. The writing gets very specific and picks up that energy that comes from a topic that is theirs. (The assumption here is that they *will* find something that interests them.) Students also begin to learn about the media that they claim for themselves—film and TV—and can begin to grasp some of the differences between light-sensitive and magnetic means of transmitting pictures and sound. Indeed, in a seminar format, students can create their own tapes and present them to the class. They often do so very skillfully, complete with handouts, and, knowing that all the members of the seminar will make a presentation, they help each other in generating response and discussion.

Yet another possibility is that if tapes of productions cover a range of time, historicity becomes a factor, and historicism can be taught and learned from context, as opposed to concept. Talking films of *Shrew*, for example, begin with the 1929 Pickford-Fairbanks production, which has the look of a silent, for all of its dialogue. The first sound film of *Dream* is the famous 1935 version. The 1936 *Romeo and Juliet* has just become commercially available, putting it within a useful spectrum that can include the flawed Castellani (1954), which has a good Juliet in Susan Shentall, the Zeffirelli film, and the Stratford, Ontario, televised version of its 1992 production, featuring Megan Porter Follows as Juliet. An advantage for teachers is that we do not have to put ourselves in the false position of defending any version of a play. The students can do that, or not, as they wish, for their reasons, not ours. They are thus allowed to work on developing their own psychology of perception rather than merely ratifying ours.

As I argued in looking at *Hamlet* openings, a fragment of the script can suggest the historical shift that occurs as films intercept a moment in time. Certainly views of war have changed in the fifty years that have incorporated wars less popular than was World War II. Again, Weimann's (1988) distinction between *locus* and *platea* becomes a useful way of approaching the historical issues. If any doubt exists that zeitgeist influences *platea* and in fact can be a large component of *platea*, four versions of Pistol's farewell should prove the point: Robert Newton (Olivier film, 1944), Brian Pringle (BBC-TV, 1980), Paul Brennan (Bogdanov, televised live performance, 1989), and Robert Stephens (Branagh film, 1989). Who is the "historical Pistol"? He is defined by the historical moment into which he emerges and by the conceptual space in which he speaks:

> Doth Fortune play the huswife with me now?
> News have I that my Nell is dead in the 'spital
> Of malady of France;
> And there my rendezvous is quite cut off.
> Old do I wax, and from my weary limbs
> Honour is cudgell'd. Well, bawd will I turn,
> And something lean to cutpurse of quick hand.
> To England will I steal, and there I'll steal;
> And patches will I get unto these cudgell'd scars
> And swear I got them in the Gallia wars. (5.1.85–94).

Pistol, of course, never had whatever honor is to begin with, so it is interesting to hear him mourn its loss. This is an unusual soliloquy by a minor character; Hume's in *I Henry VI* and Helena's in *Dream* are other examples. Pistol's is a farewell from all of the characters we have seen in the taverns since Henry IV's rueful mention of them at the end of *Richard II*. They are all swallowed up in the huge oblivion of time's passage, leaving neither a mark nor a tuppence behind.

The reference to "Doll" (F1) is emended, following Dr. Johnson, to "Nell" in each performance, but permits students so inclined to pursue the textual question and the intriguing speculation that the soliloquy was originally written for Falstaff and then switched to Pistol without the editing that would have made the lines conform to what we know of Pistol (cf. Walter, xxxviii–xxxix). *Falstaff's* mourning the loss of "honor," even if he never had it, would have reminded us of his disquisition in *Henry IV*, Part I, his dislike of Blunt's "grinning honor," of his postmortem victory over Hotspur, and of Henry V's reinvocation of the concept in the pep talk before the Battle of Agincourt. There may be, then, a textual reason Pistol's sense that he has lost his honor strikes us as strange.

These four Pistols prove two basic things to students: (1) that no "right" way to present even a soliloquy exists and (2) that the medium conditions the message. We have here two films, one made before commercial television, a televised stage play, and a straight television production. The more performance material we have available, the more able we are to look at smaller moments in production to learn about the possibilities inherent in the scripts and to measure the strengths and limitations of the conceptual spaces within which the productions occur. I suggest that our expectation does condition and to some extent control what can occur on any given medium.

In the Olivier 1944 film, made before commercial television, Robert Newton's piratical Pistol considers tossing the coin that Gower has added to Fluellen's fourpence back at Gower but pockets it instead. Pistol borrows a word from Prince Hamlet by substituting *strumpet* for *huswife*. He says *hospital* for *'spital*. He looks meaningfully at his sword as he mentions Nell's "malady of France." He decontextualizes the script by substituting *present* for *Gallia*. We notice that he wears the Constable's armor, scavenged after Henry V has killed the Constable earlier. That means that the film shows Henry V killing his half-brother, Charles de la Bret, but the film does not intend us to dwell on past history. It is 1944 and another perilous invasion of France is about to begin. The Constable had called his "the best armor in the world," and now Pistol wears it. This is another example of the film's economy—in this case, of its self-referential allusions. Pistol has been beaten—by the hilt of his own sword, which Fluellen has taken from him—but he recovers quickly, makes a quick foray through a barn, emerges with pig and rooster under his arms, and gets an actor's exit to the accompaniment of a Prokofiev-like "Pistol and the Pig." The dissolve takes with it part of the wintry landscape and absorbs it into the Magic Kingdom of the next take.

This is a cheerful, self-possessed, resilient Pistol. We have no fears for him as he roguishly makes his way through life, claiming that he is one of the king's "band of brothers." He, too, "will show his scars, / And say 'These wounds I had on Crispin's Day.' " Although Olivier's film is hardly the blatant piece of propaganda that some critics have made of it, the treatment of Pistol is not disturbing. He is a character in a farce that contrasts but does not conflict with the more sober argument of history. Certainly the film represents what John Collick (1989) calls "imperial Shakespeare," and we should not ignore its ideological assumptions, or those of film and television in any zeitgeist. To historicize the Olivier film, however, we should suggest the other ideology and what it was offering for the viewing pleasure of its audiences. Films of the execution by piano wire of the Stauffenberg plotters against Hitler in July 1944 were being shown to German troops. It is reported that they put their heads on their knees and refused to watch.

The BBC version of 1980, with Brian Pringle, gives us the soliloquy in close-up—extreme close-up. Pringle savors the word *rendezvous*. Pistol is a collector of strange words and phrases. Hotspur had used the word much earlier, and perhaps its reemergence here suggests that Pistol is a parody Hotspur, one who survives by cowardice as Hotspur had drowned in honor. Pistol, however, may have learned the word from Nym, who uses it earlier in *Henry V*, apparently to mean "last resort," as opposed to Hotspur's "a home to fly unto." Pringle takes the cue of "old do I wax" and "weary limbs" as he rises achingly to his feet. He has not been cudgeled but beaten by a heavy leek. He is startled out of his bright idea for self-fashioning by an offstage sound of ceremony, and he disappears, cut off by sudden pomp and circumstance. Obviously he does not count, is not even necessary to swell a scene. And what can we say of this Pistol? The spareness of the TV studio has given him little context, no world against which to demonstrate his small skills and large deficiencies. The close-up technique shows little more than a soap opera character disappearing. The production scarcely raises the issue of whether a character without honor can mourn its loss.

The problem with the BBC Pistol may be generic. "One of the strengths of television," says Elijah Moshinsky, "is the constant present, which is also a weakness if you are trying to build up a narrative structure. In a theatre, the space stays the same when different actors enter and leave the stage, and so a sense of continuity develops through the fixed relationships between the audience and stage. But on television, it's just a constant present" (Elsom 1989, 124). This televisual Pistol does not have the past he could have fabricated for us onstage and thus is denied both the heroic future he claims he will fabricate for himself with his scars and the probable future that his hands will not be quick enough to evade: the gallows. The wash of the studio behind the immediate action tends to erase the larger imitation of an action, the mimesis that incorporates the actors within it—Henry V and Pistol—and to obviate the ultimate issue of time itself, an issue that Shakespeare's stage consistently framed for its audience, with its heaven, hell, and space where fellows crawled briefly between. In its inability to sustain a narrative line, television reveals its weaknesses as modernist medium.

Bogdanov's Pistol, Paul Brennan, is onstage, as his voice and the audience response tell us. He has a letter relating Nell's demise, which he pulls from one of his empty holsters. The production uses paper consistently: Grandpre is writing his description of the English when he tears the paper from his typewriter and admits the futility of his image making. And Henry makes much of his commissions to Cambridge, Scroop and Grey, and of the smaller of the listings of the dead on either side. This Pistol is troublesome in that he wears the tunic of an impecunious marching band and the camouflaged pants of an infantryman. Pistol has stolen part of a Le Fer's comic opera outfit after he has been forced to cut the Frenchman's throat under the pressure of Henry's order to kill all the prisoners, but the irony does not resonate like Newton's audacious assumption of the Constable's armor. Bogdanov's eclecticism proves, as usual, that he has not looked at what soldiers really wear in battle or what they wear as veterans. The elevator operator uniforms worn by the French are designed to show that, as Zdanek Stribrny suggests, "Shakespeare lays special stress on the fact that the French lords at Agincourt refuse to lean upon their own people and rely solely on their chivalric bravery, whereas in the English host gentlemen fight side by side with their yeomen as one compact national army" (Kettle 1964, 89). Montjoy makes the point ex post facto in requesting permission "to sort our nobles from our common men." This Pistol has been forced to doff his Nazi helmet so that he can absorb a blow from Fluellen's billy club. Brennan's poverty-pinched face and complaining, Liverpool accent would have been better served by better costuming, but, then, Bogdanov's gimmicks seldom serve his actors well. They are designed to say, "Look how clever *I* am!" The effort to be timeless, by conflating elements of several times, forces us to unsuspend our disbelief beyond anything that Brecht ever intended. Bogdanov's postmodernist undercutting of early-modern scripts tends not to be deconstructive—that is, a searching for the margins of the script and the characters who live along those margins, and thus an exploration of issues obscured by a focus on establishment Shakespeare. Bogdanov's approach tends toward an obliteration of meanings, whether early modern or postmodern.

Pistol's stealing of a life preserver from the troop ship taking him back to England proves his compulsive proclivity for theft and suggests perhaps that he, like Bardolph, will ultimately be hanged for stealing something "of little price." An audience cannot dismiss this Pistol too easily, however. His accent points at the troublesome issue of class in Great Britain, and if it is a Liverpool accent, it might have even more specifically disturbing echoes. "Liverpool," says Blake Morrison,

is the city associated with the Beatles' song "Penny Lane." And the great refrain of the industrial North is that, while its people don't enjoy the material benefits of the South, they are warmer, more community-minded, stronger on family values. But in recent years images of mutual trust—the back door always open, neighbors minding each other's business, friends who would give you their last shilling—have given way to burglar alarms, glass-topped back-yard walls, and guard dogs. Neighborliness has been replaced by Neighbourhood Watch schemes; brotherhood has become the surveillance cameras of Big Brother. (1994, 51)

If so, then Shakespeare's Pistol, as delineated by Brennan, uncannily captures a postmodern moment. Morrison's article was occasioned by the murder in Liverpool, in February 1993, of toddler James Bulger by eleven-year-olds Jon Venables and Bobby Thompson.

In the Branagh film, Henry and Fluellen exchange sentimental tears about their mutual Welshness and go off arm in arm, as Henry gestures Exeter to join them. The camera pans to discover Pistol (Robert Stephens) seated, leaning against a tree. "Does fortune play the huswife with *me* now?" It has done so with Bardolph: "Fortune is Bardolph's foe, and frowns on him." Pistol's own motto has come full circle: "Si fortuna me tormenta, spero contenta." This is a Pistol without hope. He has not been cudgeled, though he says he has, but he is isolated, alone, his mates having been hanged or killed in battle. Nym has been killed while robbing a corpse. And Pistol is "cut off" from any welcome home. Here we get the post-Vietnam veteran who also begged at the end of the lane in Elizabethan England, the soldiers that Norman Rabkin describes "returned home to find their jobs gone, falling to a life of crime in a seamy and impoverished underworld that scarcely remembers the hopes that accompanied the beginning of the adventure" (1977, 293). This Pistol has been given only the context of his dissolute friends within which to establish himself. And he fails even there, if only because his friends die in the commission of crimes or are executed because of their crimes. This Pistol learns nothing, but there is nothing he can learn. He can only sit there as a small, ironic shadow cast against the king and his brotherhood and the heroism that Henry politically undercuts as soon as the necessary victory has been achieved and against the sentimentality in which the winners among the winners indulge. This Pistol, like many that we see today in the infested streets of our own cities, is below the reach of even the most effective politics.

Simply the thing he is does not guarantee this Pistol his living. No place and means exist for him. Parolles's failure in *All's Well That Ends Well* validates the male code he has failed to meet. Robert Newton's Pistol goes off to an amusing career—not socially sanctioned, true, but not one that disturbs us. He will be safely housed in the hovels of another part of the city. Stephens's Pistol is the by-product of a national purpose. He is discarded once that purpose is achieved, or abandoned for another crafted emergency, or drafted to die in it. He is not given the bright idea of valorizing his wounds, nor does he get an exit. He has no way out, but his resonance remains. The thing he is subverts the premises of the war in which he has been involved and of the peace that follows that war. Stephens's Pistol will not deploy his scars in the service of a phony heroism. It may be that his cynicism is too deep for any grasp at rationalization. Branagh's editing places the listing of those killed in the battle after Pistol's soliloquy, and so the paucity of the English dead becomes ironic. If Pistol is a synecdoche for others, the list should be longer.

Gower suggests that Pistol as type will "grace himself at his return into London under the form of a soldier. And such fellows are perfect in the great commanders' names, and they will learn you by rote where services were done; at such and such a sconce, at such a breach, at such a convoy; who came off bravely, who was shot, who disgraced, what terms the enemy stood on." And certainly, Pistol suggests as much at the end of his brief soliloquy. But Branagh's Pistol is edited down toward a very familiar and more contemporary point of view:

I had seen nothing sacred, and the things that were glorious had no glory and the sacrifices were like the stockyards at Chicago if nothing was done with the meat except to bury it. There were many words that you could not stand to hear and finally only the names of places had dignity. Certain numbers were the same way and certain dates and these with the names of the places were all you could say and have them mean anything. Abstract words such as glory, honor, courage, or hallow were obscene beside the concrete names of villages, the numbers of roads, the names of rivers, the numbers of regiments, and the dates. (Hemingway, 191)

The use of camera in the Branagh sequence is simple. That we get no deep-field shooting here and little, if any, in the film suggests that the film was designed with the cassette market in mind. As Bernice Kliman says, Branagh's "choices [are] more suggestive of TV than of film" (1989, 1). The restricted field of depth also suggests, however, that events that may seem glorious when viewed from afar are really dirty and sordid when seen more closely, and that, as Stephen Crane showed in *The Red Badge of Courage*, a soldier can see only what he can see from where he stands. For the infantryman, no big picture exists.

The four excerpts allow us to make a number of distinctions between and within the media. The stylization of the Olivier film tends toward the theatrical in a way we would not accept in a more recent film, as Branagh's blood, rain, sweat, mud, and mist show us. Olivier tends to watch events from a static camera, suggesting a fixed view of history. Branagh's camera moves, arguing no fixed premises and perhaps even a selective view of history, one inscribed by the editing of the winners, and then by all-enveloping time, as the ideological camera runs out of film. As the brief Pistol sequence shows, Olivier's style tends toward the cartoon and seems to be heavily influenced by Disney. Earlier, as Katherine pans westward, we expect her to break into "Some day, my prince will come." We notice, however, how neatly the Branagh translates to television. The smaller screen obviously conditions the field of depth that the theoretically larger screen chooses to deploy or reduce. Television is all foreground, as the BBC version shows us, but how effective is Pringle's soliloquy directly to us? Quayle had used the technique earlier, as Falstaff, and in the BBC *Hamlet*, Derek Jacobi had spoken many of his soliloquies directly to us. There, the technique emphasized his isolation from anyone, including Horatio, inside the frame. We were drawn into an uneasy relationship with this manic young man. My own sense is that we reject the too-close intimacy with Pistol. He leaves us no distance within which to formulate a response, other than a rejection based not on what he says or who he is but on the way he invades our space. That is a very subjective response, but I find the Branagh Pistol, Robert Stephens, the most effective of the four in his bitterness, hopelessness, and lack of self-pity. Another question, of course, is raised by the Bogdanov production: Does the televising of live performance in any way give us a feeling for the energetic continuum that live performance can generate? In the case of the Bogdanov, I find that the answer is no. Other live performances—Papp's *Dream* at the Delacorte in Central Park, Epstein's *Dream* at the Wilbur Theater in Boston, for example—show us an audience watching a play, thus incorporating us into the space of performance. The camera work for the Bogdanov is very awkward, giving us an occasional shot of the entire stage but concentrating mostly on close-ups of the person speaking, as if the play were a series of soliloquies. The groupings may have been effective on stage but the camera's tendency to be occasionally all-compassing and often isolating confuses a number of issues that the stage can make clear merely by blocking. We get little sense of the interdependence of Henry's enterprise or, more generally, of the middle distance that Sheldon Zitner claims is the basis of Shakespeare's drama: "What his theatre provided most often was humanity seen not in the all-defining closeup of psychology or at the far and narrowed distance of sociology or through the historical retrospect of montage but in the open middle distance of social relation" (1981, 38). The productions needed a master at televising live performances, like Peter Dews who directs the television versions of Stratford, Ontario's, productions, to make these work as television.

Implicit here, and at times explicit, is the necessity for historicizing the discussion of any production. We must try to account for the attitudes and assumptions that an audience was likely to bring to a given production when originally presented and will when re-viewed today. Some of us can remember the feelings aroused by the war against Nazi Germany and Imperial Japan and the contrast between those feelings and the ones aroused when the United States conducted a war against a Southeast Asian fragment of a country without an air force and lost the hearts and minds of many of its own citizens until finally it lost the war. Our attitude toward war, and toward specific wars, is an inevitable component of response that this play and this fragment of script force us to contact and consider.

It may be that television has made war less romantic than it once seemed to be, even after Hemingway and Remarque. It is also true, however, that Vietnam was fought by poor young men from the ghettos and farms and, for the survivors, often confirmed and intensified the cycle of poverty that had already begun to close them in. World War II encouraged its survivors in the United States to go on to college, and many did. The percentage of Vietnam veterans who took advantage of the G.I. bill was small compared to that of World War II veterans. Vietnam scooped up young men with no defenses against the draft and returned many of them in body bags or drug-ridden bags of bodies. Branagh's Pistol is that veteran as surely as Olivier's Williams, Bates, and Court are the World War II buddies sitting around their foxhole on the eve of battle. Olivier could even give Court the speech on men not dying well who die in a battle, since men before battle do have such thoughts and since the battle the next day turns out to be a victory, as World War II would turn out for the Allies. The script picks up with remarkable accuracy the emphasis of the moment into which it emerges.

REFERENCES

Collick, John. 1989. *Shakespeare, Cinema, and Society*. Manchester: Manchester University Press.

Elsom, John, ed. 1989. *Is Shakespeare Still Our Contemporary?* London: Routledge.

Hemingway, Ernest. 1929. *A Farewell to Arms*. New York: Scribner's.

Kettle, Arnold, ed. 1964. *Shakespeare in a Changing World*. New York: New Directions.

Kliman, Bernice W. 1989. "Branagh's *Henry V*." *Shakespeare on Film Newsletter* 14, no. 1, 1–2.

Morrison, Blake. 1994. "Letter from Liverpool: Children of Circumstance." *New Yorker*, 14 February, 48–60.

Rabkin, Norman. 1977. "Rabbits, Ducks, and *Henry V*." *Shakespeare Quarterly* 28, no. 3, 279–96.

Walter, J. H., ed. 1954. *King Henry V*. New Arden Shakespeare Series. London: Methuen.

Weimann, Robert. 1988. "Bi-Fold Authority in Shakespeare." *Shakespeare Quarterly* 39, no. 4, 401–17.

Zitner, Sheldon. 1981. "Wooden O's in Plastic Boxes: Shakespeare on Television." *University of Toronto Quarterly* 51, 1–12.

Selected Bibliography

Ball, Robert Hamilton. *Shakespeare on Silent Film*. London: George Allen and Unwin, 1968.

Buchman, Lorne. *Still in Movement: Shakespeare on Screen*. Oxford: Oxford University Press, 1991.

Bulman, James, ed. *Shakespeare, Theory, and Performance*. London: Routledge, 1995.

Bulman, James, and H. R. Coursen, eds. *Shakespeare on Television*. Hanover, N.H.: University Press of New England, 1988.

Bulman, James, and J. R. Mulryne, eds. *Shakespeare in Performance*. Manchester: Manchester University Press n.d.

Collick, John. *Shakespeare, Cinema, and Society*. Manchester: Manchester University Press, 1989.

Coursen, H. R. *Shakespearean Performance as Interpretation*. Newark: University of Delaware Press, 1992.

———. *Watching Shakespeare on Television*. Madison, N.J.: Fairleigh Dickinson University Press, 1993.

———. *Shakespeare in Production: Whose History?* Athens: Ohio University Press, 1996.

Crowl, Samuel. *Shakespeare Observed*. Athens: Ohio University Press, 1992.

Davies, Anthony. *Filming Shakespeare's Plays*. Cambridge: Cambridge University Press, 1988.

Davies, Anthony and Stanley Wells, eds. *Shakespeare and the Moving Image: The Plays on Film and Television*. Cambridge: Cambridge University Press, 1994.

Donaldson, Peter. *Shakespearean Films/Shakespearean Directors*. Boston: Unwin, Hyman, 1990.

Duffy, Robert A. "Gade, Olivier, Richardson: Visual Strategy in *Hamlet* Adaptation." *Literature/Film Quarterly* 4, no. 2, (1976): 141–52.

Eckert, Charles W. *Focus on Shakespearean Films*. Englewood Cliffs, N.J.: Prentice Hall, 1972.

Fenwick, Henry. *The BBC TV Shakespeare*. New York: Mayflower n.d.

Garfield, Leon. *The Animated Shakespeare*. New York: Knopf n.d.

Jorgens, Jack. *Shakespeare on Film*. Bloomington: Indiana University Press, 1977.

Kennedy, Dennis. *Looking at Shakespeare: A Visual History of Twentieth Century Performance*. Cambridge: Cambridge University Press, 1993.

Kliman, Bernice W. *"Hamlet": Film, Television, and Audio Performance*. Cranbury, N.J.: Associated University Presses, 1988.

Lusardi, James, and June Schlueter. *Reading Shakespeare in Performance: King Lear*. Cranbury, N.J.: Associated University Presses, 1991.

Manvell, Roger. *Shakespeare and the Film*. New York: Praeger, 1971.

McMurtry, Jo. *Shakespeare Films in the Classroom: A Descriptive Guide*. Hamden, Conn.: Archon, 1994.

Mullin, Michael. "Tony Richardson's *Hamlet*: Script and Screen." *Literature/Film Quarterly* 4, no. 2 (1976): 123–33.

Rothwell, Kenneth S., and Anabelle Henken Melzer. *Shakespeare on Screen*. New York: Neal-Schumann, 1990.

Skovmand, Michael, ed. *Screen Shakespeare*. Aarhus, Denmark: Aarhus University Press, 1994.

Weimann, Robert. "Bi-Fold Authority in Shakespeare." *Shakespeare Quarterly* 39, no. 4 (1988): 401–17.

Willems, Michele. *Shakespeare à la television*. Rouen: L'Université de Rouen, 1987.

Zitner, Sheldon. "Wooden O's in Plastic Boxes: Shakespeare on Television." *University of Toronto Quarterly* 51 (1981): 1–12.

Index